MASTER ● THE
Basic
ENGLISH

Second Edition

Jean Yates, M.A.
George Washington University

BARRON'S

All inquiries should be addressed to:
Barron's Educational Series, Inc.
250 Wireless Boulevard
Hauppauge, New York 11788
www.barronseduc.com

Library of Congress Control Number: 2006015564

ISBN-13: 978-0-7641-3546-0
ISBN-10: 0-7641-3546-5

Library of Congress Cataloging-in-Publication Data
Yates, Jean.
    Master the basics—English / Jean Yates. — 2nd ed.
        p. cm. — (Master the basics series)
    Includes index.
    ISBN-13: 978-0-7641-3546-0
    ISBN-10: 0-7641-3546-5
    1. English language—Textbooks for foreign speakers. 2. English
language—Grammar—Problems, exercises, etc. I. Title. II. Series.
PE1128.Y36 2006
428.2′4—dc22   2006015564

Printed in the United States of America

9 8 7 6 5 4 3

Contents

GRAMMAR

The Basics

The Parts of Speech

Special Topics

Let's Review

APPENDIX

Index

Preface

This book, designed especially for students of English as a Second Language, is one of Barron's series of grammar reference guides. It presents the essentials of English grammar in an easy-to-read outline form, and provides numerous examples of each aspect of English structure. The basics—from the mechanics of capitalization and punctuation, to the patterns of nouns, pronouns, adjectives, verbs, prepositions, adverbs, and conjunctions—are explained clearly and simply. A pre-test at the beginning of the book will help you determine what grammar you already know well, and what areas you need to study further. In addition, there are short tests at the end of the book that will help you put into practice what you have learned, and reinforce the language patterns you have mastered.

How to Use This Book

Look through the book and become familiar with the contents and numbering system of topics. This system—the symbol § + a number + a decimal number—is devised to allow you to easily refer to any topic or sub-topic and to cross-reference it with the tests and the index. You will see that each major section is identified in the Table of Contents by an § + a number. All references to this topic have the same § number throughout the book—in the pretest, in its own chapter in the text, in other sections that deal with related topics, in the exercise section, and in the index. If you are reading about a verb tense, for example, you will note that its usage is closely linked to certain adverbs. The § number will refer you to the proper adverb section for more thorough study.

Take the pretest, check your answers, and fill in the diagnostic analysis chart to pinpoint your strong and weak areas.

Start anywhere you wish. You can start with Section 1 and work straight through to the end; you can start with what you already know well, as a review; or you can start with the topics that you need to work on.

It is also up to you to decide when to do the tests. You may wish to do each test right after studying the corresponding section, or you can wait until you finish, and do all the tests at once. If you do the tests twice, you will get twice the benefit!

FIND OUT WHAT YOU KNOW

Pretest

§2 Write capital letters where necessary:

1. miss smith moved to new york on wednesday, december the twelfth.

§3 Punctuate the following sentence, and write capital letters where necessary:

2. becky my sister who studied in california is now staying in nancys apartment

§4 Identify the parts of the following sentence:

My friend gave us three tickets.

3. The subject is _____ .

4. The predicate is _____ .

5. The direct object is _____ .

6. The indirect object is _____ .

§5 Write the plural form of the following nouns:

7. man

8. lady

9. boy

10. girl

11. child

Complete the sentence with the correct noun:

12. There is one _____ in that family.
people   child   children

13. We have too much _____ .
    work   friends   noises

14. I need a new _____ .
    information   computer   discs

§6   Change the underlined nouns to pronouns:

15. <u>Sue and Carolyn</u> took <u>Bob's</u> car home.

16. <u>Tony and I</u> wanted to take <u>the flowers</u> to <u>my mother</u>.

§7   Choose the correct adjectives for the following sentences:

17. She has _____ information.
    a few   a little   many

18. He has a job at a _____ store.
    shoes   shoe   men

19. I am _____ in this book; it looks very
    _____ .
    interested   interesting

20. That show is not suitable for
    a _____ child.
    three-years-old   three-year-old   three years

21. We have _____ bills.
    too many   too much   a little

§9   Fill in the blanks with the correct verb form:

22. John (need) _____ an apartment now.

23. No, he (not/have) _____ a place to live.

24. Right now he (watch) _____ television.

25. He always (watch) _____ television at night.

26. No, he (not/have to/work) _____ at night.

27. He (work) _____ a salesman for two years.

28–33. Write a question for each of the above statements (22–27).
28. _____
29. _____
30. _____
31. _____
32. _____
33. _____

§10 Fill in the blanks with the correct verb form:

34. I (finish) _____ my report a week ago.

35. No, he (not/go) _____ to Greece last year.

36. We (should/study) _____ yesterday.

37. She was hungry at lunchtime, because she (not/eat) _____ breakfast.

38. While I (drive) _____ to the city, I ran out of gas.

39–43. Write a question for each of the above statements (34–38).
39. _____
40. _____
41. _____
42. _____
43. _____

§11 Rewrite the following sentences using a future expression:

44. I plan to work tomorrow.

_____.

45. There is a 50 percent possibility that John will move to California next month.

   _____.

46. I promise to call you soon.

   _____.

47. My friend refuses to go.

   _____.

§12 Fill in the blanks with the correct form—the gerund or the infinitive:

48. You promised (call) _____ me.

49. He enjoys (play) _____ the piano.

50. She is used to (wear) _____ glasses.

51. He used (wear) _____ glasses.

Change the following direct quotes to reported speech:

52. "She is beautiful," said my brother.

   _____.

53. "Do you want to meet her?" I asked him.

   _____.

Change the following sentence to a direct quote:

54. Joe said he had been there before.

   _____.

Change each question to a statement beginning with "I don't know":

55. Who is she?

   _____.

56. What does she want?

   _____.

§13 Choose the correct verb to complete the sentences:

57. Will you _____ me five dollars?
borrow   lend

58. Please _____ Patricia to help you.
ask   ask for

59. Are you _____ to my party?
coming   going

60. Yes, I am _____ to your party.
coming   going

61. Please don't _____ anything to his sister.
say   tell

62. She always _____ her friends.
says   tells

§14 Change these sentences from the active voice to the passive voice:

63. They made this blouse in China.

_____.

64. Somebody wrote this letter a long time ago.

_____.

§15 Give the command:

65. Tell Karen to call you.

_____.

66. Tell Wayne not to be late.

_____.

67. Suggest to the children that you play a game.

_____.

§16 Combine each pair of sentences into one sentence, beginning with I wish:

68. I don't have a car. I want a car.

_____.

69. They didn't call me. I am sorry.

_____.

Combine each pair of sentences into one sentence, beginning with if:

70. I don't have time. I want to visit you.

_____.

71. I didn't have time. I wanted to visit you.

_____.

§17 Write in the correct prepositions:

72. My house is _____ Columbus.

73. It is _____ Maple Avenue.

74. It is _____ number 702.

75. We go to work _____ bus.

76. This desk is made _____ wood.

77. He has been absent _____ school three times.

78. We aren't prepared _____ the test.

79. He is always thinking _____ his girlfriend.

80. Are you afraid _____ the dark?

81. She is married _____ my cousin.

82. The picnic was called _____ because of rain.

83. He has to get _____ his anger.

84. I am content _____ that.

85. Her dress is similar _____ mine.

86. Is he qualified _____ this job?

§18   Replace the words in parentheses with an adverb:

87. I saw her three years (before now)

_____ .

88. She called me (the week before this week)

_____ .

Write the correct form of the adverb in the blank:

89. Steve runs (fast) _____ than Jim.

90. Helen paints (carefully) _____ than
Suzanne.

91. Charles works (well) _____ of all.

§19   Fill in the blanks with conjunctions:

92. Katherine likes swimming _____ not
diving.

93. Andrew brought a hammer _____
nails.

94. Robin got up early _____ she would
get to our eight o'clock class on time.

95. I got up early, too; _____ , I didn't get
there on time.

96. Terry slept until nine o'clock; _____ ,
he didn't get to class on time either.

§20   Fill in each blank with the most appropriate word or
expression:

97. To operate this machine, first, push the "start"
button. _____ , set the clock.
After   Next   Also   Besides

98. You should accept that job. It pays well.
_____ , it offers great benefits.
Plus   However   On the other hand   Still

99. She doesn't work here. _____ , I've
     never heard of her.
     Instead   Nevertheless   Plus   As a matter of fact

100. If I get the job I'll buy an apartment.
     _____ , I'll look for a room to rent.
     However   Instead   Otherwise   Consequently

§21   Write the following amount as it should be read or
       said:

101. $48,823.92 _____

§22   Write the following calendar year as it should be read
       or said:

102. 1996 _____

§23   Write the time indicated on the clock as it should be
       read or said:

103.

_____

§24   Fill in the blank with best answer:

104. 30°F is _____ .
     cold weather   pleasant weather   hot weather

Answers to Pretest

1. Miss Smith moved to New York on Wednesday, December the twelfth.
2. Becky, my sister who studied in California, is now staying in Nancy's apartment.
3. My friend
4. gave
5. three tickets
6. us
7. men
8. ladies
9. boys
10. girls
11. children
12. child
13. work
14. computer
15. They   his
16. We   them   her
17. a little
18. shoe
19. interested   interesting
20. three-year-old
21. too many
22. needs
23. does not have / doesn't have
24. is watching
25. watches
26. does not have to work / doesn't have to work
27. has worked / has been working
28. What does John need?
29. Does he have a place to live?
30. What is he doing?
31. When does he watch television? / What does he do at night?
32. Does he have to work at night?
33. How long has he worked as a salesman? / How long has he been working as a salesman?
34. finished
35. did not go / didn't go
36. should have studied

37. had not eaten / hadn't eaten
38. was driving
39. When did you finish your report?
40. Did he go to Greece last year?
41. What should you have done yesterday? / When should you have studied?
42. Why was she hungry?
43. When did you run out of gas? / What happened while you were driving to the city?
44. I am going to work tomorrow. / I am working tomorrow.
45. John may move to California next month. / John might move to California next month. / Maybe John will move to California next month.
46. I will call you soon. / I'll call you soon.
47. My friend won't go. / My friend will not go.
48. to call
49. playing
50. wearing
51. to wear
52. My brother said she was beautiful. / My brother said that she was beautiful.
53. I asked him if he wanted to meet her.
54. Joe said, "I've been there before." / "I have been there before," said Joe.
55. I don't know who she is.
56. I don't know what she wants.
57. lend
58. ask
59. coming
60. coming
61. say
62. tells
63. This blouse was made in China.
64. This letter was written a long time ago.
65. Call me, Karen.
66. Don't be late, Wayne.
67. Let's play a game!
68. I wish I had a car.
69. I wish they had called me.
70. If I had time, I would visit you.
71. If I had had time, I would have visited you.
72. in
73. on
74. at
75. by
76. of

77. from
78. for
79. about / of
80. of
81. to
82. off
83. over
84. with
85. to
86. for
87. ago
88. last week
89. faster
90. more carefully
91. the best
92. but
93. and
94. so that
95. however / nevertheless
96. therefore
97. Next
98. Plus
99. As a matter of fact
100. Otherwise
101. forty-eight thousand, eight hundred and twenty-three dollars and ninety-two cents
102. nineteen ninety-six
103. six-oh-five / five after six / five past six
104. cold weather

DIAGNOSTIC ANALYSIS

Section	Question Numbers	Number of Answers	
		Correct	Incorrect
§2. Capitalization	1		
§3. Punctuation	2		
§4. Sentences	3, 4, 5, 6		
§5. Nouns	7, 8, 9, 10, 11, 12, 13, 14		
§6. Pronouns	15, 16		
§7. Adjectives	17, 18, 19, 20, 21		
§9. Verbs—Present Time	22, 23, 24, 25, 26, 27, 28, 29, 30, 31, 32, 33		
§10. Verbs—Past Time	34, 35, 36, 37, 38, 39, 40, 41, 42, 43		
§11. Verbs—Future Time	44, 45, 46, 47		
§12. Verbs—Additional Patterns	48, 49, 50, 51, 52, 53, 54, 55, 56		
§13. Verbs—Special Usage	57, 58, 59, 60, 61, 62		
§14. Verbs—Passive Voice	63, 64		
§15. Verbs—Imperative Mood	65, 66, 67		
§16. Verbs—Subjunctive Mood	68, 69, 70, 71		
§17. Prepositions	72, 73, 74, 75, 76, 77, 78, 79, 80, 81, 82, 83, 84, 85, 86		
§18. Adverbs	87, 88, 89, 90, 91		
§19. Conjunctions	92, 93, 94, 95, 96		
§20. Discourse Markers	97, 98, 99, 100		
§21. Numbers	101		
§22. Dates	102		
§23. Time	103		
§24. Weather	104		
TOTAL QUESTIONS:	104		

Use the following scale to see how you did.

95–104 correct	Excellent	78–82 correct	Below Average
89–94 correct	Very Good	Fewer than 78	Low Proficiency
83–88 correct	Average	correct	

GRAMMAR

The Basics

§1.

Letters and Words

English has an alphabet of 5 vowel letters

> a, e, i, o, u

and 21 consonant letters

> b, c, d, f, g, h, j, k, l, m, n, p, q, r, s, t, v, w, x, y, z

Each word is one example of a *part of speech.* In general,

nouns name people, places, and things

EXAMPLES

> **nurse   town   books**

pronouns are substitutes for nouns

EXAMPLES

> **I you he she it we they us him her them**

adjectives describe nouns

EXAMPLES

> **pretty   tall   new   red**

verbs define states of being or actions

EXAMPLES

> **is are sing have went buying gone**

prepositions relate words to additional information

EXAMPLES

> **for of with by to in out**

adverbs tell where, when, and how the action or state occurs

EXAMPLES

here today fast happily

conjunctions connect and relate various elements of a sentence

EXAMPLES

and but so however

Abbreviations

An *abbreviation* is a shortened form of a word. Abbreviations are often used in informal writing.

EXAMPLES

Mon. for Monday
Sept. for September
ch. for chapter

In formal writing, it is better not to abbreviate most words. The above words, for example—Monday, September, and chapter—should be written out completely. The following words, however, are always abbreviated:

Time Expressions

A.D. *anno Domini*—the years counted for present time
B.C. before Christ—the years counted backward from present time
A.M. *ante meridiem*—before 12 o'clock noon
12:30 A.M. = 12:30 in the morning
P.M. *post meridiem*—after 12 o'clock noon
12:30 P.M. = 12:30 in the afternoon

Personal Titles

Mr. the title for a man
Mr. John Jackson   Mr. Jackson
Mrs. the title for a married woman
Mrs. Margaret Barnes   Mrs. Barnes
Ms. the business title for a married or unmarried woman
Ms. Janice Best   Ms. Best

(Miss, the title for an unmarried woman or young girl, is not followed by a period.)

Dr.   the title for a man or woman who has earned a doctorate degree
    Dr. Pat Reeves   Dr. Reeves

Rev.   the title for a member of the clergy
    Rev. James Thurston   Rev. Thurston

Sr.   senior, used after a man's name when his son has the same name
    Mr. Solomon Thomas, Sr.

Jr.   junior, used after a man's name when his father has the same name
    Mr. Solomon Thomas, Jr.

Credentials

Ph.D. Doctor of Philosophy, used after the name of a person who has earned that degree
    Sally Benson, Ph.D.
    Randy Thorne, Ph.D.

M.D.   Doctor of Medicine, used after the name of a medical doctor
    Cynthia Travis, M.D.
    Daniel Thornton, M.D.

D.D.S. Doctor of Dental Surgery, used after the name of a dentist
    Rose Ann Smithson, D.D.S.
    Dennis Hamilton, D.D.S.

LL.D. Doctor of Laws, used after the name of a lawyer who has earned that degree
    Thomas O'Neill, LL.D.
    Teresa Marshall, LL.D.

Choose one title or the other:
Dr. Donald Lawrence   or   Donald Lawrence, **M.D.**

Latin Abbreviations

cf.   *confer*—compare
e.g.   *exempli gratia*—for example
et al.   *et alii*—and others
etc.   *et cetera*—and so forth
i.e.   *id est*—that is
N.B.   *nota bene*—note well

On an Invitation

R.S.V.P.   *répondez s'il vous plaît*—please reply

§2.

Capitalization

Each alphabet letter has two forms

Lower Case—a, b, c, d, e, f, g, h, i, j, k, l, m, n, o, p, q, r, s, t, u, v, w, x, y, z

Upper Case—A, B, C, D, E, F, G, H, I, J, K, L, M, N, O, P, Q, R, S, T, U, V, W, X, Y, Z

Upper case letters are also called *capitals*. Capital letters are used for:

the first letter of the first word of a sentence
That is our house.

proper nouns and their abbreviations
We live in the **U**nited **S**tates of **A**merica.
We live in the **USA**.

major words in titles
Master the Basics: English

the pronoun **I**.

§3.

Punctuation

Punctuation symbols are written marks that help make meaning clear.

The **period** (.) is used: at the end of most sentences
It is raining.

in many abbreviations
etc.   lb.   Mr.

in numbers, and is called a
decimal point
3.50   4.6   9.99

The **question mark** (?) is used: at the end of a question
Where is Bob?

The **exclamation point** (!) is used: at the end of an exclamation and at the end of some commands
Here he is!
Come here now!

The **comma** (,) is used: to separate elements of a sentence to avoid confusion
If you leave, Sam can rest.

between items in a series
I like ice cream, cake, pie, and all other rich desserts.

with dates
October 2, 1977

with titles
Marta Ruiz, R.N.

with numbers
4,978   5,325,000

The **semi-colon** (;) is used: to separate closely related independent clauses
He is my son; I love him.

She is my friend; besides, I love her.

between items in a series, when commas have already been used
I like ice cream with chocolate, cherries, and whipped cream; cookies, cake, and pie; and all other rich desserts.

The **colon** (:) is used: to call attention to an explanation or list
They need the following: bread, milk, sugar, flour, and salt.

The **dash** (—) is used: to emphasize information within a sentence
Everything they need—bread, milk, sugar, flour, and salt—is at the corner store.

Quotation marks (" ") are used: to indicate exactly what someone said or wrote
Tom said, "You must be crazy!"

Parentheses ( ) are used: to give another form of the same expression
The Yorktown Dance Team (YDT)
Self-contained Underwater Breathing Apparatus (scuba)

The **apostrophe** (') is used: to indicate possession
Mary's book

to form a contraction
I'm   don't   haven't   they're

The **hyphen** (-) is used: to connect the parts of a compound word
seventy-eight   make-up

to connect certain prefixes with words
re-use   pre-approve

§4.

Sentences

The basic unit of written and spoken English is the sentence. A *sentence* is a meaningful combination of words. The first word of a sentence begins with a capital letter, and the last word is followed by a period, a question mark, or an exclamation point.

§4.1 THE SENTENCE

A sentence is an *independent clause;* it
* has a *subject*—a noun and its modifiers
* has a *predicate*—a verb and its modifiers
* expresses a complete idea.

§4.1-1 The Subject

The *subject* is the person, place, or thing we are talking or writing about. It can be singular or plural.

EXAMPLES

Singular Subjects	Plural Subjects
John	John and Bill
He	They
My house	My house and my car
Swimming	Swimming and diving

It is the subject for certain common expressions
   (a) with the weather
      It is windy.
      It is snowing.
      It is hot.

   (b) with time
      It is ten o'clock.
      It is late.

   (c) with distance
      It is a long way.

   (d) with adjectives or nouns followed by infinitives
      It is nice to see you.
      It is sad to say good-bye.
      It is a shame to lose it.

§4.1-2
The Predicate

The *predicate* is a verb that tells what the subject is or does. The form of the verb must be appropriate for the subject.

The verb can be:

4.1-2.1 LINKING

A *linking* verb connects the subject to a *complement*—a word that describes the subject. The complement can be a noun or adjective.

Common linking verbs are *be, become, get* (when it means *become*), *appear, seem, feel, smell, sound,* and *taste*.

EXAMPLES

Subject	Predicate	Complement
John	is	my brother.
My house	seems	empty.
Swimming	sounded	good.

4.1-2.2 TRANSITIVE

A *transitive* verb must have a *direct object*—a noun or pronoun that tells *whom* or *what* the verb points to.

EXAMPLES

Subject	Predicate	Direct Object
John	likes	Susan.
My house	needed	an air conditioner.

4.1-2.3 TRANSITIVE WITH AN INDIRECT OBJECT

An *indirect object* is the person who is the receiver of the direct object.

Common verbs that can have indirect objects are *give, show, tell, teach, buy,* and *send.*

EXAMPLES

Subject	Predicate	Indirect Object	Direct Object
John	gave	Susan	a ring.
She	is telling	her mother	the secret.
We	will send	them	presents.

4.1-2.4 INTRANSITIVE

An *intransitive* verb does not have an object.

EXAMPLES

Subject	Predicate
John	travels.
My car	runs.

§4.2 SENTENCE PATTERNS

The most common sentence patterns are:

(a) Subject	+	Linking Verb	+	Noun Complement
Mary		is		a doctor.
(b) Subject	+	Linking Verb	+	Adjective Complement
Mary		is		intelligent.
(c) Subject	+	Transitive Verb	+	Direct Object
Mary		helps		sick people.
(d) Subject	+	Transitive Verb + Indirect Object +		Direct Object
Mary		gives sick people		medicine.
(e) Subject	+	Intransitive Verb		
Mary		works.		

§4.3 TYPES OF SENTENCES

§4.3-1 Declarative

A *declarative* sentence is a statement that gives information or ideas. It ends with a period.

EXAMPLE
    Mary helps sick people.

§4.3-2 Interrogative

An *interrogative* sentence asks a question. It ends with a question mark.

1. An interrogative sentence may begin with a question word:

Who   asks for the name of a person or people, the subject of the answer sentence
Who is Chan?   **Chan** is my brother.

Whom   asks for the name of a person or people, the object of the answer sentence
Whom did you talk to? I talked to **Chan**.

Whom is used in formal speaking and in writing. Informally, **Who** is used in place of **Whom.**
Who did you talk to?   I talked to **Chan**.

Whose   asks for the name of the owner of something
Whose book is this?   That is **Chan's** book.

What   asks for the name of a place or thing, or of places or things
What is that?   It is **our garden**.
What is this?   It is **a book**.
What are Maine and
  Ohio?   They are **states**.
What are these?   They are **flowers**.

Which   asks for a choice between things
Which hat do you   I want **the red one**.
  want?
Which are your bags? **These bags** are mine.

When   asks for a time
When is the party?   The party is **next Saturday**.

Where   asks for a place
Where is the party?   The party is **at my house**.

Why   asks for a reason
Why did you buy that? I bought it **because I needed it**.

What   asks for a reason
...for   **What** did you buy   I bought it **because that for**?   **I needed it**.

How come	asks for a reason informally	
	How come you bought that?	I bought it **because I needed it**.

How	asks for the manner of the action	
	How does she drive?	She drives **carefully**.

How many	asks for a number	
	How many boxes are there?	There are **three** boxes.

How much	asks for an amount	
	How much money is there?	There is **a little** money.

How + adjective	asks for the intensity of the adjective	
	How heavy is it?	It is **very heavy**.

How + adverb	asks for the intensity of the adverb	
	How fast does she type?	She types **very fast**.

2. A question may ask for a "yes" or "no" answer. The word order is:

Form of *Be* or Auxiliary Verb +	Subject +	Main Verb +	Complement or Object
Are	you		sick?
Is	she		here?
Do	they	like	ice cream?
Does	he	work?	

§4.3-3 Exclamatory

An *exclamatory* sentence expresses surprise or another emotion. It ends with an exclamation point.

Exclamatory sentences often begin with **What** or **How**.

EXAMPLES
> **What** a beautiful dress!
> **How** nice of you to say that!

An exclamatory sentence may be a statement spoken with special emphasis.

EXAMPLES
> I am hungry!
> She is a wonderful teacher!
> You didn't call me!

§4.3-4
Imperative

An *imperative* sentence is a command. It tells someone what to do or not to do. An imperative sentence may end with a period or an exclamation point.

The subject may be "you"—either singular or plural—but it is not expressed.

EXAMPLES
> Turn right on Oak Street.
> Open the boxes.
> Come here!
> Drive carefully!
> Don't touch that wine!

The subject could also be "we" or "you and I"—also not expressed.

EXAMPLES
> Let's go to the movies.
> Let's not waste time.

The Parts of Speech

§5.

Nouns

A *noun* is a word that names one or more people, animals, places, things, or abstractions. *Abstractions* are things you cannot touch.

> A noun that names a person or people answers the question, "Who?"
>
> A noun that names one or more animals, places, or things answers the question, "What?"

§5.1 COUNTABLE NOUNS

Nouns that can be counted have two forms: *singular* and *plural*.

§5.1-1 Singular Nouns

A *singular* noun names *one* person, animal, place, thing, or abstraction.

Person	Place	Thing	Abstraction
girl	town	house	idea
boy	airport	piano	science
doctor	area	radio	problem

Collective Nouns

A *collective* noun is a singular noun that names a group of people with a common interest.

EXAMPLES

team	a group of players working together
class	a group of students studying together
family	a group of people related by blood
office	a group of people who work for the same boss

To use a singular noun,
    (a) always use a *noun determiner* (*a/an, the, one, this, that, any, each, every, another, either, neither, my, your, his, her, our, their,* or a **possessive noun**)—see **§5.1** and **§7.1**.

    (b) use a *singular verb* (he/she/it form)—see **§8**.

EXAMPLES

Noun Determiner	Singular Noun	Singular Verb
a	book	is
the	book	has
my	book	weighs
my	team	wins
a	family	has
the	class	is

§5.1-2
Plural Nouns

A *plural* noun names *two or more* people, animals, places, things, or abstractions.
    To make plurals,

1. add **-s** to most nouns:

People	Places	Things	Abstractions
girls	towns	houses	ideas
boys	airports	pianos	sciences
doctors	areas	radios	problems

2. add **-es** to the following nouns that end in *-o:*

People	Things	Abstractions
heroes	tomatoes	tornadoes
	potatoes	echoes
	mosquitoes	

3. add **-es** to nouns ending in *ch, sh, ss,* and *x:*

People	Places	Things	Abstractions
witches	churches	watches	crashes
		brushes	messes
		dresses	
		boxes	

4. for nouns ending in *y* after a consonant, drop the *y* and add **ies**:

People	Places	Things	Abstractions
lady/ladies	city/cities	body/bodies	philosophy/philosophies
baby/babies	university/ universities	factory/factories	study/studies

5. for nouns ending in *f* or *fe*, drop the *f(e)* and add **ves**:

People	Things	Abstractions
wife/wives	knife/knives	life/lives
	leaf/leaves	
	shelf/shelves	

6. change the form of several common nouns:

People		Things	
one man	three men	one foot	three feet
one woman	three women	one tooth	three teeth
one child	three children	one mouse	three mice
one person	three people		

7. use the singular form for the plural of several nouns:

Animals		Abstractions	
one deer	two deer	one series	two series
one sheep	two sheep	one species	two species
one fish	two fish		

8. use Latin plurals for certain Latin nouns:

Things		Abstractions	
one memorandum	two memoranda	one criterion	two criteria
		one phenomenon	two phenomena
one thesis	two theses	one crisis	two crises
		one stimulus	two stimuli

To use plural nouns,
 (a) a *noun determiner* is optional. You can use *the, zero,* all numbers except *one, these, those, any, no, either, neither, other, some, both, few, enough, plenty, of, a lot of, lots of, many, all, my, your, his, her, its, our, their,* or a possessive noun—see §5.1 and §7.1.

 (b) When there is no noun determiner, the meaning **"all"** is implied.

EXAMPLES

Her flowers are beautiful.	(Only **her** flowers)
Flowers are beautiful.	(**All** flowers)
These exercises are fun.	(Only **these** exercises)
Exercises are fun.	(**All** exercises)

(c) use a plural verb (*we/you/they* form)—see **§8**.

EXAMPLES

Noun Determiner	Plural Noun	Plural Verb	
The	girls	are	here.
My	friends	have	jobs.
These	exercises	help.	
Her	flowers	are	beautiful.
	Exercises	help.	
	Flowers	are	beautiful.

§5.2 NON-COUNT NOUNS

§5.2-1 Common Examples

A *non-count* noun names

1. a group or collection of diverse things:

furniture	tables, chairs, beds, etc.
jewelry	necklaces, bracelets, rings, watches, etc.
mail	letters, postcards, packages, etc.
equipment	necessities for a project
machinery	different machines
hardware	tools and supplies
makeup	lipstick, powder, mascara, etc.
money	bills and change
change	nickels, dimes, quarters, and pennies

2. an item made up of parts that are too small to count:

hair	many tiny strands
sugar	many tiny grains
rice	many tiny grains
salt	many tiny grains
sand	many tiny grains
coffee	many tiny granules
tea	many tiny leaves

corn	many small kernels
dirt	many small particles
dust	many small particles
flour	many small particles
grass	many small blades

3. an activity or abstraction made up of variable parts:

work	activities of physical or mental concentration
housework	cleaning, dusting, doing laundry, etc.
homework	assignments of reading, writing, listening, researching, etc.
advice	suggestions to help someone
information	facts of interest
news	important events
music	series of notes, sounds, songs

4. liquids:
   water
   milk
   soup
   juice
   coffee
   tea

5. food and other useful commodities:
   bread
   meat
   chicken
   fish
   cheese
   cotton
   wool
   copper
   glass
   rubber
   soap

6. environmental phenomena:
   air
   land
   oxygen
   smoke
   steam
   wind
   heat

7. human qualities:
   honesty
   beauty
   intelligence
   patience
   kindness
   generosity
   courage
   independence
   pride
   selfishness

8. conditions:
   health
   sickness
   wealth
   poverty
   education
   anger
   luck

9. subjects of study:
   psychology
   biology
   medicine
   law
   science
   religion
   English

§5.2-2 Using Non-Count Nouns

To use non-count nouns,

(a) a *noun determiner* is optional. You can use *the, this, that, any, no, either, neither, some, little, enough, a lot of, lots of, plenty of, much, all, my, your, his, her, its, our, their,* or a possessive noun—see **§5.1** and **§7.1**.

(b) When there is no noun determiner, the meaning "all" is implied.

EXAMPLES
This coffee is delicious. (Only **this** coffee)
Coffee is delicious. (**All** coffee)

(c) use a *singular verb* (*he/she/it* form) — see **§8**.

EXAMPLES

Noun Determiner	Non-Count Noun	Singular Verb	
Our	homework	is	difficult.
A lot of	medicine	makes	me sick.
	Homework	is	necessary.
	Medicine	costs	a lot.

§5.2-3 Nouns That Can Be Count or Non-Count

A few nouns can be *count* in certain situations, and *non-count* in others.

count:	one coffee	one cup of coffee
non-count:	coffee	the beans or granules used for making a cup of coffee
count:	one chicken	an animal
non-count:	chicken	the meat of a chicken
count:	one glass	a container that holds liquids
	glasses	lenses for improving sight
non-count:	glass	the material a glass is made of
count:	one iron	an appliance used for pressing clothes
non-count:	iron	a metal
count:	one paper	a newspaper; a report
non-count:	paper	the material a report is written on
count:	one time	one occasion
non-count:	time	the present, past, and future

§5.3 PROPER NOUNS

Proper nouns are specific names of individual people, groups of people, places, and things. They are written with capital letters. The article *the* is used with certain proper nouns, but not with others. See **§7.14**.

EXAMPLES

Mary Smith	the name of a person
Mr. Jones	the name of a person
New York	the name of a state

Springfield	the name of a city
Oak Street	the name of a street
Canadian	the name of a nationality
November	the name of a month
Saturday	the name of a day
Thanksgiving	the name of a holiday
English	the name of a language
the United States	the name of a country
the Book Club	the name of an organization
the Arlington Library	the name of an institution
the Capitol	the name of a building

§5.4 APPOSITIVES

An *appositive* is a noun that follows a noun and renames it. Put a comma *before* the appositive, and a comma or a period *after* the appositive.

EXAMPLES
Mary, **my sister**, is a doctor.
Mary liked her teacher, **Mrs. Smith**.
Our neighbors, **the Cordovas**, are delightful.
Rice, **her favorite food**, is good for her.

§5.5 POSSESSIVE NOUNS

§5.5-1 "Whose?"

A *possessive* noun tells who "has" something. It answers the question, **"Whose?"**

To make a noun possessive,
(a) add **'s** to a singular noun:

the book that Mary owns	Whose book?	**Mary's**
the friend that Mary has	Whose friend?	**Mary's**
the car that my friend has	Whose car?	**my friend's**
the dog that Charles owns	Whose dog?	**Charles's**
the dog that Charles Adams owns	Whose dog?	Charles **Adams's**
the stereo that Joe Perez has	Whose stereo?	Joe **Perez's**
the bone that the dog has	Whose bone?	the **dog's**
the basketball that the boy has	Whose basketball?	the **boy's**

    (b) add **'s** to a plural noun that does not end in *s:*

the money that the people have	Whose money?	the **people's**
the toys that the children have	Whose toys?	the **children's**
the shirts that the men own	Whose shirts?	the **men's**
the shoes that belong to the women	Whose shoes?	the **women's**

    (c) add **'** to a plural noun that ends in *s:*

the party that the ladies have	Whose party?	the **ladies'**
the basketball that belongs to the boys	Whose basketball?	the **boys'**
the room where the teachers relax	Whose room?	the **teachers'**
the house that belongs to the Adamses	Whose house?	the **Adamses'**
the car that belongs to the Perezes	Whose car?	the **Perezes'**

    (d) use ***a*** + (noun) + ***of*** + **the possessive noun** to indicate that the item owned is only one of several:

| a book that Mary has | Whose book? | **a** book **of Mary's** |
| a friend that my sister has | Whose friend? | **a** friend **of my sister's** |

§5.5-2 Using Possessive Nouns

Use the possessive form to show ownership by people. Do not use *of the* with people.

EXAMPLES
John's book
Mr. Harris's car
The Lewis's house

    Use either the possessive form or the prepositional phrase *of the* with other living or natural things.

EXAMPLES

the dog's leg		the leg of the dog
the tiger's tail		the tail of the tiger
the plant's leaves	or	the leaves of the plant
the sun's rays		the rays of the sun
the river's mouth		the mouth of the river

Use either the possessive form or the prepositional phrase *of the* with collective nouns.

EXAMPLES

the company's president	the president of the company
the team's captain	the captain of the team
the committee's agenda	the agenda of the committee
a family's celebration	the celebration of a family

Use the possessive form—or a prepositional phrase—with certain time expressions.

EXAMPLES

today's date	the date of today
the year's end	the end of the year
the day's work	the work of the day
tomorrow's agenda	the agenda for tomorrow
next week's lesson	the lesson for next week

Do not use the possessive form for other nonliving things. Show possession with *of the*.

EXAMPLES

the door of the car
the legs of the table
the color of her dress
the rooms of the house
the name of that street

§5.6
COMPARING NOUNS

§5.6-1
Comparing Nouns by Number or Amount

To make a positive comparison of plural or non-count nouns, use:

more + noun + *than* + noun

or

more + noun + *than* + subject + (verb)

The verb is optional.

I have **more** pencils **than** pens.
I have **more** pencils **than** you do.

I have **more** sugar **than** flour.
I have **more** sugar **than** she does.

To make a negative comparison of plural nouns, use:
fewer + noun + *than*

I have **fewer** pens **than** pencils.
I have **fewer** pens **than** she does.

To make a negative comparison of non-count nouns, use:
less + noun + *than*

I have **less** flour **than** sugar.
I have **less** flour **than** she does.

To show equality with plural nouns, use:
as many + noun + *as*

I have **as many** notebooks **as** books.
I have **as many** notebooks **as** he does.

You can also use:
the same number of + noun + *as*

I have **the same number of** notebooks **as**
books.
I have **the same number of** notebooks **as**
he does.

To show equality with non-count nouns, use:
as much + noun + *as*

I have **as much** vinegar **as** oil.
I have **as much** vinegar **as** you do.

You can also use:
the same amount of + noun + *as*

I have **the same amount of** vinegar **as** oil.
I have **the same amount of** vinegar **as**
you do.

§5.6-2 Expressing Equality of Size, Weight, Shape, and Color

For singular, plural and non-count nouns, use:
  the same + noun + *as*

EXAMPLES
My dress is **the same size as** your dress.
Our dresses are **the same size**.

My shoes are **the same size as** your shoes.
Our shoes are **the same size.**

My furniture is **the same size as** your furniture.
Our furniture is **the same size.**

Your baby is **the same weight** as her baby.
Your babies are **the same weight**.

He is **the same height** as his father.
They are **the same height**.

Her skirt is **the same length** as the model's.
Their skirts are **the same length**.

This pond is **the same depth** as that one.
They are **the same depth**.

This tree is **the same shape as** that tree.
The trees are **the same shape**.

Their uniforms are **the same color as** ours.
They are **the same color**.

§5.6-3 Expressing Absolute Equality

To show that two nouns are equal in every way, use:
  exactly like + noun   or   *exactly alike*
  the same as + noun   *the same*

EXAMPLES
Your dress is **exactly like** my dress.
Our dresses are **exactly alike**.

Your dress is **the same as** my dress.
Our dresses are **the same**.

Her earrings are **exactly like** yours.
Your earrings are **exactly alike**.

Her earrings are **the same as** yours.
Your earrings are **the same**.

His furniture is **exactly like** hers.
Their furniture is **exactly alike**.

His furniture is **the same as** hers.
Their furniture is **the same**.

§5.6-4
The Same +
Noun

the same + noun = the actual noun previously thought
about or spoken about

EXAMPLES
I saw some beautiful shoes in the window.
You did? I saw **the same shoes**.

There is a young lady waiting for you.
She is **the same lady** who was here before.

I lost my suitcase.
Now I have to wear **the same clothes** for a week.

§6.

Pronouns

A *pronoun* is a substitute for a noun. Use the pronoun when the noun has already been named, to avoid repeating it.

**§6.1
SUBJECT
PRONOUNS**

A *subject pronoun* replaces a noun that is the subject of a sentence—the *person, place,* or *thing* we are talking about. It answers the question, **"Who?"** for a person, and **"What?"** for an animal, thing, or abstraction—see **§4.1**.

I	= the speaker	**I** am Mary.
you	= the person spoken to	**You** are Susana.
he	= another person, who is male	**He** is David.
she	= another person, who is female	**She** is Patricia.
we	= I and you, he, she, and/or they	**We** are Mary and Susana.
you	= you and he, she, and/or they	**You** are Susana and David.
they	= other people	**They** are David and Patricia.
it	= an animal, thing, or abstraction	**It** is Rover. **It** is a book. **It** is information.
they	= one or more animals, things, or abstractions.	**They** are dogs. **They** are books. **They** are announcements.

EXAMPLES

Question	Response
Who is the teacher?	**Sara** is the teacher.
When does **she** begin the class?	**She** begins at eight.
When does **she** go home?	**She** goes home at four-thirty.
Who are the students?	**Steve and Tom** are the students.
Is Steve from St. Louis?	**He and Tom** are from St. Louis.
	They are from St. Louis.
Who is taking them home?	**Sara and I** are taking them home.
	She and I are taking them home.
What time are **you** taking them?	**We** are taking them at four-thirty.

42

Sometimes the pronouns *you* and *they* do not refer to a specific person or people, but to people in general, or all people.

EXAMPLES

Question	Meaning	Answer
Do **you** buy medicine at the supermarket?	Do people buy medicine at the supermarket?	Yes. **You** (can) buy medicine at the supermarket.
Where do **you** get your keys?	Where do people get their keys?	**You** get your keys at the office.
How do **you** get to Route 7?	How does one get to Route 7?	**You** drive straight ahead, then turn left.
Do **they** sell medicine at the supermarket?	Is medicine sold at the supermarket?	Yes. **They** sell medicine at the supermarket.
Do **they** give you your keys at the office?	Are keys given out at the office?	Yes. **They** give you your keys at the office.

§6.2 OBJECT PRONOUNS

An *object pronoun* replaces a noun that is a direct object, an indirect object, or an object of a preposition. It answers the question, **"Who(m)?"** for people, and **"What?"** for things—see **§4.1**.

Subject Pronoun	Object Pronoun
I	me
you	you
he	him
she	her
it	it
we	us
they	them

§6.2-1 Direct Object Pronouns

John called **Mary**. (I am Mary.)   John called me.
John called **Susana**. (You are Susana.) John called you.
John called **Patricia**. (She is Patricia.) John called her.
John called **David**. (He is David.) John called him.
John called **Mary and Susan.** John called us.
     John called me and you.

John called **Susana and Patricia**. John called you.
     John called you and her.

John called **Patricia and David.**   John called **them.**
                                           John called **her**
                                              and him.

John got **the check.**   John got **it.**
John got **the checks.**   John got **them.**

EXAMPLES

Question	Answer
Who(m) did you see?	I saw **Betty.**
When did you see **her**?	I saw **her** yesterday.
Did you see **Sam**?	Yes, I saw **him**, too.
	I saw **her** and **him** yesterday.
	I saw **Betty** and **him.**
	I saw **her** and **Sam.**
	I saw **them** yesterday.
Did they see **you and your** **friend**?	No, they didn't see **us.**
	They didn't see **me and him.**
	They didn't see **him and me.**

§6.2-2 Object-of-Preposition Pronouns

to	**Mary**	= to **me**
for	**Susana**	= for **you**
from	**Patricia**	= from **her**
with	**David**	= with **him**
about	**Mary and Susana**	= about **us**
without	**Susana and Patricia**	= without **you**
of	**Patricia and David**	= of **them**

EXAMPLES

Question	Answer
Are you going with **Cathy** **and Ali**?	Yes. I am going with **her and him.**
	I am going with **them.**
Did Bob leave without **you** **and Georges**?	Yes. He left without **me and him.**
	He left without **us.**
Who(m) is that present for?	It's for **my mother and Ines.**
	It's for **her and Ines.**
	It's for **them.**

§6.2-3 Indirect Object Pronouns

Kim gave the book to **Mary.**   Kim gave **me** the book.
Kim gave the book to **Susana.**   Kim gave **you** the book.
Kim gave the book to **Patricia.**   Kim gave **her** the book.
Kim gave the book to **David.**   Kim gave **him** the book.

Kim gave the book to **David and Mary**.	Kim gave **us** the book. Kim gave **David and me** the book.
Kim gave the book to **Susana and Patricia**.	Kim gave **you** the book. Kim gave **you and her** the book.
Kim gave the book to **Patricia and David**.	Kim gave **them** the book. Kim gave **her and him** the book.

EXAMPLES

Question	Answer
Who(m) did you send the letter to?	I sent **my friend** the letter. I sent **him** the letter.
Did you send it to **him and his sister**?	No. I didn't send **her** the letter. I didn't send **them** the letter. I sent **him** the letter.
Who wrote **you** the answer?	She wrote **me and my brother** the answer. She wrote **me and him** the answer. She wrote **us** the answer.

§6.2-4 Using Two Object Pronouns Together

When there is an indirect object pronoun before the direct object, the direct object must be in noun—not pronoun—form.

EXAMPLES	**Do Not Use:**
He gave me the book.	He gave me it.
We told them the story.	We told them it.
I'll show you my new dresses.	I'll show you them.

To use the direct object pronoun with an indirect object pronoun, use a preposition.

EXAMPLES	
He gave me the book.	He gave it **to me**.
We told them the story.	We told it **to them**.
I'll show you my new dresses.	I'll show them **to you**.

§6.3 RECIPROCAL PRONOUNS

The *reciprocal pronoun* **each other** refers to a relationship between two people or groups.

EXAMPLES
Jane and I are friends.
I talk to Jane; Jane talks to me.   We talk to **each other**.

The doctors and nurses work together.
The doctors help the nurses, and
the nurses help the doctors.   They help **each other**.

One another is used to refer to a relationship among three
or more people.

EXAMPLES
The doctors and nurses help **one another**.
Jane, Carolyn, and Mia talked to **one another** about the
problem.

§6.4 INTENSIVE AND REFLEXIVE PRONOUNS

myself	**ourselves**
yourself	**yourselves**
himself	**themselves**
herself	
itself	

§6.4-1 Intensive Pronouns

An *intensive pronoun* restates a subject noun or pronoun,
to emphasize it.

EXAMPLES
I vote "no" **myself**.
You know that **yourself**.
Julie went to the store **herself**.
Mark did it **himself**.
Emily and I made this cake **ourselves**.
Did you and Jack build the house **yourselves**?
The robbers **themselves** called the police.

§6.4-2 Reflexive Pronouns

A *reflexive pronoun* is an object pronoun that refers back
to the subject. The subject and the object are the same
person or thing.

EXAMPLES
I cut **myself**.
Did you cure **yourself**?

He needs to help **himself**.
She sent a letter to **herself**.
This door locks **itself**.
We gave **ourselves** a party.
Did you make **yourselves** comfortable?
They are hurting **themselves**.

The preposition *by* + a reflexive pronoun means "alone."

Statement	Meaning
I did it **by myself**.	Nobody helped me.
She is **by herself**.	She is alone.
They played **by themselves**.	Nobody else played with them.

§6.5 POSSESSIVE PRONOUNS

A *possessive pronoun* replaces a possessive noun. It answers the question, **"Whose?"** — see **§5**.

Whose book is it?

The book is **Mary's**.	The book is **mine**.
The book is **Susana's**.	The book is **yours**.
The book is **David's**.	The book is **his**.
The book is **Patricia's**.	The book is **hers**.
The book is **Mary's and Susana's**.	The book is **ours**.
The book is **Susana's and Patricia's**.	The book is **yours**.
The book is **Patricia's and David's**.	The book is **theirs**.

To show possession, you can also use

It belongs to + noun or object pronoun

Whose book is it?

It belongs to me.	It's **mine**.
It belongs to you.	It's **yours**.
It belongs to her.	It's **hers**.
It belongs to him.	It's **his**.
It belongs to her and me.	It's **ours**.
It belongs to me and him.	It's **ours**.
It belongs to us.	It's **ours**.
It belongs to her and him.	It's **theirs**.
It belongs to them.	It's **theirs**.

§6.6 RELATIVE PRONOUNS

A *relative pronoun*

who, whom, whose, which, that

replaces a noun in an adjective clause. It answers the questions

"Who...?" "Whom...?" "Whose...?" "Which...?" "What...?" and "What kind of...?"

Who is he?	He is a man. He came to our house. He is the man **who** came to our house.
From **whom** did you receive the gift?	The lady is Mrs. Smith. I received the gift from her. The lady from **whom** I received the gift is Mrs. Smith.
Whose dog is this?	The girl is my niece. This is her dog. The girl **whose** dog this is is my niece.
What kind of book do you want?	I want a book. The book has pictures. I want a book **that** has pictures.
What book do you want?	The book **that** I want is the one with pictures.

Note: The pronoun in the last example can be deleted: The book ( ) I want is the one with pictures.

§6.7 DEMONSTRATIVE PRONOUNS

§6.7-1 Indicating a Specific Noun

A *demonstrative pronoun* indicates a specific noun. It answers the questions

"Which?" "Which one?" and "Which ones?"

This replaces a singular or
non-count noun that is nearby.
It is here.

This is my watch.
This is my jewelry.

These replaces a plural noun that
is nearby. They are here.

These are my
watches.

That replaces a singular or
non-count noun that is farther
away. It is there.

That is your watch.
That is your jewelry.

Those replaces a plural noun that
is farther away. They are there.

Those are your
watches.

§6.7-2 Using *One*

One refers to a specific item already named.

Question	Answer
Which dress do you want?	I want the red one.
	I want **this one**.
	I don't want **that one**.
Which (one) is yours?	**This** is mine.
	This one is mine.
It can be plural.	
Which dresses do you want?	I want the cotton **ones**.
	I want **these**.
	I don't want the wool **ones**.
	I don't want **those**.
Which (ones) are yours?	**These** are mine.

Note: Do not use *ones* after *these* and *those*.

§6.8 INDEFINITE PRONOUNS

An *indefinite pronoun* refers to a noun that is not specific.

§6.8-1 Singular Indefinite Pronouns

(a) Referring only to **people**:

anybody	(one of all people)	**Anybody** can do it.
anyone	(one of all people)	Is **anyone** there?
not anybody	(not one person)	There **isn't anybody** in the house.
not anyone	(not one person)	There **isn't anyone** in the store.
nobody	(not one person)	**Nobody** can do it.

no one	(not one person)	**No one** is at home.
somebody	(one person)	**Somebody** can help us.
someone	(one person)	**Someone** is in the office.

(b) Referring only to **places**:

anywhere	(one of all places)	I can go **anywhere**.
not anywhere	(not one place)	I can**not** go **anywhere**. The ring is **not anywhere** in this house.
nowhere	(not one place)	The ring is **nowhere** in this house.
somewhere	(one place)	I will find it **somewhere**.

(c) Referring only to **things**:

anything	(one of all things)	**Anything** is better than nothing.
not anything	(no thing)	There **isn't anything** to eat.
nothing	(no thing)	There is **nothing** to eat.
something	(one thing)	There is **something** in this box.

(d) Referring to **people** or **things**:

one	(one)	Is there a doctor in the house? Yes, I am **one**. Does anybody have a book? Yes, I have **one**.
another (one)	(one more)	She has two children. She wants **another**.
	(a different one)	She has a book. She wants **another one**.
any	(one, no preference)	Which lawyer do you prefer? **Any** will be O.K. What book do you want? **Any** is fine.
each	(all, one by one)	What do the children have? **Each** has a balloon.
either	(one or the other)	Do you want an apple or a banana? **Either** is fine.
neither	(not one nor the other)	Which coat is yours? **Neither** is mine.

§6.8-2
Plural
Indefinite
Pronouns

Plural indefinite pronouns may refer to people or things.

none	(zero)	How many books are there?
		There are **none**.
not any	(zero)	How many teachers are there?
		There aren't **any**.
any number over one	(two to infinity)	How many chairs are there?
		There are **twelve**.
some	(more than one)	How many girls are there?
		There are **some**.
both	(the two)	Which pen is yours?
		Both are mine.
either	(these or those)	Which do you want, CDs or tapes?
		Either are fine.
neither	(not these or those)	Which dishes are yours —these or those?
		Neither are mine.
others	(different ones)	Are these all you have?
		No. I have **others**.
few, very few	(not enough)	How many participants are there?
		There are **few**.
a few	(three or four)	How many people are there?
		There are **a few**.
several	(four or five)	How many children are there?
		There are **several**.
enough	(the needed number)	How many cars are there?
		There are **enough**.
a lot	(a large number)	How many sandwiches are there?
		There are **a lot**.
not many	(not a large number)	How many plates are there?
		There are **not many**.

too many	(more than is good)	How many mistakes are there? There are **too many**.
all	(100 percent)	Which photographs are good? **All** are good.

§6.8-3 Non-Count Indefinite Pronouns

none	(no amount)	How much traffic is there? There is **none**.
either	(one or the other)	Do you want furniture or jewelry? **Either** is good.
neither	(not one or the other)	Do you want tea or coffee? **Neither** is good for me.
some	(more than none)	How much pollution is there? There is **some**.
little, very little	(not enough)	How much money is there? There is **little**.
a little	(a small quantity)	How much information is there? There is **a little**.
enough	(the needed amount)	How much work is there? There is **enough**.
a lot	(a large amount)	How much music is there? There is **a lot**.
too much	(more than is good)	How much advice is there? There is **too much**.

§6.8-4
Another /
The Other /
Others

Compare *another/the other/others*:

Singular		Plural	
another = one more or a different one		**others** = more or different ones (but not all of them)	
$ one	$ $ $ $ another	$$$ some	$ $ $ $ $ others
the other = the only remaining one		**the others** = all of the remaining ones	
$ one	$ the other	$$$ some	$$$$$ the others

§7.

Adjectives

Adjectives give information about nouns.

There are two kinds of adjectives: *noun determiners* and *descriptive adjectives.*

Noun determiners identify and limit nouns. They have specific relationships with singular nouns, plural nouns, and non-count nouns.

Descriptive adjectives have the same form for singular, plural, and non-count nouns. Their use is optional.

Use the following patterns:

Noun Determiner (required)	+	Descriptive Adjective (optional)	+	Singular Noun
a		beautiful		**watch**
Noun Determiner (optional)	+	Descriptive Adjective (optional)	+	Plural Noun
these		beautiful		**watches**
Noun Determiner (optional)	+	Descriptive Adjective (optional)	+	Non-Count Noun
this		beautiful		**jewelry**

EXAMPLES

Correct Forms	Do Not Use:
Singular Nouns	
I have a watch.	I have watch.
I have a beautiful watch.	
I have the watch.	
I have this watch.	
Plural Nouns	
I have watches.	I have a watches.
I have beautiful watches.	I have this watches.
I have the watches.	
I have these watches.	
Non-count Nouns	
I have jewelry.	I have a jewelry.
I have beautiful jewelry.	I have these jewelry.
I have the jewelry.	I have jewelries.
I have this jewelry.	

§7.1
NOUN
DETERMINERS

§7.1-1
Articles—
a, an, the

An *article* helps identify a noun.

(a) *A* or *an* is used only before a singular noun and identifies it as one of many, not a special one. It answers the question, **"What is it?"** or **"Who is it?"**

Use *a* before a singular noun that begins with a consonant sound.

a man	**a** street	**a** cassette	**a** problem
a nurse	**a** building	**a** box	**a** thought
	a university*		

*university begins with a vowel letter, but is pronounced with the consonant sound, **y**u.

Use **an** before a singular noun that begins with a vowel sound.

an artist	**an** area	**an** apple	**an** idea
an optimist	**an** estate	**an** orange	**an** operation
		an R.S.V.P.*	

*R is a consonant, but is pronounced with the vowel sound, **a**r.

When there is a descriptive adjective, choose *a* or *an* according to the first sound of the adjective.

a nice lady	**a** big city	**a** red belt	**a** pretty dress
an intelligent lady	**an** old city	**an** orange belt	**an** ugly dress

(b) *The* indicates a specific singular, plural, or non-count noun.

the table	the tables	the furniture

The answers the question, **"What (noun)?"** or **"Which one(s)?"**
Use *the*

1. when there is only one to choose from:

Question	Answer	Meaning
Which door?	*the* door	the only door
Which keys?	*the* keys	the only keys
What zoo?	*the* zoo	the (only) zoo in the city

2. when the listener knows which item:

Question	Answer	Meaning
Which book?	*the* book	the book you gave me
What letters?	*the* letters	the letters John wrote to us
What dress?	*the* dress	the dress we saw in the shop
Which car?	*the* car	our car
What jewelry?	*the* jewelry	the jewelry I gave you

(c) Compare *a/an* with *the*:

What is it?	It's *an* apple.
Which apple is it?	It's *the* apple you gave me.
What is it?	It's *a* school.
What school is it?	It's *the* school our children go to.
What is it?	It's *a* problem.
What problem is it?	It's *the* problem I told you about.
Who is she?	She's *a* girl.
Which girl is she?	She's *the* girl I like.

(d) *The* with proper nouns:
To be sure about these, learn each proper noun as you need it.
Do not use *the* with certain singular proper nouns. For example:
Mary
Mary Jones
Mrs. Jones
President Smith
Texas
South America
Korea
Chicago
Central Park
Hudson Bay
Memorial Bridge
Madison High School

Virginia Tech
Oak Street
January
Monday
Kim's Dry Cleaners

Use **the** before other singular proper nouns. For example,
the Secretary of Labor
the President of the United States
the Equator
the Catskills
the White House
the Smithsonian
the University of Wisconsin
the New Jersey Turnpike
the Brooklyn Bridge
the Chesapeake Bay
the White Company
the United Kingdom
the Western Hemisphere

Use **the** before plural proper nouns. For example,
the United States
the Netherlands
the Philippines
the Andes
the Rocky Mountains
the Great Lakes
the United Nations
the Smiths, **the** Joneses

(e) Special cases of no article and **the**:
at home = in a person's own home
at the home of = in someone else's home

at school = attending classes
at the school = visiting a school

at church = worshipping
at the church = visiting the church

in jail = detained by law
at the jail = visiting the jail

at work = working

home = to a person's own home
to the home of = to someone else's home

to school = to the school for study
to the school = to a school for a visit

to church = to the church for worship
to the church = to a church for a visit

to jail = to be locked up
to the jail = to the jail for a visit

to work = to a place for work

EXAMPLES
She won't be **at home** today. The meeting is **at the home** of her sister.
My son came **home** from **school** early yesterday because he was sick. He didn't go to **school** today. I went to **the school** this morning to talk to the teacher.

North, south, east, and west are directions. **They** are used with verbs that indicate movement in that direction. **The** before each word indicates a section of a larger place.

EXAMPLES
Go **north**, and you will find that building. It is in **the north** of the city.
The birds fly **south** every winter. The weather is much warmer in **the south**.
His parents were not happy in **the west**, so they moved back **east**.

Breakfast, lunch, and dinner are meals in general.
The breakfast, **the** lunch, and **the** dinner mean specific meals.

EXAMPLES
I usually don't eat **breakfast**. **The breakfast** your mother made was delicious.
We are having **lunch** at the office today. **The lunch** Max brought looks good.
Let's eat **dinner** at that restaurant. **The dinner** we had there last week was great.

last night = the night before today
the last night = the final night

last week = the week before this one
the last week = the final week

last year = the year before this one
the last year = the final year

EXAMPLES

Jack called me **last night**. He said that Friday was **the last night** of his conference.

We had our exam **last week**. It was **the last week** of classes.

I bought a car **last year**; 1997 will be **the last year** I have to make payments on it.

in office = serving as an elected official
in the office = located in a room

EXAMPLES

Her husband has been **in office** for five years. He spends a lot of time **in the office** writing letters to his supporters.

§7.1-2 Numbers

(a) *Cardinal* numbers answer the question **"How many?"**

0 (zero, no) requires a plural noun.

There are **zero** apple**s** in the basket.
There are **no** apple**s** in the basket.

1 (one) describes a singular noun.

There is **one** table in the room.

All other numbers describe plural nouns.

There are **two** chairs.
There are **forty-six** people.
There are **fifty** states in the United States.

(See **§20** for a complete number chart.)

(b) An *ordinal* number tells the relative position of a singular or plural noun. Always use the article ***the*** before an ordinal number.

The ordinal numbers for 1, 2, 3, and for combinations with 1, 2, and 3, are:

the first	the 1st	**the** twenty-**first**	the 21st
the second	the 2nd	**the** thirty-**second**	the 32nd
the third	the 3rd	**the** sixty-**third**	the 63rd

The ordinal numbers for 5, 8, 9, 12, and for combinations with 5, 8, and 9 are:

the fifth	the 5th	**the** forty-**fifth**	the 45th
the eighth	the 8th	**the** eighty-**eighth**	the 88th
the ninth	the 9th	**the** twenty-**ninth**	the 29th
the twelfth	the 12th		

All other ordinal numbers are the cardinal number + **th**:

the fourth	the 4th	**the** twenty-fourth	the 24th
the sixth	the 6th	**the** seventy-sixth	the 76th
the seventh	the 7th	**the** thirty-seventh	the 37th
the fifteenth	the 15th		

EXAMPLES

January is the **first** month of the year.

The **third** day of the week is Tuesday.

The **first** three days of the month are the **first**, the **second**, and the **third**.

Her birthday is on the twenty-seven**th** of December, the twelf**th** month of the year. — see §**21**.

§7.1-3
Possessive Adjectives

A *possessive* adjective indicates the owner of the following noun. It answers the question **"Whose?"**

Whose book is it?

It's *Mary's* book.	(I am Mary)	It's **my** book.
It's *Susana's* book.	(You are Susans)	It's **your** book.
It's *David's* book.	(He is David)	It's **his** book.
It's *Patricia's* book.	(She is Patricia)	It's **her** book.
It's *Mary and Susana's* book.		It's **our** book.
It's *Susana and Patricia's* book.		It's **your** book.
It's *Patricia and David's* book.		It's **their** book.

§7.1-4
Demonstrative Adjectives

A *demonstrative* adjective points out a specific noun. It answers the question **"Which?"**

This indicates a singular or non-count noun that is nearby:

This watch is expensive.

This jewelry is expensive.

That indicates a singular or non-count noun that is farther away:

    That watch is expensive.
    That jewelry is expensive.

These indicates a plural noun that is nearby:

    These watches are expensive.

Those indicates a plural noun that is farther away:

    Those watches are expensive.

§7.1-5
More Noun Determiners

Use adjectives marked *s* with singular nouns, *pl* with plural nouns, *nc* with non-count nouns—see **§5.1** and **5.2**.

any	*s*	one, but not a special one	I will take **any** book.
	pl	more than one, but not special ones	I will take **any** books.
	nc	an unspecific amount	I will take **any** information.
not any	*pl*	zero	I do **not** want **any** presents.
	nc	no amount	I do **not** want **any** money.
no	*pl*	zero	I have **no** books.
	nc	no amount	I have **no** information.
each	*s*	100 percent, one by one	She collects **each** test.
every	*s*	100 percent, one by one	She collects **every** test.
another	*s*	one more	I want **another** cookie.
	s	a different one	I want **another** doctor.
other	*pl*	different, more	She has **other** friends.
	nc	different, more	She has **other** jewelry.
the other	*s*	not this one, that one	He wants **the other** car.
	nc	not this, that	She wants **the other** jewelry.
either	*s*	this one or that one	He wants **either** car.
	pl	these or those	He wants **either** books.
	nc	this or that	He wants **either** furniture.

neither	s	not this one or that one	He wants **neither** car.
	pl	not these or those	He wants **neither** these nor those.
	nc	not this or that	He wants **neither** furniture.
some	pl	more than one	She has **some** pennies.
	nc	more than nothing	He has **some** money.
both	pl	the two	We like **both** dresses.
very few	pl	almost no	He eats **very few** vegetables.
few	pl	not many	They have **few** doctors.
a few	pl	three or four	They have **a few** helpers.
quite a few	pl	enough, or more	There are **quite a few** people.
very little	nc	almost no	She drinks **very little** milk.
little	nc	a small amount	He eats **little** meat.
a little	nc	a small amount, but enough	We have **a little** furniture.
quite a bit of	nc	enough, or more	There is **quite a bit** of work.
enough	pl	the necessary number	I have **enough** clothes.
	nc	the necessary amount	He doesn't have **enough** time.
plenty of	pl	enough, or more	They have **plenty of** toys.
	nc	enough, or more	She has **plenty of** time.
a lot of	pl	a large number	There are **a lot of** cars.
	nc	a large amount	There is **a lot of** traffic.
lots of	pl	a large number	There are **lots of** cars.
	nc	a large amount	There is **lots of** traffic.
quite a lot of	pl	a large number	There are **quite a lot of** leaves.
	nc	a large amount	There is **quite a lot of** crime.
How many?	pl	What number of?	**How many** lamps are there?
not many	pl	a small number of	There are **not many** dishes.
many	pl	a large number of	We have **many** friends.

a good many	*pl*	a large number of	We have **a good many** parties.
a great many	*pl*	a very large number of	There are **a great many** ideas.
too many	*pl*	more than desirable	There are **too many** calls.
How much?	*nc*	What amount of?	**How much** time is there?
not much	*nc*	a small amount of	There is **not much** china.
too much	*nc*	more than desirable	She wears **too much** makeup.
a good deal of	*nc*	a large amount of	There is **a good deal of** food.
a great deal of	*nc*	a very large amount of	There is **a great deal of** heat.
all	*pl*	100 percent, in general	**All** things change.
no determiner	*pl*	100 percent, in general	Things change.
all	*nc*	100 percent, in general	**All** time is valuable.
no determiner	*nc*	100 percent, in general	Time is valuable.
all the	*pl*	100 percent of specific things	**All the** leaves (in our yard) have fallen.
	nc	100 percent of a specific amount	**All the** money (we have) is in the bank.

§7.2 DESCRIPTIVE ADJECTIVES

A *descriptive* adjective tells the size, shape, age, color, origin, material, or the speaker's opinion of a noun. It is the same for singular, plural, and non-count nouns.

Its place is before the noun:

a **big** table	**big** tables	**big** furniture
this **big** table	these **big** tables	this **big** furniture
my **big** table	my **big** tables	my **big** furniture

after a form of *be* or other *linking verb*—see §4.1-2:

The table *is* **big**.	The tables *are* **big**.	The furniture *seems* **big**.
The apple *is* **good**.	The apples *are* **good**.	The fruit *smells* **good**.
The bracelet *is* **pretty**.	The bracelets *are* **pretty**.	The jewelry *looks* **pretty**.

§7.2-1
Proper
Descriptive
Adjectives

A proper adjective identifies a noun as a part of an official place or group. It is written with a capital letter.

EXAMPLES
an **American** flag
the **Mexican** students
my **Italian** shoes
her **European** friends
the **Eastern** seaboard
a **Jewish** holiday
the **Hispanic** community

§7.2-2
Nouns Used
as Adjectives

A noun can describe another noun, and is placed before it, like an adjective. It is never plural, even when its reference is plural.

EXAMPLES
a **glass** jar	a jar made of glass
a **plastic** bag	a bag made of plastic
paper dolls	dolls made of paper
mosquito bites	the bites of mosquitoes
a **school** bus	a bus for a school
a **jewelry** box	a box for jewelry
a **bottle** opener	a tool for opening bottles
a **shoe** store	a store that sells shoes
a **dress** shop	a shop that sells dresses
an **apple** pie	a pie made of apples
an **earring** box	a box for earrings

Some noun + noun combinations are written as one word.

EXAMPLES
dishwasher
motorcycle
trashcan
drugstore

Certain adjectives are formed by adding **ed** to a noun. (See **§8**, page 74 for spelling with **ed** suffixes). These adjectives are often preceded by a color or a number, and are written with hyphens.

EXAMPLES
head	a **red-headed** boy
leg	a **three-legged** stool
point	a **six-pointed** star

§7.2-3
Verbs Used as Adjectives

Present participle forms of verbs, which end in *ing*, can describe nouns.

> **sleeping** babies
> a **caring** mother
> **daring** acrobats
> a **terrifying** experience
> an **interesting** story

Past participle forms of verbs can describe nouns.

> **ironed** clothes
> **dried** flowers
> **saved** money
> **deserted** streets
> a **spoken** language
> a **broken** plate
> **lost** and **found** clothing

Participles that describe people can be confusing. Remember:

the *ing* form is the **cause**;	the *ed* form is the **effect**.
When the teacher is **boring**,	the students are **bored**.
If the movie is **exciting**,	the audience is **excited**.
If the actor is **fascinating**,	the people are **fascinated**.
When the news is **surprising**,	the people are **surprised**.
If the lesson is **confusing**,	the students are **confused**.
If the message is **threatening**,	the reader feels **threatened**.
If the voice is **frightening**,	the listener feels **frightened**.
If the book is **interesting**,	the reader is **interested**.

§7.2-4
Prepositions Used as Adjectives

Certain prepositions (**§17**) can be used as adjectives.

EXAMPLES
the **in** crowd
a **through** street
the **down** staircase

§7.2-5 Compound Adjectives

A *compound* adjective is a combination of two or more words joined by hyphens and used to describe a noun.

EXAMPLES
a **ten-pound** baby
the **six-foot** man
my **two-hundred-dollar** shoes
an **all-night** party
a **well-built** house
an **up-to-date** analysis
a '**round-the-clock** schedule

§7.2-6 Comparing Descriptive Adjectives

Adjectives change to show differences in nouns.

To strengthen an adjective:		To weaken an adjective:
1. add *er* to a one-syllable adjective		put *not as* before the adjective

cheap	cheap**er**	not as cheap
clean	clean**er**	not as clean
cold	cold**er**	not as cold
dark	dark**er**	not as dark
fair	fair**er**	not as fair
fast	fast**er**	not as fast
light	light**er**	not as light
long	long**er**	not as long
near	near**er**	not as near
neat	neat**er**	not as neat
plain	plain**er**	not as plain
short	short**er**	not as short
slow	slow**er**	not as slow
small	small**er**	not as small
soon	soon**er**	not as soon
sweet	sweet**er**	not as sweet

To strengthen		To weaken
2. add *r* to one-syllable adjectives that end in *e*		put *not as* before the adjective

nice	nice**r**	not as nice
close	close**r**	not as close
fine	fine**r**	not as fine
cute	cute**r**	not as cute
late	late**r**	not as late
loose	loose**r**	not as loose

3. double the last consonant, then add *er* to one-syllable adjectives that end in a consonant + vowel + consonant

     put ***not as*** before the adjective

big	big**ger**	not as big
thin	thin**ner**	not as thin
fat	fat**ter**	not as fat
hot	hot**ter**	not as hot
fit	fit**ter**	not as fit

4. drop the *y* and add *ier* to two-syllable adjectives that end in *y*

     put ***not as*** before the adjective

happy	happ**ier**	not as happy
crazy	craz**ier**	not as crazy
funny	funn**ier**	not as funny
lonely	lonel**ier**	not as lonely
lovely	lovel**ier**	not as lovely
easy	eas**ier**	not as easy
lazy	laz**ier**	not as lazy
noisy	nois**ier**	not as noisy

5. add *er* to the following two-syllable adjectives

     put ***not as*** before the adjective

able	abl**er**	not as able
cruel	cruel**er**	not as cruel
gentle	gentl**er**	not as gentle
narrow	narrow**er**	not as narrow
quiet	quiet**er**	not as quiet
simple	simpl**er**	not as simple

6. put ***more*** before other two-or-more-syllable adjectives

     use ***not as*** or ***less*** before the adjective

capable	**more** capable	not as capable **less** capable
careful	**more** careful	not as careful **less** careful
cautious	**more** cautious	not as cautious **less** cautious
common	**more** common	not as common **less** common
decent	**more** decent	not as decent **less** decent
dependable	**more** dependable	not as dependable **less** dependable

difficult	**more** difficult	not as difficult **less** difficult
expensive	**more** expensive	not as expensive **less** expensive
famous	**more** famous	not as famous **less** famous
gracious	**more** gracious	not as gracious **less** gracious
grateful	**more** grateful	not as grateful **less** grateful
handsome	**more** handsome	not as handsome **less** handsome
idle	**more** idle	not as idle **less** idle
important	**more** important	not as important **less** important
jealous	**more** jealous	not as jealous **less** jealous
modest	**more** modest	not as modest **less** modest
patient	**more** patient	not as patient **less** patient
pleasant	**more** pleasant	not as pleasant **less** pleasant
polite	**more** polite	not as polite **less** polite
popular	**more** popular	not as popular **less** popular
responsible	**more** responsible	not as responsible **less** responsible
ridiculous	**more** ridiculous	not as ridiculous **less** ridiculous
thankful	**more** thankful	not as thankful **less** thankful
trustworthy	**more** trustworthy	not as trustworthy **less** trustworthy
truthful	**more** truthful	not as truthful **less** truthful
wonderful	**more** wonderful	not as wonderful **less** wonderful

7. use an irregular form for the following adjectives:

bad	**worse**	not as bad
far	**farther** (in distance)	not as far
far	**further** (in depth)	not as far
good	**better**	not as good

| little | **less** | not as much |
| many | **more** | not as many |

To compare two nouns, use the **positive comparative form of the adjective +** *than*:

A car is **slower than** a train.
This vase is **finer than** that one.
John is **bigger than** his brother.
The book is **funnier than** the movie.
These children are **more polite than** those.
My doctor is **more patient** than his partners.
Maria's new car is **more expensive than** mine.
Is it **better than** yours?

For a negative comparison, use *not as. . . as* or *less. . . than*:

A train is **not as slow as** a car.
That vase is **not as fine as** this one.
John's brother is **not as big as** he is.
The movie is **not as funny as** the book.
Those children are **not as polite as** these.
My doctor's partners are **not as patient as** he is.
My car is **less expensive than** Mary's.
It's not **as good as** yours.

8. to describe a gradual process, use the same comparative adjective two times, with *and*.

The old car went **slower and slower**.
The balloon got **bigger and bigger**.
Her grades are **better and better**.
The weather is getting **colder and colder**.
The girl is **more and more beautiful** every day.

9. More comparisons

as (adjective) as
          Your bag is **as heavy as** mine.
          Your dress is **as pretty as** mine.
          Her shoes are **not as big as** yours.
similar to
     equal to in some ways
          Your bag is **similar to** mine.
different from
     not the same as
          Your dress is **different from** mine.

different than
> not the same as
>> Your dress is **different than** mine.

§7.2-7 Superlative Adjectives

A *superlative* adjective distinguishes one noun from three or more. To make an adjective superlative

1. put **the** before the adjective, and add **st** instead of **r**:

the slow**est**	the nic**est**	the big**gest**	the funn**iest**
the fast**est**	the cut**est**	the fatt**est**	the eas**iest**

2. add **the most** instead of **more** before the adjective:

the most important	**the most** expensive	**the most** ridiculous
the most wonderful	**the most** responsible	**the most** untrustworthy

3. use the irregular form for the following adjectives:

good	**the best**
bad	**the worst**
far	**the farthest** (in distance)
far	**the furthest** (in depth)
many	**the most**
little	**the least**

To make a superlative negative, put **the least** before the adjective:

the least funny	**the least** expensive
the least polite	**the least** important

To express superlatives, use the following patterns:

He is **the tallest** of the three boys.	He is the tallest **of all**.
That is **the funniest** movie I have ever seen.	It is the funniest **of all**.
Fred is **the most handsome** actor in the play.	He is the most handsome **of all**.
This is **the most important** part of the story.	This is the most important **of all**.
It was **the worst** storm this year.	It was the worst **of all**.
He is **the least polite** boy in the school.	He is the least polite **of all**.
That is **the least important** part of the report.	It is the least important **of all**.

§7.3 ORDER OF ADJECTIVES

1. To describe a noun with several adjectives, use the following order. It is better not to use more than three descriptive adjectives together.

First,	a noun determiner	*a, the, my, this,* etc.
then,	a subjective descriptive adjective (the speaker's opinion)	*wonderful, crazy, tired,* etc.
then,	factual descriptive adjectives:	
	size	*big, small, huge,* etc.
	shape	*round, square,* etc.
	age	*young, new, old,* etc.
	color	*red, blue, yellow,* etc.
	origin	*American, Belgian,* etc.
	material	*wood, silk, glass,* etc.
finally,	the noun	*chair, chairs, furniture,* etc.

EXAMPLES

Three valuable old Chinese vases
My favorite pink silk blouse
Some beautiful old Mexican doors
A cheap little blue dress
A few wrinkled old black-and-white photographs
All the friendly new neighbors
A lot of pretty yellow silk ribbons

2. Adjective order exceptions:
   (a) The adjective ***else***, which means "another" or "different," is placed after certain indefinite pronouns. It answers the questions, **"Who else?" "What else?"** and **"Where else?"**

Remember that *some* = positive
not any = negative

Question	Answer	Meaning
Who else is here?	I don't see **anybody else**.	I don't see another person.
	I don't see **anyone else**.	I don't see another person.
	Nobody else is here.	No other person is here.
	No one else is here.	No other person is here.
	I think **somebody else** is here.	I think another person is here.
	I think **someone else** is here.	I think another person is here.

What else do you want?	I don't want **anything else**.	I don't want another thing.
	I want **nothing else**.	I don't want another thing.
	Bring me **something else**.	Bring me another thing.
	I need **little else**.	I only need a few other things.
	I don't need **much else**.	I only need a few other things.
Where else did he go?	He didn't go **anywhere else**.	He didn't go to another place.
	I think he went **somewhere else**.	I think he went to another place.

(b) Descriptive adjectives can also follow the indefinite pronouns

> *anybody, anyone, anything, anywhere*
> *nobody, no one, nothing,*
> *somebody, someone, something, somewhere*
> *little, not much*

when they answer the question **"What kind of?"**

Question	Answer	Meaning
What kind of typist do you need?	I need **somebody good**.	a person who is good
What kind of things did they do?	They did **nothing interesting**.	not anything that was interesting
What kind of furniture do they have?	They don't have **anything nice**.	not anything that is nice
What kind of car does he need?	He needs **something cheap**.	a car that is cheap
What kind of place is she going to for her vacation?	She is going **somewhere warm**.	a place that is warm

(c) *Enough* can precede or follow a noun.
   I have **enough plates** for twenty people.
   I have **plates enough** for twenty people.
   He doesn't have **enough money** to buy a car.
   He has **money enough** to buy a car.

§8.

Verbs—Introduction

A *verb* tells the state or action of a subject.
  Verbs have three *moods:*
- the *indicative,* for most statements and questions
- the *imperative,* for commands
- the *subjunctive,* for expressing wishes and certain untrue situations

  Verbs have two *voices:*
- the *active,* for most statements and questions
    In an *active voice* sentence, the subject is the performer of the action of the verb.
    An active voice sentence emphasizes the subject of the sentence.
- the *passive,* for emphasizing the object
    In a *passive voice* sentence, the subject is the receiver of the action of the verb.

  Verbs have a number of *tenses.* The verb *tense* indicates the time of the action. In certain tenses, verbs change according to the subject of the sentence.
    The verb *be* changes in the present, the past, the present progressive, and the past progressive tenses.
    All other verbs change in the he/she/it form in the present tense and the present perfect tense.

  The *basic verb* = the *dictionary form*
  The *infinitive* = **to** + the basic verb
  The *present participle* = the basic verb + **ing**
  The *past form* = the basic verb + **ed** (Irregular past forms are listed on pp. 330–332 of the appendix.)
  The *past participle* = the basic verb + **ed** (Irregular past participles are listed on pp. 330–332 of the appendix.)

SPELLING OF WORDS WITH *ING* AND *ED* SUFFIXES

Verb		*-ING* Present Participles/ Gerunds		*-ED* Past Participles/ Past Tense Forms/ Certain Nouns Used as Adjectives
ends in 2 consonants	start end	add *ing*	starting ending	add *ed*	started ended
ends in 2 vowels + a consonant	clean rain	add *ing*	cleaning raining	add *ed*	cleaned rained
ends in *w* or *x*	sew fix	add *ing*	sewing fixing	add *ed*	sewed fixed
two syllables, first syllable stressed	listen open master	add *ing*	listening opening mastering	add *ed*	listened opened mastered
ends in vowel + *y*	play obey	add *ing*	playing obeying	add *ed*	played obeyed
ends in consonant + *y*	carry study try cry	add *ing*	carrying studying trying crying	drop *y*, add *ied*	carried studied tried cried
ends in *ee*	agree free see	add *ing*	agreeing freeing seeing	add *d*	agreed freed (saw)
ends in *ie*	die lie	drop *ie*, add *ying*	dying lying	add *d*	died lied
ends in *e*	tape dance	drop *e*, add *ing*	taping dancing	add *d*	taped danced
one syllable, ends in vowel + consonant	shop beg sit get	double the consonant add *ing*	shopping begging sitting getting	double the consonant add *ed*	shopped begged (sat) (got)
two syllables, ends in vowel + consonant, second syllable stressed	occur deter permit	double the consonant add *ing*	occurring deterring permitting	double the consonant add *ed*	occurred deterred permitted

§9.

Verbs—Present Time

§9.1
PRESENT
TENSE

The present tense is used:
- to state facts
- to state habitual action.

It is not used to state present action—see **§9.2.**

§9.1-1
The Verb *Be*

The verb **be** is different from all other English verbs.

1. The present tense forms are:

Singular		Plural	
I	**am**	we	**are**
you	**are**	you	**are**
he	**is**	they	**are**
she	**is**		
it	**is**		

Am, **is**, and **are** can be combined with the subject to make one word. This is a *contraction*. An apostrophe (') takes the place of the lost letter.

Singular		Plural	
I am	**I'm**	we are	**we're**
you are	**you're**	you are	**you're**
he is	**he's**	they are	**they're**
she is	**she's**		
Sue is	**Sue's**		
it is	**it's**		

To make forms of **be** negative, add **not**. Most negatives can be contracted two ways. Use either way.

	Subject + *not*	Verb + *not*
I am not	**I'm not**	
you are not	**you're not**	**you aren't**
he is not	**he's not**	**he isn't**
she is not	**she's not**	**she isn't**
it is not	**it's not**	**it isn't**
we are not	**we're not**	**we aren't**
you are not	**you're not**	**you aren't**
they are not	**they're not**	**they aren't**

To make questions, put the verb before the subject.

Affirmative	Negative	
Am I?	**Am** I **not**? (formal)	
	Aren't I? (informal)	
Is he?	**Isn't** he?	
Is she?	**Isn't** she?	
Is it?	**Isn't** it?	
Are we?	**Aren't** we?	
Are you?	**Aren't** you?	
Are they?	**Aren't** they?	

To show a surprised response, use **subject + verb + ?**

Statement	Surprised Response
You are the best student in the class.	**I am?**
Ronald isn't here yet.	**He isn't? (He's not?)**
We're not sisters.	**You're not? (You aren't?)**

Questions are often answered with a short form:

Affirmative	Negative	
Yes, **I am.**	No, **I'm not.**	
Yes, **he is.**	No, **he's not.**	No, **he isn't.**
Yes, **she is.**	No, **she's not.**	No, **she isn't.**
Yes, **it is.**	No, **it's not.**	No, **it isn't.**
Yes, **we are.**	No, **we're not.**	No, **we aren't.**
Yes, **you are.**	No, **you're not.**	No, **you aren't.**
Yes, **they are.**	No, **they're not.**	No, **they aren't.**

2. Using *be*:

   Be connects the subject of a sentence with a fact about the subject. It has several different meanings.

   (a) *Be* identifies the following noun or pronoun as the same person, place, thing, or abstraction as the subject.

Question	Answer		
Who **are** *you?*	*I*	**am**	*Joseph Carlson.*
Who **is** *she?*	*She*	**is**	*the doctor.*
Who **are** *you?*	*We*	**are**	*your assistants.*
Who **are** *your friends?*	*They*	**are**	*Alex and Sam.*
What **is** *your name?*	*My name*	**is**	*Bill Andrews.*
What **are** *their names?*	*Their names*	**are**	*Michelle and Bonnie.*
What **is** *this?*	*It*	**is**	*a notebook.*
What **is** *that?*	*It*	**is**	*the wind.*
What **are** *these?*	*They*	**are**	*thumbtacks.*
What **are** *those?*	*They*	**are**	*hangers.*

(b) **Be** + a *possessive noun, pronoun,* or *adjective* identifies the owner of the subject.

Question	Answer	
Whose (coat) **is** this?	That (coat) **is**	*Mary's.*
Whose hat **is** this?	It **'s**	*hers.*
Whose (shoes) **are** these?	They **are**	*my shoes.*
Whose gloves **are** those?	They**'re**	*Larry's.*
	They**'re**	*his.*

(c) **Be** + a *descriptive adjective* describes the subject or tells its condition.

Question	Answer	
What **are** you *like?*	I**'m**	*athletic.*
What **is** your friend *like?*	She **is**	*serious.*
What **is** her house *like?*	It **is**	*big.*
What **are** the teachers *like?*	They**'re**	*patient.*
What color **is** the dress?	It **is**	*blue.*
What color **are** his eyes?	They**'re**	*brown.*
How **are** you?	I**'m**	*fine.*
How **is** Annette?	She**'s**	*sick.*
How **are** your parents?	They**'re**	*better.*

(d) **Be** + an *adverb* or *prepositional phrase* identifies the location, origin, or time of the subject.

Question	Answer	
	Location	
Where **is** the car?	It**'s** *there.*	It**'s** *in the garage.*
Where **are** my keys?	They**'re** *here.*	They**'re** *in my hand.*
	Origin	
Where **are** you *from?*	I**'m** *from Virginia.*	
Where **is** he *from?*	He**'s** *from Ohio.*	
Where **are** they *from?*	They**'re** *from Egypt.*	
Where **is** your jewelry *from?*	It**'s** *from Afghanistan.*	
	Time	
When **is** the test?	It**'s** *soon.*	It**'s** *on Monday.*
When **are** the exams?	They **are** *later.*	They **are** *in December.*
What time **is** the party?	It**'s** *at 9 o'clock.*	It**'s** *at night.*
What time **is** our meeting?	It**'s** *at 10:30.*	It**'s** *in the morning.*

(e) The subject **there** + **be** indicates the existence of the following noun.
Use **there is** for a singular or non-count noun.

	Singular Noun
What **is there** in the room?	**There is** *a lamp.*
Is there *a rug?*	Yes, **there is.**
Is there *a piano?*	No, **there isn't.**

	Non-Count Noun
Is there *any food* in the kitchen?	Yes, **there is.**
What **is there** in the refrigerator?	**There is** *milk.*
Is there *any cheese?*	Yes, **there is.**
Is there *any yogurt?*	No, **there isn't.**
How much cheese **is there**?	**There is** *plenty.*

Use **there are** for a plural noun:

How many *children* are there in the family?   **There are** *three* children.
There are *three* boy*s*.

Use **there are** to indicate 0 (zero):

How many girls **are there**?   **There aren't** *any* girls
There are *no* girls.

(f) Use **it** + **is** to indicate the present time and the present weather conditions.

Question	**Answer**
What time **is it?**	**It is** *four o'clock.*
	It is *10:30* A.M.
	It is *midnight.*
How **is** the weather?	**It's** *fine.*
	It's *warm.*
	It's *windy.*
	It's not *raining.*
	It isn't *cold.*

§9.1-2
The Present Tense of Verbs Other than *Be*

All verbs except *be* and models (§9.1-3) form the present tense according to the charts below:

1. Use the *basic verb* with the subjects *I, you, we,* and *they.*
   Use **do** + subject + *basic verb* to make a question.
   Use **do** + *basic verb* to make an emphatic response.
   Use **do** + **not** (**don't**) + *basic verb* to make a negative.
   Use **do** or **don't** without the basic verb to make a short answer.

Statement			I/You/We/They		**work.**
Question		**Do**	I/you/we/they		**work?**
Short Answer	Yes,		I/you/we/they	**do.**	
Negative			I/You/We/They	**do not**	**work.**
Negative Short Answer	No,		I/you/we/they	**don't.**	

For most verbs, use the basic verb + **s** with the subjects *he, she,* and *it.*

Use **does** + subject + basic verb to make a question.

Use **does** + **not** (**doesn't**) + basic verb to make a negative.

Use **does** or **doesn't** without the basic verb to make a short answer.

Statement			He/She/It/		**works.**
Question		**Does**	he/she/it		**work?**
Short Answer	Yes,		he/she/it	**does.**	
Negative			He/She/It/	**does not**	**work.**
Negative Short Answer	No,		he/she/it	**doesn't.**	

2. To spell the *he, she, it* form,
   (a) add **s** to most basic verbs:

he	work**s**	live**s**	rise**s**
she	put**s**	smile**s**	praise**s**
it	laugh**s**	come**s**	lose**s**

   (b) add **es** to verbs ending in *o, ch, sh, ss,* and *x:*

John	go**es**	watch**es**	kiss**es**	box**es**
Ann	do**es**	wash**es**	miss**es**	fax**es**

   (c) for verbs ending in *y* after a consonant, drop the *y* and add **ies**:

cry	The baby	cr**ies**
fly	The airplane	fl**ies**
study	Susana	stud**ies**
testify	Terry	testif**ies**

   (d) use **has** for the verb *have:*

Question	Answer
What **does** she **have** in her hair?	She **has** a ribbon.
What color car **does** he **have**?	He **has** a red car.
What **does** his new car **have**?	It **has** air-conditioning and a sun-roof.

3. Questions and statements
   (a) Use verbs in the present tense to ask for or to state facts.

Question	Short Answer	Long Answer
Do I **need** a license?	Yes, you **do**.	You **need** a license.
	No, you **don't**.	You **don't need** a license.
Do you **have** a ticket?	Yes, I **do**.	I **have** a ticket.
	No, I **don't**.	I **don't have** a ticket.
Do we **need** an appointment?	Yes, you **do**.	You **need** an appointment.
	No, you **don't**.	You **don't need** an appointment.
Do you **need** help?	Yes, we **do**.	We **need** help.
	No, we **don't**.	We **don't** need help.
Do they **live** here?	Yes, they **do**.	They **live** here.
	No, they **don't**.	They **don't live** here.
Does he **have** time?	Yes, he **does**.	He **has** time.
	No, he **doesn't**.	He **doesn't have** time.

To show a surprised response, use the **subject + form of do + ?**

Statement	Surprised Response
I don't like it.	**You don't?**
He doesn't live here.	**He doesn't?**
We don't have any money.	**You don't?**
They have a new baby.	**They do?**
She works in that office.	**She does?**

   (b) Use information questions with the present tense to learn facts.

Question word + **do/does** + subject + **basic verb**

   (1) A *linking verb*, a verb that connects the subject with an adjective or noun that describes the subject, is used—see **§4**.

Question	Answer
	subject + linking verb + adjective
How **do** you **feel?**	I **feel** *tired.*
How **does** she **seem**?	She **seems** *happy.*
How **does** the food **taste**?	It **tastes** *great.*
How **does** it **smell**?	It **smells** *delicious.*
How **does** the chorus **sound**?	It **sounds** *good.*
How **does** the house **look**?	It **looks** *beautiful.*
How **do** I **look**?	You **look** *wonderful.*

Add *like* before a noun:

Question	Answer
	subject + linking verb + noun
Who **do** I **look like**?	You **look like** *your mother—* see **§13**.
Who **does** she **sound like**?	She **sounds like** *a rock star.*
What **does** the music **sound like**?	It **sounds like** *a full orchestra.*
What **does** the dessert **taste like**?	It **tastes like** *oranges and coconut.*
What **does** the perfume **smell like**?	It **smells like** *gardenias.*

    (2) A *direct object* after the verb answers the question—see **§4**.

Question	Answer
What **do** you **want**?	I **want** *a new car.*
What **does** he **want**?	He **wants** *a cookie.*
What **do** you **want**?	We **want** *jobs.*
What **do** they **want**?	They **want** *help.*
Which color **do** you **like**?	I **like** *red.*
Which color **does** she **like**?	She **likes** *blue.*
How much jewelry **do** you **have**?	I **have** *a little.*
How much money **does** he **have**?	He **has** *a lot.*
How many books **do** they **want**?	They **want** *100 books.*
How many tickets **do** you **need**?	We **need** *five tickets.*

    (3) A *prepositional phrase* after the verb answers the question—see **§17**.

Question	Answer
Where **do** you **live**?	I **live** *in the city.*
Where **does** Mike **work**?	He **works** *at the university.*
Who **do** they **study** *with*?	They **study** *with their tutor.*
Who **does** she **talk** *to*?	She **talks** *to her friends.*
What school **do** they **go** *to*?	They **go** *to Spring Hill School.*
What **does** he **write** *with*?	He **writes** *with a pencil.*

    (4) An *adverb* after the verb answers the question— see **§18**.

Question	Answer
Where **do** you **live**?	I **live** *nearby.*
Where **does** Mike **work**?	He **works** *far away.*
How **do** they **speak** English?	They **speak** *well.*
How **does** Jackie **drive**?	She **drives** *fast.*

(5) A *frequency adverb* before the verb expresses general or habitual action—see **§18.4**.

Question	Answer
When **do** you **wear** a coat?	I *never* **wear** a coat.
When **do** you **go** out?	I *rarely* **go** out.
When **does** he **call** you?	He *seldom* **calls** me.
When **does** she **visit** you?	She *hardly ever* **visits** me.
How often **do** you **take** trips?	We *occasionally* **take** trips.
When **do** you **dance**?	I *often* **dance**.
When **do** you **eat** early?	We *frequently* **eat** early.
How often **does** she **help** them?	She *usually* **helps** them.
How often **do** they **arrive** on time?	They *always* **arrive** on time.

The adverb *sometimes* is an exception. Place it either before the subject or at the end of the phrase.

How often **does** he **wear** a coat?	*Sometimes* he **wears** a coat.
	He **wears** a coat *sometimes*.

When no time expression is used,
a positive statement = *sometimes*
a negative statement = *never*

Question	Answer	Meaning
Do you **drink** coffee?	Yes, I **do**.	*Sometimes* I drink coffee.
	I **drink** coffee.	
	No, I **don't**.	I *never* drink coffee.
	I **don't drink** coffee.	
Does she **wear** glasses?	Yes, she **does**.	She wears glasses *sometimes*.
	She **wears** glasses.	
	No, she **doesn't**.	She *never* wears glasses.
	She **doesn't** wear glasses.	

(6) You can also express a usual or habitual activity with an *adverbial* or *prepositional phrase*. Place it at the end of the sentence.

Question	Answer
When **do** you **wear** a coat?	I **wear** a coat *in the winter*.
When **do** you **exercise**?	We **exercise** *in the morning*.
When **do** you **rest**?	We **rest** *in the afternoon*.
When **does** he **celebrate** his birthday?	He **celebrates** his birthday *in July*.
When **do** they **write** letters?	They **write** letters *on weekends*.
When **do** they **stay** home?	They **stay** home *on holidays*.

When **do** we **have** class?	We **have** class *on Mondays.*
When **does** she **study**?	She **studies** *at night.*
When **does** the movie **start**?	It **starts** *at 9 o'clock.*

How often **do** you **exercise**?	I **exercise** *every day.*
How often **do** you **go** to the store?	I **go** *every other day.*
How often **do** you **see** her?	I **see** her *once a week.*
How often **does** she **take** the medicine?	She **takes** it *every three hours.*
How often **does** he **cook**?	He **cooks** *once in a while.*

To emphasize the time expression you can place it before the subject.

Question	Answer
What **do** you **wear** in the winter?	*In the winter* I **wear** a coat.
What **do** they **do** on weekends?	*On weekends* they **write** letters.
What **do** you **do** every day?	*Every day* I **go** to the store.
What **does** she **do** at night?	*At night* she **studies**.

(7) *Because* + **subject** + **verb** answers the question.

Question	Answer
Why **do** you **eat** hot dogs?	I **eat** hot dogs *because I like them.*
Why **does** he **study** so much?	He **studies** *because he wants to learn.*

(8) Using the information questions *Who* and *What*:

Who

(a) "**Who...?**" (in formal English, "**Whom...?**") refers to the object in the answer.
Use the pattern: Who(m) + **do/does** + subject + verb (+ preposition).

Question	Answer
Who(m) do you talk to?	I talk to **Jack**.
Who(m) do we call?	We call **Sara**.
Who(m) do they need?	They need **the teacher**.
Who(m) does she want?	She wants **Val**.

(b) "**Who...**" refers to the subject in the answer.
Use the pattern: Who + *he, she, it* verb. (Do not use *do* or *does* in the question.)

Question	Answer
Who talks to Jack?	**I** talk to Jack.
Who calls Sara?	**We** call Sara.
Who needs the teacher?	**They** need the teacher.
Who wants Val?	**She** wants Val.

Who likes ice cream?	**I** like ice cream.
Who works on Wednesdays?	**We** work on Wednesdays.
Who sings well?	**They** sing very well.
Who lives here?	**Mary** lives here.
Who travels a lot?	**Bill** travels a lot.

Who with a subject answer is always followed by a singular verb, even when the answer is plural.

Who likes ice cream?	**I** do.	**He** does.	**We** do.	**They** do.

Use ***do*** or ***does*** for short answers and for negative questions and answers.

Question	Short Answer
Who likes ice cream?	*I* **do**.
Who works on Wednesdays?	*We* **do**.
Who sings well?	*They* **do**.
Who lives here?	*Mary* **does**.
Who travels a lot?	*Bill* **does**.

Negative Question	Short Answer	Long Answer
Who doesn't like ice cream?	*I* **don't**.	*I* **don't like** ice cream.
Who doesn't work on Wednesdays?	*We* **don't**.	*We* **don't work** on Wednesdays.
Who doesn't travel a lot?	*Bill* **doesn't**.	*Bill* **doesn't travel** a lot.

Compare:

Hans calls Carol.		
Who(m) does Hans call?	He calls ***Carol***.	
Who calls Carol?	***Hans*** calls her.	*Hans* **does**.

What

    (a) **"What...?** refers to the direct object in the answer.
        Use ***do*** or ***does*** in the question:

Question	Answer
What do you like?	I like **ice cream**.
What does she like?	She likes **museums**.
What do they want?	They want **a new car**.

    (b) When **"What?" "Which?"** or **"Whose?"** refer to the subject in the answer, do not use ***do/does*** in the question.

Question	Answer
What works?	**Nothing** works.
What goes here?	**The dishes** go there.
What happens now?	**The excitement** happens now.
What comes next?	**The sad part** comes next.
What causes the flu?	**Germs** cause the flu.
What animals live on the farm?	**Cows and chickens** live on the farm.
Which cars park here?	**Small cars** park here.
Whose dress needs ironing?	**Ann's** dress needs ironing.

What with a subject answer is always followed by a singular verb, even when the answer is plural:

What goes here?	**The toaster** goes there.
	The dishes go there.

Use **do/does** in short answers and in negative questions and answers:

Question	Answer
What *works?*	**Nothing** *does.*
What *doesn't work?*	**The car** *doesn't.*
What *happens* now?	**The excitement** *does.*
What *comes* next?	**The sad part** *does.*
What *causes* the flu?	**Germs** *do.*
What animals *live* on the farm?	**Cows and chickens** *do.*
Which cars *park* here?	**Small cars** *do.*
Whose dress *needs* ironing?	**Ann's** dress *does.*

§9.1-3 Modal Auxiliaries in the Present Tense

A *modal auxiliary* is a word that comes before a verb and modifies its meaning.

The form is simple: use the same form for all persons. Usage is tricky:

- a modal may have a different meaning in another tense
- a modal may have a different meaning in the negative
- a modal may require a different modal as a response
- some modals have negative contractions; others don't
- certain expressions with *be* and *have* have modal meanings, but use the normal forms of those verbs.

Present Tense Modals

1. **Can** expresses *ability*.

Statement			I/You/He/She/It/We/They	can	work.
Question		Can	I/you/he/she/it/we/they		work?
Short Answer	Yes,		I/you/he/she/it/we/they	can.	
Negative			I/You/He/She/It/We/They	cannot/can't	work.
Negative Short Answer	No,		I/you/he/she/it/we/they	can't.	

Question	Answer	Meaning
What **can** you do?	I **can** play the piano.	I am able to play the piano.
What **can** she do?	She **can** play the guitar.	She is able to play the guitar.
Can he play the cello?	No, he **cannot**. No, he **can't**.	He is not able to play it.
Can they sing?	Yes, they **can**.	They are able to sing.

2. *May* and *might* express possibility. They both mean *"I don't know if."*

Statement	I/You/He/She/It/We/They	may/might	work.
Question (not possible)			
Negative	I/You/He/She/It/We/They	may/might not	work.
Contraction (not possible)			

Question	Answer	Meaning
Is he sick?	He **may** be sick. He **might** be sick.	I don't know if he is sick.
Do you have the flu?	I **may** have the flu. I **might** have the flu. I **may not** have the flu. I **might not** have the flu.	I don't know if I have the flu; I need to ask the doctor.

Another word with the same meaning is *maybe*, placed before the subject:

Maybe I am sick.
Maybe I have the flu.

3. *May* and *can* ask for and give *permission.* They have the same meaning, but *may* is more formal.

Statement			You/He/She/They	may	work.
Question		May	I/he/she/we/they		work?
Short Answer	Yes,		you/he/she/they	may.	
Negative			You/He/She/They	may not	work.
Negative Short Answer	No,		you/he/she/they	may not.	

Question	Answer	Meaning
May we have the day off?	Yes, you **may**.	You have my permission.
	No, you **may not**.	You do not have my permission.
May I borrow your book?	Yes, you **may**.	You have my permission.
	No, you **may not**.	You do not have my permission.
Can I borrow your book?	Yes, you **can**.	You have my permission.
	No, you **can't**.	You do not have my permission.

4. *Can*, *could*, *will*, and *would* ask for *assistance*.
   Use *please* before the verb or at the end of the phrase:

Question	Answer
Can you *please* open the door?	Sure!
Could you *please* open the door?	I'll be glad to!
Will you open the door, *please?*	Yes, I **will**.
Would you open the door, *please?*	I'm sorry. I can't help you./Yes, I **will**.

5. *Should*, *ought to*, and *had better* express *advice*.

Statement			I/You/He/She/It/We/They	**should**	**work.**
Question		**Should**	I/you/he/she/it/we/they		**work?**
Short Answer	Yes,		I/you/he/she/it/we/they	**should.**	
Negative			I/You/He/She/It/We/They	**shouldn't**	**work.**
Negative Short Answer	No,		I/you/he/she/it/we/they	**shouldn't.**	

Statement		I/You/He/She/It/We/They	**ought to**	**work.**
Question (use <u>should</u>)				
Short Answer (use <u>should</u>)				
Negative		I/You/He/She/It/We/They	**ought not to**	**work.**
Negative Short Answer (use <u>should</u>)				

Statement		I/You/He/She/It/We/They	**had better**	**work.**
Question (use <u>should</u>)				
Short Answer	Yes,	I/you/he/she/it/we/they	**'d better.**	
Negative		I/You/He/She/It/We/They	**had better not**	**work.**
Negative Short Answer	No,	I/you/he/she/it/we/they	**'d better not.**	

Advice	Meaning
You **should** arrive on time. You **ought to** arrive on time.	It is important that you arrive on time.
You **shouldn't** go alone. You **ought not** to go alone.	It is important that you not go alone.
You **had better** arrive on time. You**'d better not** arrive late.	It is very important that you arrive on time.

6. **Must** and **have to** express *necessity* or *requirement*. **Must** is a modal; **have to** is conjugated like *have*. Use **have to** or **has to** (not *must*) for questions and negative statements.

Statement			I/You/He/She/It/We/They		**must**	**work.**
Question (use *have to*)						
Short Answer (use *have to*)						
Negative (use *have to*)						

Statement			I/You/We/They		**have to**	**work.**
Question		**Do**	I/you/we/they		**have to**	**work?**
Short Answer	Yes,		I/you/we/they	**do.**		
Negative			I/You/We/They	**don't**	**have to**	**work.**
Negative Short Answer	No,		I/you/we/they	**don't.**		

Statement			He/She/It		**has to**	**work.**
Question		**Does**	he/she/it/		**have to**	**work?**
Short Answer	Yes,		he/she/it/	**does.**		
Negative			He/She/It	**doesn't**	**have to**	**work.**
Negative Short Answer	No,		he/she/it	**doesn't.**		

Question	Answer	Meaning
What do you **have to** do? What do you **have to** do?	I **have to** study. I **must** study.	It is necessary for me to study.
Do you **have to** study?	I **don't have to** study.	It is not necessary for me to study.

7. **Must not** expresses *prohibition*.

Statement		I/You/He/She/It/We/They	**must not**	**work.**
Question (Use *may*)				
Short Answer	No,	I/you/he/she/it/we/they	**mustn't.**	

Warning	Meaning
You **must not** cross the street here.	Do not cross the street here; it is dangerous.
She **must not** drive without a license.	Don't allow her to drive without a license.
They **mustn't** make any noise.	Do not allow them to make any noise.

8. *Must* can mean *probably*.

Statement	I/You/He/She/It/We/They	must	be lost.
Question (not possible)			
Negative	I/You/He/She/It/We/They	must not	be lost.

Question	Answer	Meaning
Why isn't he here?	He **must** be lost.	He is probably lost.
Why is she coughing?	She **must** have a cold.	She probably has a cold.
Why do they speak so well?	They **must** practice a lot.	They probably practice a lot.
Why is he resting?	He **must not*** be busy.	He's probably not busy.

*Do not contract **must not** when the meaning is *probably*.

9. *Would like to* expresses desire, politely.

Statement			I/You/He/She/We/They	would	like to work.
Question		Would	you/he/she/they		like to work?
Short Answer	Yes,		I/you/he/she/we/they	would.	
Negative			I/You/He/She/We/They	wouldn't	like to work.
Negative Short Answer	No,		I/you/he/she/we/they	wouldn't.	

Question	Answer	Meaning
What **would** you **like** to do?	**I'd like** to walk.	I want to walk.
What **would** your friend **like** to do?	She**'d like** to rest.	She wants to rest.
Would you **like** a cup of coffee?	Yes, I **would**, thanks.	Yes, please.
Would you **like** a sandwich?	No, thank you. I **wouldn't**.	No, thank you.

10. *Would rather* expresses preference.

Statement			I/You/He/She/We/They	would rather		work.
Question		Would	you/he/she/they	rather		work?
Short Answer	Yes,		I/you/he/she/we/they	would.		
Negative			I/You/He/She/We/They	would rather	not	work.
Negative Short Answer	No,		I/you/he/whe/we/they	wouldn't.		

Question	Answer	Meaning
Would you **rather** dance or watch TV?	I **would rather** dance.	
What **would** you **rather** do?	I**'d rather** dance.	I prefer to dance.
What **would** they **rather** do?	They**'d rather** watch TV.	They prefer to watch TV.
Would your friend **rather** dance?	Yes, he **would**.	He prefers to dance.
	No, he **wouldn't**.	He prefers not to dance.

§9.2
PRESENT PROGRESSIVE TENSE

Use the *present progressive tense*—not the present tense—to express action in progress now.

To make the present progressive tense, use a form of *be* + a **present participle** (a basic verb + **ing**). (See p. 74.)

Statement			I	am		working.
Question		**Am**	I			working?
Short Answer	Yes,		I	am.		
Negative			I	am ('m)	not	working.
Negative Short Answer	No,		I	'm	not.	

Statement			You/We/They	are		working.
Question		**Are**	you/we/they			working?
Short Answer	Yes,		you/we/they	are.		
Negative			You/We/They	are	not	working.
Negative Short Answer	No,		you/we/they	aren't.		

Statement			He/She/It	is		working.
Question		**Is**	he/she/it			working?
Short Answer	Yes,		he/she/it	is.		
Negative			He/She/It/	is	not	working.
Negative Short Answer	No,		he/she/it	isn't.		

Present progressive action began in the past and is not finished.

Use *now, at this time, at the moment, this week, this month, this year, this summer, this afternoon, this evening,* or *tonight* (when the meaning is "now") after the present participle.

Question	Answer	Meaning
What **are** you do**ing**?	I **am** study**ing**.	It is 3:00. I began to study at 2:30; I am not finished.
Who **is** talk**ing**?	Joe **is** talk**ing**.	Joe began to talk ten minutes ago. He is not finished.
What **are** they do**ing** this summer?	They **are** work**ing**.	It is July. They started to work in June. They are not finished.

§9.2-1 Separated Progressive Forms

Use *still* with the present progressive to emphasize the length of the action. Use *not anymore* to tell that the action finally stopped.

Still and *not* separate *be* from the present participle.

> *Pattern:* subject + *be* + *still* + present participle.
> subject + *be* + *not* + present participle + *anymore*.

Question	Answer	Meaning
Are they **still** sleeping?	Yes, they are. They are **still** sleeping.	They continue to be asleep.
Are you **still** working?	No, I'm not. I'm **not** working **anymore**.	I stopped working. I no longer work.

Adverbs that intensify the action of the verb always separate *be* and the *ing* form—see **§18.6**.

We are **really** enjoying our vacation.

He is **hardly** working.

Do not use frequency adverbs, such as *sometimes, never, occasionally, seldom,* etc.—see **§18.4**—with the present progressive.

Informally, *always* used with the present progressive indicates annoyance or worry. It separates *be* from the *ing* form.

Statement	Meaning
He is **always calling** me.	I am annoyed that he calls.
She is **always talking** in class.	It bothers me that she talks in class.
They are **always telling** secrets.	It annoys me that they tell secrets.
He is **always scratching** his arms.	I think he might have the measles.
She is **always sneezing**.	Maybe she has an allergy.

Adverbs and prepositional phrases that tell the time, location, or manner of the action can be placed either between *be* and the *ing* form or at the end of the phrase.

EXAMPLES

She is **now** working on her master's degree.	or She is working on her master's degree **now**.
He is **at present** studying law.	He is studying law **at present**.
We are **here** playing tennis.	We are playing tennis **here**.
They are **at home** waiting for us.	They are waiting for us **at home**.
They are **outside** playing.	They are playing **outside**.
They are **in the house** cooking.	They are cooking **in the house**.
I am **alone** reading in the library.	I am reading in the library **alone**.
They are **happily** playing outside.	They are playing outside **happily**.

§9.2-2 Non-Progressive Verbs

Certain verbs express facts that do not require conscious effort. Use the present tense—not the present progressive—for these verbs.

(a) verbs similar in meaning to *be:*

> *be, exist, appear, seem, smell, taste*

EXAMPLES   **Do Not Use:**

Who **is** she?	She **is** a teacher.	She is being a teacher.
How **does** it **seem** to you?	It **seems** unfair.	It is seeming unfair.
How **is** this perfume?	It **smells** good.	It is smelling good.
Do you **like** the ice cream?	It **tastes** good.	It is tasting good.

(b) verbs that express knowledge, state of mind, or opinion:

> *believe, know, think, understand, remember, forget*

EXAMPLES

Do Not Use:

Do you **believe** in ghosts?	I **don't believe** in ghosts.	I am not believing in ghosts.
Does he **know** the secret?	He **doesn't know** it.	He isn't knowing it.
What **does** your mother **think**?	She **thinks** it's wonderful.	She is thinking it's wonderful.
Do you **understand** the lesson?	Yes. I **understand** it.	I am understanding it.
Does she **remember** me?	No. She **doesn't remember** you.	She isn't remembering you.

(c) verbs that express possession:

have, own, contain

EXAMPLES

Do Not Use:

Do you **have** a car?	Yes. I **have** a car.	I am having a car.
Does he **own** a house?	He **owns** a house.	He is owning a house.
What **does** this box contain?	It **contains** books.	It is containing books.

(d) verbs that express automatic use of the senses:

see, hear, smell

EXAMPLES

Do Not Use:

What **do** you **see**?	I **see** what is in front of me.	I am seeing what is in front front of me.
Do you **hear** a strange noise?	No. I **don't** hear anything.	I am not hearing anything.
Do you **smell** something burning?	Yes. I **smell** smoke.	I am smelling smoke.

(e) verbs that express desire, necessity, or preference:

want, need, prefer, like, love, hate

EXAMPLES

Do Not Use:

What **does** he **want**?	He **wants** a cold drink.	He is wanting a cold drink.
Do they **need** anything?	They **need** books.	They are needing books.
What color **does** she **prefer**?	She **prefers** red.	She is preferring red.
What kind of ice cream **do** you **like**?	I **like** chocolate ice cream.	I am liking chocolate ice cream.
Does he **love** her?	Yes. He **loves** her.	He is loving her.
Does she **like** the apartment?	No. She **hates** it.	She is hating it.

When these verbs express a conscious effort or action, they are used in the present progressive, and have a different meaning.

being	acting on purpose, or pretending
thinking	concentrating one's mind
remembering	concentrating one's mind on a past event
seeing a person	dating a person
smelling	consciously trying to detect or distinguish an odor
loving	enjoying a temporary experience
hating	disliking a temporary experience

EXAMPLES	**Meaning:**
He **is being** difficult.	He is not cooperating.
I **am thinking** about you.	My mind is concentrated on you.
She **is remembering** her wedding.	She is thinking about the day she got married.
She **is seeing** someone special.	She is dating a special person.
We **are smelling** all the perfumes.	We are sniffing all the perfumes to distinguish them.
They **are loving** every minute of their vacation.	They are enjoying their vacation.
She **is hating** her stay in the hospital.	She is unhappy in the hospital.

When **have** means "to temporarily experience," it can be used in the present progressive.

EXAMPLES	**Meaning:**
We are **having** lunch.	We are eating lunch.
She is **having** a good time.	She is enjoying the occasion.
They are **having** fun.	They are enjoying the occasion.
He is **having** trouble parking.	He can't find a parking space.
They are **having** an argument.	They are arguing.
We are **having** a meeting.	We are meeting with each other.
She is **having** a party.	She is entertaining friends.

§9.3 PRESENT PERFECT TENSE

The *present perfect tense* explains the present in terms of past experience at an unspecified time.

    Use a present tense form of **have** + the **past participle** of a verb.

Statement			I/You/We/They	have	worked.
Question		**Have**	I/you/we/they		worked?
Short Answer	Yes,		I/you/we/they	have.	
Negative			I/You/We/They	have not	worked.
Negative Short Answer	No,		I/you/we/they	haven't.	

Statement			He/She/It	has	worked.
Question		**Has**	he/she/it		worked?
Short Answer	Yes,		he/she/it	has.	
Negative			He/She/It	has not	worked.
Negative Short Answer	No,		he/she/it	hasn't.	

For the present perfect,

(a) to express an action that started in the past and is still occurring, use

> *for* + a length of time
> *since* + a specific time or date

Question	Answer	Meaning
How long **have** you **lived** here?	I **have lived** here *for four years.*	I began to live here in the past and I stilll live here.
	I **have lived** here *since 1992.*	

(b) to indicate experience, use

> *ever* and *never* before the past participle
> *before, once, twice, three times, many times*
> at the end of the phrase

Question	Answer	
Have you *ever* **driven** a truck?	Yes, I **have**.	I **have driven** a truck *before*.
	No, I **haven't**.	I **have** *never* **driven** a truck.
How many times **have** you **been** in Mexico?	I **have been** in Mexico *four times*.	
How many times **has** he **seen** that movie?	He **has seen** it *five times*.	

(c) to explain a present condition, use **already** or **not yet**.

> *Pattern:* **have** + **already** + **past participle**
> **have** + **not**   + **past participle** + **yet**

Condition		Reason
I am not hungry	*because*	I **have** *already* **eaten**.
He does not want to see that movie	*because*	he **has** *already* **seen** it.
We are tired	*because*	we **have** not **slept** *yet*.
She is hungry	*because*	she **has** not **eaten** *yet*.

(d) to indicate that the action is not finished, use **so far** or **not yet** at the end of the phrase.

Question	Answer	Meaning
What **have** you **done** *(so far)*?	I **have taken** half of my medicine.	I plan to take the other half later.
How far **has** he **walked**?	He **has walked** four miles.	He plans to walk more.
Have you **finished** eating dinner *yet*?	We **haven't finished** *yet*.	We are still eating dinner.

(e) to indicate expectation of an action, use **yet** at the end of the phrase.

Question	Answer	Meaning
Have you **seen** him?	I **haven't seen** him *yet*.	I expect to see him later.
Has she **cooked** dinner?	She **hasn't cooked** dinner *yet*.	She plans to cook dinner later.
Have they **arrived** *yet*?	No, they **haven't**.	They are not here. We expect them later.

(f) to indicate that an action happened a very short time ago, use **just** or **finally**.

> *Pattern*: **have** + **just**   + **past participle**
> **have** + **finally** + **past participle**

Question	Answer
Have they **arrived** yet?	Yes, they **have**. They **have** *just* **arrived**.
What **has happened**?	The president **has** *just* **left**.
	Our team **has** *just* **won** the tournament.
	We **have** *finally* **finished**.

§9.4 PRESENT PERFECT PROGRESSIVE TENSE

The *present perfect progressive* emphasizes action in progress in the past.

Use the present tense of **have** + **been** + **present participle**.

Use *all day*, *all night*, *all week*, *all year*, *for* (a length of time), *since* (an exact time).

Statement			I/You/We/They	have	been working.
Question		**Have**	I/you/we/they		been working?
Short Answer	Yes,		I/you/we/they	have.	
Negative			I/You/We/They	have not	been working.
Negative Short Answer	No,		I/you/we/they	haven't.	

Statement			He/She/It	has	been working.
Question		**Has**	he/she/it		been working?
Short Answer	Yes,		he/she/it	has.	
Negative			He/She/It	has not	been working.
Negative Short Answer	No,		he/she/it/	hasn't.	

Question	Answer
What **have** you **been doing** all day?	I've **been studying**.
How long **has** he **been driving**?	He **has been driving** for six hours.
Where **have** they **been hiding**?	They **have been hiding** in the garage since ten o'clock this morning.
Where **have** you **been staying**?	We've **been staying** with my sister.

§10.

Verbs—Past Time

§10.1
PAST TENSE

The *past tense* indicates a situation or action that started and ended before now.

Use *before, then, yesterday, last night, last week, last month, last year, five minutes ago, after that* at the beginning or the end of the phrase.

§10.1-1
The Past Tense of *Be*

The past tense forms of *be* are:

Statement			I/He/She/It	**was**	*there.*
Question		**Was**	I/he/she/it		*there?*
Short Answer	Yes,		I/he/she/it	**was.**	
Negative			I/he/she/it	**was not**	*there.*
Negative Short Answer	No,		I/he/she/it	**wasn't.**	

Statement			You/We/They	**were**	*there.*
Question		**Were**	you/we/they		*there?*
Short Answer	Yes,		you/we/they	**were.**	
Negative			You/We/They	**were not**	*there.*
Negative Short Answer	No,		you/we/they	**weren't.**	

Question	Answer
What **was** that noise last night?	That **was** *the wind.*
Whose coat **was** this before?	It **was** *my sister's* coat.
What **was** your mother like then?	She **was** *brilliant.*
What color **was** this dress before you washed it?	It **was** *blue.*
When **was** the test?	It **was** *yesterday.*
What **was** there in the room before?	There **was** *a lamp.*
What time **was** it when he called?	It **was** *five-thirty.*
How **was** the weather last week?	It **was** *rainy.*
Was the test hard?	Yes, it **was.**
Was it long?	No, it **wasn't.**
How **were** you last night?	I **was** *sick.*
Where **were** you?	I **was** *at home.*
Were you alone?	Yes, I **was.**
Were you lonely?	No, I **wasn't.**

Where **were** your keys? They **were** *in my pocket.*
How many people **were** there? There **were** *ten* people.
Were my friends there? Yes, they **were**.
Were they unhappy? No, they **weren't**.

§10.1-2 The Past Tense of Verbs Other than *Be*

The past tense form of all other verbs is the same for all persons.

- Use the **subject** + a **past tense** form for a positive statement.
- Use *did* + a **basic verb** for questions, negatives, and short answers.

Statement			I/You/He/She/It/We/They		worked.
Question		**Did**	I/you/he/she/it/we/they		work?
Short Answer	Yes,		I/you/he/she/it/we/they	did.	
Negative			I/You/He/She/It/We/They	did not	work.
Negative Short Answer	No,		I/you/he/she/it/we/they	didn't.	

To make the past tense form of many verbs, add *ed* to the basic verb, or *d* to a verb that ends in *e*.

ed	*d*
walk**ed**	danc**ed**
help**ed**	chang**ed**
laugh**ed**	believ**ed**

When the basic verb ends in *y* after a consonant, drop the *y* and add *ied*.

cry	cr**ied**
try	tr**ied**
study	stud**ied**
testify	testif**ied**

For other spellings with *ed*, see page 74. Many verbs have irregular past tense forms. A list of common irregular verbs is on pp. 330–332 of the appendix.

EXAMPLES

Question	Affirmative Answer	Negative Answer
What **did** you **do**?	I **ran** to the store.	I **didn't run**.
What **did** he **do**?	He **went** to the movies.	He **didn't go**.
What **did** you **do**?	We **read** in the afternoon.	We **didn't read**.
What **did** they **do**?	They **slept** nine hours.	They **didn't sleep**.

Question	Affirmative Short Answer	Negative Short Answer
Did you **run**?	Yes, I **did**.	No, I **didn't**.
Did he **go**?	Yes, he **did**.	No, he **didn't**.
Did you **read**?	Yes, we **did**.	No, we **didn't**.
Did they **sleep**?	Yes, they **did**.	No, they **didn't**.

§10.1-3 Modals in the Past

Meaning	Present	Past	Past Negative
ability	can	could	couldn't
permission	may	was allowed to	wasn't allowed to
		could	couldn't
possibility	may	may have + past participle	may not have
	might	might have + past participle	might not have
advice	should	should have + past participle	should not have + past participle
necessity	have to	had to	didn't have to
	must		
probability	must	must have + past participle	must not have + past participle

Question	Short Answer	Long Answer
(1) ability		
Were you **able to** work?	Yes, I **was**.	I was able to work.
	No, I **wasn't**.	I wasn't able to work.
Could you work?	Yes, I could.	I **could** work.
	No, I couldn't.	I **couldn't** work.
(2) permission		
Was she **allowed to** work?	Yes, she **was**.	She **was allowed to** work.
	No, She **wasn't**.	She **wasn't allowed to.**
(3) possibility		
Did he work?	He **may have**.	He **may have** worked.
	He **may not have**.	He **may not have** worked.
	He **might have**.	He **might have** worked.
	He **might not have**.	He **might not have** worked.
(4) advice		
Should we **have** worked?	Yes, you **should have**.	You **should have** worked.
	No, you **shouldn't have**.	You **shouldn't have** worked.
(5) necessity		
Did they **have to** work?	Yes, they **did**.	They **had to** work.
	No, they **didn't**.	They **didn't have to** work.

(6) probability

| **Did** he work? | Yes, he **must have**. | He **must have** worked. |
| | No, he **must not have**. | He **must not have** worked. |

§10.2 PAST PROGRESSIVE TENSE

The *past progressive* describes an action in progress when something else happened.

Use the past of *be* + a **present participle**.

Statement			I/He/She/It	**was**	**working**.
Question		**Was**	I/he/she/it		**working**?
Short Answer	Yes,		I/he/she/it	**was**.	
Negative			I/He/She/It	**was not**	**working**.
Negative Short Answer	No,		I/he/she/it	**wasn't**.	

Statement			You/We/They	**were**	**working**.
Question		**Were**	you/we/they		**working**?
Short Answer	Yes,		you/we/they	**were**.	
Negative			You/We/They	**were not**	**working**.
Negative Short Answer	No,		you/we/they	**weren't**.	

Always relate the past progressive action with a time or an event in the past tense.

Question	Past Time or Event	Past Progressive Action
What **were** you **doing**	*at ten o'clock?*	I **was sleeping**.
What **was** he **doing**	*at that time?*	He **was working**.
What **was** she **doing**	*when I arrived?*	She **was sleeping**.
What **were** they **doing**	*when it started to rain?*	They **were having a picnic**.
What **were** you **doing**	*then?*	We **were dancing**.

Another pattern is as follows:

| ***when*** |
| ***while*** + subject + **present participle** + comma + past event |
| ***as*** |

EXAMPLES

When they **were eating**,	the phone rang.
When we **were dancing**,	John called.
While they **were having a picnic**,	it started to rain.
As I **was walking to the store**,	I fell down.

Compare the past progressive tense with the past tense:

Statement	Meaning
My friends **were laughing** when I arrived at the party.	They started laughing before I arrived.
My friends **laughed** when I arrived at the party.	They began to laugh when I arrived.
She **was crying** when he left.	She started to cry before he left.
She **cried** when he left.	She started to cry after he left.

Describe two past progressive events that were happening *at the same time* as follows:

When they **were dancing**, we **were watching** television.
While you **were talking** on the phone, I **was washing** the dishes.
As he **was walking** down the street, he **was singing**.

§10.2-1 Separated Progressive Forms

Still and *not* always separate the *be* from the *ing* form—see **§18.2**.

They *were* **still** *talking* on the phone when I left.
When I got home, they *were* **not** *talking* on the phone **anymore**.

Adverbs of intensity—see **§18.7**—also come between the *be* form and the *ing* form.

He was **hardly** paying attention.
She was **really** trying.

Adverbs of location, time, and manner—see **§18.1, 18.2, and 18.5**—can come between the *be* and *ing* forms or at the end of the phrase.

EXAMPLES

He *was* **there** *watching* TV.	He *was watching* TV **there**.
She *was* **in bed** *sleeping*.	She *was sleeping* **in bed**.
We *were* **later** *walking* down the street.	We *were walking* down the street **later**.
I *was* **slowly** *driving* home.	I *was driving* home **slowly**.

§10.2-2 Non-Progressive Verbs in the Past

Verbs that express facts that did not require conscious effort are not used in the past progressive, even when they have a progressive meaning. Use the **past tense** for most instances of the following verbs (see §9.2-2):

(a) verbs similar in meaning to *be:*

be, exist, appear, seem, smell, taste

EXAMPLES		**Do Not Use:**
Who **was** the teacher?	Miss Smith **was** the teacher.	Miss Smith was being the teacher.
How **did** it **seem** to you?	It **seemed** unfair.	It was seeming unfair.
Was it true?	It **appeared** to be true.	It was appearing to be true.
Did you **like** my perfume?	It **smelled** good.	It was smelling good.
How **were** the pies?	They **tasted** good.	They were tasting good.

(b) verbs that express knowledge, state of mind, or opinion:

believe, know, think, understand, remember, forget

EXAMPLES		**Do Not Use:**
Did you believe her?	I **believed** her.	I was believing her.
Did you know him then?	I **didn't know** him.	I wasn't knowing him.
What **did** they **think** about your haircut?	They **thought** it was beautiful.	They were thinking it was beautiful.
Did you **understand** the lecture?	I **didn't** understand it.	I wasn't understanding it.
Did she **remember** her promise?	She **didn't remember** it.	She wasn't remembering it.
	She **forgot** it.	She was forgetting it.

(c) verbs that express possession:

have, own, contain

EXAMPLES		**Do Not Use:**
Did you have enough money?	No. I **didn't have** enough.	No. I wasn't having enough.
Did she **own** a car?	Yes. She **owned** a car.	Yes. She was owning a car.
What **did** the bottle **contain**?	It **contained** poison.	It was containing poison.

(d) verbs that express automatic use of the senses:

see, hear, smell

EXAMPLES		**Do Not Use:**
What **did** you **see** in the picture?	I **saw** three women.	I was seeing three women.
Did you **hear** the news?	Yes. I **heard** it.	Yes. I was hearing it.
Did you **smell** smoke?	No. I **didn't smell** anything.	No. I wasn't smelling anything.

(e) verbs that express desire, necessity, or preference:

want, need, prefer, like, love, hate

EXAMPLES		**Do Not Use:**
What **did** they **want**?	They **wanted** to buy a diamond.	They were wanting to buy a diamond.
Did you **need** a towel?	No. I **didn't need** one.	No. I wasn't needing one.
Which one **did** you **prefer**?	I **preferred** the red one.	I was preferring the red one.
Did you **like** her dress?	Yes. I **liked** it.	Yes. I was liking it.
Did she **love** him?	No. She **didn't love** him.	No. She wasn't loving him.

When these verbs express a conscious effort or action in the past, they are used in the past progressive, and have a different meaning.

being	acting on purpose, or pretending
thinking	concentrating one's mind
remembering	concentrating one's mind on a past event
seeing a person	dating a person
smelling	consciously trying to detect or distinguish an odor
loving	enjoying a temporary experience
hating	disliking a temporary experience
having	experiencing a temporary occasion

EXAMPLES	**Meaning:**
She **was being** silly.	She was behaving in a silly manner.
He **was being** so kind to me.	He was treating me kindly.
We **were thinking** about you.	Our minds were concentrated on you.
They **were remembering** old times.	They were reminiscing about old times.
He **was seeing** her regularly.	He was dating her regularly.
The dogs **were smelling** the boxes.	The dogs were trying to detect a scent.
They **were loving** their vacation until she got sick.	They were enjoying their vacation until she got sick.
I **was having** dinner when you called.	I was eating dinner when you called.
She **was having** a good time.	She was enjoying the occasion.
We **were having** fun.	We were enjoying the occasion.
Were you **having trouble** with the machine?	Were you experiencing difficulties with the machine?
They **were having** an argument.	They were arguing.
We **were having** a meeting.	We were meeting together.
They **were having** a party.	They were celebrating.

§10.2-3
Was Going To. . .

Was going to + *basic verb* indicates past intentions. Use with *but...*

Statement	Meaning
I **was going to** *call* Mary, **but** I fell asleep.	I planned to call Mary, *but didn't* because I was asleep.
He **was going to** *go* to the party, **but** he got sick.	He planned to go to the party. He *didn't go* because he was sick.
They **were going to** *get* married, **but** her mother disapproved.	They planned to get married. They *didn't* because her mother disapproved.

§10.3
USED TO. . .

Used to + *basic verb* indicates a fact in the past that is not true now.

The form is the same for all persons.

Statement	Meaning
She **used to** *be* the mayor.	She was the mayor before; she is not the mayor now.
We **used to** *be* friends.	We were friends before; we are not friends now.
I **used to** *live* in Europe.	I lived in Europe before; I don't live in Europe now.
He **used to** *smoke*.	He was a smoker; now he never smokes.
They **used to** *visit* me.	They visited me regularly before; now they never visit me.

The **past tense + a past time expression** may be used as an alternative to "used to."

EXAMPLES
I **used to play** with dolls.   =   I **played** with dolls **then**.
They **used to call** me.   =   They **called** me **in those days**.

§10.4
WOULD

Would + *basic verb* indicates "usually" or "always" in the past.

The form is the same for all persons. Use *would* to reminisce about the past.

EXAMPLE
"When we were children, on Sundays we **would** always **go** to our grandmother's house. I **would play** with my cousin. My grandmother **would** always **make** a big dinner, and the

whole family **would eat** at her big table. After dinner, we **would** all **wash** the dishes, and it was fun. My mother **would** always **talk** to her mother in the kitchen for a long time, and then we **would go** home."

A **frequency expression** + the **past tense** may be used as an alternative to this use of *would*.

EXAMPLES

We **would visit** on Sundays.	=	We **often visited** on Sundays.
They **would read** stories to us.	=	They **usually read** stories to us.
He **would** never **help** me.	=	He **never helped** me.

§10.5 PAST PERFECT TENSE

The *past perfect* relates two past actions. Like a "flashback" in a movie, it tells a past event that happened before another past event.
Use *had* + **past participle.**

Statement			I/You/He/She/It/We/They	had	worked.
Question		Had	I/you/he/she/it/we/they		worked?
Short Answer	Yes,		I/you/he/she/it/we/they	had.	
Negative			I/You/He/She/It/We/They	had not	worked.
Negative Short Answer	No,		I/you/he/she/it/we/they	hadn't.	

Use the past perfect with *for, since, before, ever, never, once, twice, already, yet, so far, by then, just, finally*.

(a) Use the **past perfect** with the first event. Use the **past tense** with the later event.

EXAMPLES

We **lived** in New York from 1990 to 1995. We **moved** to Los Angeles in 1995.

We **had lived** in New York *for five years* when we moved to Los Angeles.

Jane **went** to Mexico three times last year. She **went** back this year.

Jane **had gone** to Mexico three times *before* this trip.

Steve **took** his first trip to Hong Kong last summer.
Steve **had** *never* **been** in Hong Kong *before* last summer.

John **ate** lunch at one o'clock. At one-thirty, Mr. Smith invited John to eat with him.
John **had** *already* **eaten** lunch when Mr. Smith invited him.

(b) To emphasize the *result* of the first action, mention the later event first.

EXAMPLES
Tai won the election on Friday. On Saturday he had a big party.
Tai had a party because he **had** *finally* **won** the election.

Mike didn't read the newspaper. He didn't know the news.
Mike didn't know the news because he **hadn't read** the paper *yet*.

Kathleen didn't do her homework yesterday. She couldn't go to the party last night.
Kathleen couldn't go to the party because she **hadn't done** her homework.

Brenda didn't study for the test. She failed the test.
Brenda failed the test because she **hadn't studied.**

§10.6 PAST PERFECT PROGRESSIVE TENSE

The *past perfect progressive* emphasizes action that was in progress before another past event.
Use *had been* + present participle.

Statement			I/You/He/She/It/We/They	had	been working.
Question		Had	I/you/he/she/it/we/they		been working?
Short Answer	Yes,		I/you/he/she/it/we/they	had.	
Negative			I/You/He/She/It/We/They	had not	been working.
Negative Short Answer	No,		I/you/he/she/it/we/they	hadn't.	

EXAMPLES

Question	Answer
What **had** you **been doing** before you started to work?	I **had been studying** *for five years.*
Where **had** she **been living** before she bought this house?	She **had been living** in an apartment *for a long time.*
How long **had** he **been driving** when he fell asleep?	He **had been driving** *for three hours.*

§11.

Verbs—Future Time

The *future* tenses express expectation of action.

Use *later, tonight, tomorrow, day after tomorrow, next Tuesday, next week, next January, next month, next year, soon, some time, ten years from now, at ten o'clock,* before the subject or after the verb.

There are several ways to express future time.

§11.1 PRESENT PROGRESSIVE USED FOR THE FUTURE

Use the present progressive tense with a future time expression.

Question	Answer
What **are** you **doing** tomorrow?	I **am** study**ing** tomorrow.
What **is** she **doing** next week?	She **is** fly**ing** to San Antonio next week.
What **is** he **speaking** about next Friday?	He **is** speak**ing** about health care next Friday.
What **are** you **wearing** to the party tonight?	We **are** wear**ing** blue jeans tonight.
When **are** they **coming** home?	They **are** com**ing** home next month.
Are you **working** tomorrow?	Yes, I **am**.
Is she **coming** home next week?	No, she **isn't**.

§11.2 BE GOING TO . . .

Use a form of *be + going to + a basic verb*.

Question	Answer
What **are** you **going to do** tomorrow?	I **am going to study** tomorrow.
What **is** she **going to do** next week?	She **is going to fly** to San Antonio.
What **is** he **going to speak** about next Friday?	He **is going to speak** about health care next Friday.
What **are** you **going to wear** to the party?	We **are going to wear** jeans.
When **are** they **going to come** home?	They **are going to come** home next month.

Short answers and negatives are the same as for the present progressive.

Question	Answer
Are you **going to study** medicine?	Yes, **I am**. No, **I'm not**.
Is he **going to call** you tonight?	Yes, **he is**. No, **he isn't**.
Are they **going to eat**?	Yes, **they are**. No, **they aren't**.

§11.3 *WILL* AND OTHER MODAL AUXILIARIES

Use a modal auxiliary: *may, might, should*, or *will* + a basic verb to express possibility, probability, promises, or predictions. The forms are the same for all persons.

1. Use *may, might*, or *maybe* when there is a 50 percent possibility of the action.

Question	Answer	Negative Answer
What are you doing tomorrow?	I **may** work. I **might** work. **Maybe** I **will** work.	I **may not** work. I **might not** work. **Maybe** I **won't** work.
What is he going to do tomorrow?	He **may** work. He **might** work. **Maybe** he **will** work.	He **may not** work. He **might not** work. **Maybe** he **won't** work

Question	Short Answer	Negative Short Answer
Are they going to work tomorrow?	They **may**. They **might**. **Maybe**.	They **may not**. They **might not**. **Maybe not**.

2. Use *should* to express expectation (99 percent possibility).

Question	Answer
What time are you going to get here?	We **should** get there around eight o'clock.
When are you going to know the answer?	I **should** know it tomorrow morning.

3. Use *will probably* when there is a 90 percent possibility of the action.

Question	Answer
Are you working tomorrow?	I **will probably** work.
Is he going to work tomorrow?	He **will probably** work.

4. Use *probably won't* when there is a 10 percent possibility of the action.

Question	Answer
Are you working tomorrow?	I **probably won't** work.
Is he going to work tomorrow?	He **probably won't** work.

5. Use **will** + **you** to request action.
Will you (please) work tomorrow?
Will you help me next week?

6. Use **will** to make a promise or commitment.

Question	Answer	Short Answer
Will you please work tomorrow?	I **will** work.	Yes, I **will.**
Will your son help?	My son **will** help, too.	Yes, he **will.**

7. Use **won't** to refuse to act.

Question	Answer	Short Answer
Will you work for me?	I **won't** work for you	No, I **won't.**
Will he help me?	He **won't** help you.	No, he **won't.**

8. Use **will** to predict the future.

Question	Answer
What **will** happen in the twenty-first century?	We **will** travel to the moon for a vacation.
	My baby **will** be a doctor.

9. Other **modals** in the future are:

Meaning	Present	Future	Future Negative
ability	can	**will be able to**	**won't be able to**
permission	may	**will be allowed to**	**won't be allowed to**
assistance	can	**will be able to**	**won't be able to**
	will	**will be glad to**	**won't be able to**
necessity	must	**will have to**	**won't have to**
	have to	**will have to**	**won't have to**
desire	would like	**will want to**	**won't want to**

EXAMPLES
I can't sleep. After I take my medicine, I **will be able to sleep**.
He can't play the piano, and he **won't be able to play**
   unless he practices.
You may not leave the room during the test. You **will be allowed to leave** when the test is over.
She doesn't have to take the test now, but she **will have to take** it before next semester.
I wouldn't like to eat now, but I **will want to eat** before I go
   to bed.

§11.4 PRESENT TENSE USED FOR THE FUTURE

(a) Use the present tense for a scheduled future event.

Question	Answer
When **is** the party?	It **is** tomorrow.
What time **does** the movie **start**?	It **starts** at seven o'clock.
When **do** they **leave** for the beach?	They **leave** next week

(b) Use a present tense verb after **before, after, as soon as**, and **when** to express future time.

Pattern:

Future Tense	Time Expression	Present Tense
I **am going to leave**	*before*	he **gets here**.
He **is speaking**	*after*	the chairman **speaks**.
She **will come**	*as soon as*	she **finishes**.
They **should be** here	*when*	you **arrive**.
I **might cry**	*when*	I **say** goodbye.

§11.5 FUTURE PROGRESSIVE TENSE

The *future progressive* tense expresses action that will be in progress in the future.

To make the *future progressive* tense, use **will be** + a **present participle**.

Statement			I/you/he/she/it we/they	will be	working.
Question		Will		be	working?
Short Answer	Yes,			will.	
Negative				won't be	working.
Negative Short Answer	No,			won't.	

Future progressive action may or may not have already begun; it will not be finished at the indicated future time.

Question	Answer
What **will you be doing** tomorrow at noon?	I **will be studying**.
What **will your sister be doing** then?	She **will be taking** an exam.
What **will your friends be doing** this summer?	They **will be relaxing**.
What **will your son be doing** next year?	He **will be going** to college.
Where **will he be studying**?	He **will be studying** at the university.

§11.6 FUTURE PERFECT TENSE

The future perfect tense is used to express action that will be finished at a specific time in the future.

Use *will have* + **past participle** + *by* + | a specific date
a specific time
a specific event

EXAMPLES
I **will have finished** my exams **by** June 1st.
We **will have read** the reports **by** ten o'clock.
She **will have lost** ten pounds **by** her wedding day.

Use *by the time* or *when* + subject + present tense verb + subject + *will have* + **past participle**

EXAMPLES
By the time I see you, I **will have graduated**.
When I get home, I **will have finished** my exams.
By the time you read this, I **will have left**.

§11.7 FUTURE PERFECT PROGRESSIVE TENSE

The *future perfect progressive* expresses action that will have been in progress for a certain length of time at a specific time in the future.

Use subject + *will have been* + **present participle**

EXAMPLES
I am going to cook from 8 A.M. until 8 P.M.
You are going to come home at 6 P.M.

At 9:00 A.M., I **will be cooking**.
At noon, I **will still be cooking**. I **will have been cooking** for four hours.
At 3:00 P.M., I **will have been cooking** for seven hours.
When you come home at 6:00 P.M., I **will have been cooking** for ten hours.
By the time I go to bed, I **will have been cooking** for 12 hours. After this party, I don't think I will ever want to cook again.

§12.

Verbs—Additional Patterns

§12.1
VERBS USED
AS NOUNS

§12.1-1
The Gerund Form

The *gerund* form is the present participle (basic verb + *ing*) used as a subject or a direct object of a sentence, or as an object of a preposition.

Gerund Subject	Gerund Object	Gerund Object of Preposition
Singing is fun.	I like **singing**.	I am fond of **singing**.

1. Certain verbs are followed by gerund objects:
   admit, appreciate, avoid, consider, deny, discuss, enjoy, finish, imagine, keep, mind, miss, postpone, quit, recall, resist, risk, stop, suggest, tolerate

EXAMPLES

consider	He is considering **taking** the train.
discuss	Did you discuss **visiting** Canada?
enjoy	We enjoy **traveling**.
finish	They are going to finish **cleaning** soon.
keep (on)	He kept (on) **talking** to me.
mind	Do you mind **helping**?
postpone	We will postpone **going**.
quit	They have quit **smoking**.
stop	It has stopped **snowing**.

2. Use *go* + gerund for certain activities:
   go   *boating, bowling, camping, dancing, fishing, hiking, jogging, running, sailing, shopping, skating, skiing, swimming*

EXAMPLES
Please **go bowling** with us.
We are going to **go camping**.
They **went fishing** last week.

113

He **has** never **gone sailing** before.
They have to **go shopping**.

3. Use *feel like* + gerund to express desire to do something <u>now</u>.

What do you **feel like doing**?   I **feel like dancing**.
What does he **feel like doing**?   He **feels like taking** a nap.
What do you all **feel like doing**?   We **feel like going shopping**.

4. Use *would you mind* + gerund to make a very polite request.

Question	Meaning
Would you mind **moving** over?	Please move over.
Would you mind **helping** me?	Please help me.
Would you mind **closing** the window?	Please close the window.

5. Use a gerund after a preposition.

Thank you	*for*	**helping**.
I did it	*by*	**working** quickly.
She is tired	*of*	**living** there.
I want to keep	*on*	**studying**.
He is thinking	*about*	**quitting**.

6. Use a gerund after a possessive noun or pronoun.

I love *Carolyn's* **singing**.
He appreciates *my* **being** here.
We appreciated *his* **helping** us.
They regret *your* **moving** so far away.

§12.1-2 The Infinitive Form

The *infinitive* (*to* + a basic verb) can be used as a subject or a direct object of a sentence.

Infinitive Subject	Infinitive Object
To win the lottery would be fun.	They wanted **to win** the game.

1. Certain verbs are followed by infinitive objects:
   afford, agree, appear, beg, claim, decide, expect, forget, hope, intend, learn, manage, mean, need, offer, plan, pretend, promise, refuse, seem, try, wait, want

EXAMPLES

Let's agree **to meet** next month.
I'm learning **to swim**.
He didn't mean **to hurt** you.
We need **to try** harder.
They are offering **to help** us.

2. Use the infinitive (or *in order* + infinitive) to tell the reason for the action:

I went to the store **to buy** milk.	I went to the store **in order to buy** milk.
They are studying **to get** good grades.	They are studying **in order to get** good grades.

3. Use the infinitive after *too + adjective* and *enough + adjective.*

She is *too young* **to drive**.
She is *tall enough* **to drive**.
She is *not old enough* **to drive**.

4. Use the infinitive after *be supposed* to mean "expected."

You are supposed **to wear** a hat.
It is supposed **to rain**.

5. Use the infinitive after *be glad* and *be sorry.*

I'm glad **to meet** you.
I was glad **to help** him.
She will be glad **to hear** that.
I am sorry **to hear** your news.
He was sorry **to tell** her.

6. Use the infinitive after *it takes* + an amount of time to mean *the amount of time is necessary.*

It takes three hours **to drive** home.
It took ten minutes **to write** the letter.

7. Use the infinitive after a verb + noun or direct object pronoun—see **§15.5**.

    (a) to express a desire for action by another person:
        I *want Loan* **to call** me.
        I *want her* **to call** me.

I *want Charles* **to study** more.
I *want him* **to study** more.

I don't *want Mom and Dad* **to know** the truth.
I don't *want my parents* **to know** the truth.
I don't *want them* **to know** the truth.

(b) to request action:
Ask *Loan* **to call** me.
Ask *her* **to call** me.

Tell Charles **to study** more.
Tell him **to study** more.

I don't want to *ask my parents* **to help** me.
I don't want to *ask them* **to help** me.

§12.1-3
Gerunds vs. Infinitives

1. Certain verbs may be followed by either a gerund or an infinitive and have the same meaning.

begin, continue, hate, like, love

EXAMPLES
They began **studying** last night.
They began **to study** last night.

We want to continue **reading**.
We want to continue **to read**.

She hates **washing** dishes.
She hates **to wash** dishes.

He likes **going** to school.
He likes **to go** to school.

I love **dancing**.
I love **to dance**.

2. After a descriptive adjective (§7.2),

(a) normally, use the infinitive:
It is nice **to see** you.
It is important **to finish** early.
It was great **to be** there.

(b) Informally, you can use *it was* + descriptive adjective + gerund when you say good-bye to someone.
It was nice **knowing** you.
It was fun **working** with you.
It was great **seeing** you.

3. stop
Stop + gerund and *stop* + infinitive have different meanings.

Statement	Meaning
Please **stop talking**.	Don't talk any more.
Please **stop to talk**.	Stop (what you are doing) and talk to me.

4. try
Try + gerund and *try* + infinitive have different meanings.

Try + gerund means "consider as a solution."
I couldn't open the door, so I **tried using** a different key.
He decided to **try taking** aspirin for his headache.

Try + infinitive means "make an effort."
Please **try to sleep**.
I need to **try to practice** every day.

5. *Used to* and *be used to*
Used to + infinitive expresses past action that is no longer true.
I **used to live** in Chicago.   I lived in Chicago before; I don't live there now.

Be used to + gerund expresses present custom.
I **am used to living** in Chicago.   I live in Chicago, and I am accustomed to it.

Get used to + gerund expresses adjustment.
I have to **get used to waking up** at 6:00 A.M.
I can't **get used to going** to bed before eleven o'clock.

6. *Remember* and *forget*
Remember + infinitive = the thought is the cause of the action.
I remembered **to turn off** the iron.

Forget + infinitive = the lack of thought causes the lack of action.
I forgot **to turn off** the iron.

Remember + gerund = the memory is of the action.
I remember **turning off** the iron.

Not forget + gerund = the memory is of the action.
I will never forget **shaking hands** with the president!

7. Consider

Consider + direct object + infinitive = believe about
  someone or something
I consider him **to be** very intelligent.
I consider her **to be** my friend.
Consider + gerund = think about in order to decide
You should consider **taking** that course.
We are considering **going** to that play.

8. Imagine

Imagine + direct object + infinitive = possibly believe about
someone or something
I imagine her **to be** a lot of fun.
I don't imagine him **to be** a very good cook.

Imagine + gerund = dream about
I can imagine **skiing** down those mountains.
I can't imagine **living** with him.

9. Come

Come may be followed by a basic verb or an infinitive in the
imperative or the future tenses, with the same meaning.
Come see us.   **Come to see** us.
They will **come visit** soon.   They will **come to visit** soon.

In other tenses, *come* is followed by an *infinitive*.
You **came to see** us.
They **came to visit**.
We **have come to tell** you a secret.

10. Help

Help is followed by a basic verb instead of a gerund or
infinitive.
Please **help clean** the floor.
I have to **help sell** tickets.
They **helped shovel** the snow.

A direct object may be used.
Please **help** me **clean** the floor.
I have to **help** them **sell** tickets.
They **helped** us **shovel** the snow.

11. *Make* + direct object + basic verb = to force
Have + direct object + basic verb = to arrange
Let + direct object + basic verb = to allow

EXAMPLES	Meaning:
She **makes** him go outside	She forces him to go outside.
She **has** him go outside.	She arranges for him to go outside.
She **lets** him go outside.	She allows him to go outside.
They **made** her cut her hair.	They forced her to cut her hair.
They **had** her cut her hair.	They arranged for her to cut her hair.
They **let** her cut her hair.	They allowed her to cut her hair.

§12.2 QUOTED AND REPORTED SPEECH

1. **Direct Quotes**

To repeat someone's exact words, use quotation marks before the quote and after the comma, period, question mark, or exclamation point.

EXAMPLES
Bob said, **"It's snowing!"**
Mary said, **"I'm not going to go to school."**
"I will not shovel snow," said Mary.
I said, **"It snowed yesterday, too."**

If the quote comes first, end the quote with a comma instead of a period. However, do not change question marks or exclamation points.

EXAMPLES
"She's sick," said Mieko.
"Should we call the doctor?" she asked.
"Let's go to the hospital!" cried Kim.

If the quote is second, use a comma after the introduction.

EXAMPLES
Mieko said, "She's sick."
She asked, "Should we call the doctor?"
Kim cried, "Let's go to the hospital!"

2. **Reported Speech**
To tell what someone said, use:

Subject + Past Verb + (*that*) + Subject + Verb in an earlier tense

A present or future statement changes to the past:
Bob said, "It's snowing."
Bob said (that) it **was snowing**.

Bob said, "Mary works hard at school."
Bob said (that) Mary **worked** hard at school.

Mary said "I'm not going to go to school."
Mary said (that) she **wasn't going to go** to school.

Mary said "I will not shovel snow."
Mary said (that) she **would** not **shovel** snow.

A past or present perfect tense statement changes to the past perfect:
I answered, "It snowed yesterday."
I answered that it **had snowed** the day before.

Bob said, "Mary worked hard at school."
Bob said (that) Mary **had worked** hard at school.

I said, "It has snowed five times this winter."
I said (that) it **had snowed** five times this winter.

3. Direct Quotes of Questions
To repeat exactly what someone asked, use quotation marks.

Yes or No Questions:
"Are you going to work?" asked Mary.
"Will you help me?" asked Patsy.
"Have you eaten breakfast?" asked Abu.

Information Questions:
"What are you doing?" asked Bob.
"Why did Judy leave?" I asked.
"Where have they been?" Jane asked.

4. Reported Questions
To tell what someone asked:

Yes or No Questions:

Subject + Verb + *if* + Subject + Verb in an earlier tense

Mary asked if I **was going** to work.
Patsy asked if we **would help** her.
Abu asked if I **had eaten** breakfast.

Information Questions:

> Subject + Verb + Question Word + Subject + Verb in an
> earlier tense

Bob asked what I **was doing**.
I asked why Judy **had left**.
Jane asked where they **had been**.

§12.3 INCLUDED QUESTIONS AND STATEMENTS

To ask questions within questions, use:

Question Phrase	+	Question Word	+	Subject	+	Verb + ?
Do you know		who		that man		is?
Can you tell me		where		the White House		is?
Will you find out		when		they		are coming?
Do you know		why		he		did that?

To answer these questions, use:

Answer Phrase	+	Question Word	+	Subject	+	Verb
I don't know		who		that man		is.
I can't tell you		where		the White House		is.
I can't find out		when		they		are coming.
I don't care		when		they		are coming.

When the included question or answer refers to future action, you can use:

> Question Phrase or Answer Phrase +
> Question Word + Infinitive

EXAMPLES

Do you know what we should do?

Can you tell me how I can get there?

Will you find out when we should arrive?

Do you know who(m) I can call?

Can you tell her where she should go?

Do you know what **to do**?

Can you tell me how **to get** there?

Will you find out when **to arrive**?

Do you know who(m) **to call**?

Can you tell her where **to go**?

I don't know what we should do.	I don't know what **to do**.
I can't tell you how you can get there.	I can't tell you how **to get** there.
I will find out when we should arrive.	I will find out when **to arrive**.
I don't know who(m) you should call.	I don't know who(m) **to call**.
I don't know where I should go.	I don't know where **to go**.

§12.4 TAG QUESTIONS

A *tag question* is often added to a statement, asking the listener to agree with, or confirm the speaker's statement. When you want your listener to agree with you

(a) after a positive statement, use a negative tag.

Be

Statement	Tag Question	Response of Agreement	Response of Disagreement
positive	**negative**		
I am crazy	am I not? aren't I?	Yes, you are.	No, you aren't.
I'm studying hard,	aren't I?		
You are smart,	aren't you?	Yes, I am.	No, I'm not.
You are studying,	aren't you?		
We are lost,	aren't we?	Yes, we are.	No, we aren't.
They are wonderful,	aren't they?	Yes, they are.	No, they aren't.
She is sweet,	isn't she?	Yes, she is.	No, she isn't.
He is nice,	isn't he?	Yes, he is.	No, he isn't.
It is interesting,	isn't it?	Yes, it is.	No, it isn't.

All Other Verbs

Statement	Tag Question	Response of Agreement	Response of Disagreement
positive	**negative**		
I work hard,	don't I?	Yes, you do.	No, you don't.
You study a lot,	don't you?	Yes, I do.	No, I don't.
We try our best,	don't we?	Yes, you do.	No, you don't.
They live here,	don't they?	Yes, they do.	No, they don't.
She works hard,	doesn't she?	Yes, she does.	No, she doesn't.
He studies a lot,	doesn't he?	Yes, he does.	No, he doesn't.
It works,	doesn't it?	Yes, it does.	No, it doesn't.

(b) after a negative statement use a positive tag.

Be

Statement	Tag Question	Response of Agreement	Response of Disagreement
negative	**positive**		
I'm not crazy,	am I?	No, you aren't.	Yes, you are.
You aren't late,	are you?	No, I'm not.	Yes, I am.
We aren't ready,	are we?	No, we aren't.	Yes, we are.
They aren't honest,	are they?	No, they aren't.	Yes, they are.
She isn't helpful,	is she?	No, she isn't.	Yes, she is.
He isn't sorry,	is he?	No, he isn't.	Yes, he is.

All Other Verbs

Statement	Tag Question	Response of Agreement	Response of Disagreement
negative	**positive**		
I don't need that,	do I?	No, you don't.	Yes, you do.
You don't care,	do you?	No, I don't.	Yes, I do.
We don't want that,	do we?	No, we don't.	Yes, we do.
They don't look good,	do they?	No, they don't.	Yes, they do.

Follow the same patterns for other tenses.

Statement	Tag Question	Response of Agreement	Response of Disagreement
negative	**positive**		
You were here,	weren't you?	Yes, I was.	No, I wasn't
He smiled at me,	didn't he?	Yes, he did.	No, he didn't.
We have been there,	haven't we?	Yes, we have.	No, we haven't.
They had seen it,	hadn't they?	Yes, they had.	No, they hadn't.

Statement	Tag Question	Response of Agreement	Response of Disagreement
negative	**positive**		
You weren't here,	were you?	No, I wasn't.	Yes, I was.
He didn't smile at me,	did he?	No, he didn't.	Yes, he did.
We haven't been there,	have we?	No, we haven't.	Yes, we have.
They hadn't seen it,	had they?	No, they hadn't.	Yes, they had.

§12.5 USING VERBS WITH INDIRECT OBJECTS

There are several patterns for sentences that have indirect objects—see **§6.2-3**.

1. After the verbs *bring, give, hand, lend, offer, owe, pass, pay, sell, send, serve, take, show, read, sing, teach, tell, write* use:

> verb + direct + preposition + indirect
>   object   *to*   object
>   (noun or pronoun)

or

> verb + indirect + direct
>   object   object noun
>   (do not use pronoun)

EXAMPLES

He brings *flowers* to me.	He brings me *flowers*.
I sold *the car* to him.	I sold him *the* car.
They have told *the truth* to us.	They have told us *the truth*.
She is going to serve *lamb* to us.	She is going to serve us *lamb*.

Possible:	**Do Not Use:**
He brings *them* to me.	He brings me *them*.
I sold *it* to him.	I sold him *it*.
They have told *it* to us.	They have told us *it*.
She is going to serve *it* to us.	She is going to serve us *it*.

Use the same patterns with the preposition *for* after the verbs *bake, buy, build, cook, do, draw, find, get, make, save*.

EXAMPLES

She is baking *a cake* for him.	She is baking him *a cake*.
He bought *a ring* for her.	He bought her *a ring*.
They have drawn *pictures* for me.	They have drawn me *pictures*.
Please save *a seat* for me.	Please save me *a seat*.

Possible:	**Do Not Use:**
She is baking *it* for him.	She is baking him *it.*
He bought *it* for her.	He bought her *it.*
They have drawn *them* for me.	They have drawn me *them.*
Please save *it* for me.	Please save me *it.*

2. After the following verbs, only the first pattern is possible:

with *to*	*admit, announce, describe, explain, introduce, mention, prove, recommend, repeat, report, say, suggest*
with *for*	*answer, cash, change, close, open*

	Do Not Use:
She is describing the house to him.	She is describing him the house.
We explained the lesson to them.	We explained them the lesson.
I mentioned the party to her.	I mentioned her the party.
Can you change a twenty for me?	Can you change me a twenty?
Please answer this question for me.	Please answer me this question.

After **ask**, only the second pattern is possible:

	Do Not Use:
May I ask you a question?	May I ask a question to you?
Did you ask him a question?	Did you ask a question to him?

§13.

Verbs—Special Usage

1. *Get* + adjective
Use *get*—to mean "become"—before an adjective.
Commonly used adjectives with *get* include:

> get angry, get mad, get anxious, get nervous, get
>   excited, get worried
> get tall, get big, get old, get fat, get thin, get gray, get bald
> get rich, get poor, get busy
> get hungry, get thirsty, get cold, get hot
> get sleepy, get tired, get sick, get well, get dizzy, get
>   better, get worse
> get late, get dark, get light, get wet, get dry

Other examples:
> I **get cold** in the evenings.
> Are you going to **get involved**?
> He **gets excited** at football games.
> Are you **getting bored**?
> It is **getting dark**.
> We **got confused** without the map.
> They **got lost**, too.
> Did you **get married**?
> No, but we **got engaged**.

2. **Have** or **get** something **done**
To express that somebody else is doing something for you, use:

> **have** + noun + past participle
> or **get** + noun + past participle

EXAMPLES

Statement	Meaning
I **have** my hair **done**. I **get** my hair **done**.	Somebody else does my hair.
We **have** our grass **cut** every week. We **get** our grass **cut** every week.	Somebody else cuts our grass.

She **had** her curtains **made** last year.	Somebody else made her curtains.
She **got** her curtains **made** last year.	
He **has** his oil changed often.	Somebody else changes his oil.
He **gets** his oil changed often.	

3. *Ask* and *ask for*

ask + *indirect object* = to direct a question to somebody

Ask *Mary* if she is sick.

I need to **ask** *her* when she is leaving.

Did you **ask** *him* who his friend is?

ask for + *direct object* = to request or order something

Ask for a *hamburger* with onions.

I need to **ask for** more *money*.

Did you **ask for** *help*?

4. *Borrow* and *lend*

borrow = to receive a loan

May I please **borrow** a dollar (from you)?	Yes, you may **borrow** it.

lend = to give a loan

Will you **lend** me a dollar?	Yes, I will you **lend** you a dollar.

5. *Speak* and *talk*

speak = use a language

       give a serious message

       give a public speech

He doesn't **speak** Russian.

The teacher **spoke** to me about my son's behavior.

The president is going to **speak** on television.

talk = to converse

I hope we can **talk** soon.

She **talks** to her mother on the phone every day.

6. *Go* and *come, take* and *bring*

go = movement to a place where neither the speaker nor listener is

Please **go** to the store.

I'm **going** to Janet's house.

My friends **went** home.

come = movement to where the listener is
> I want to **come** see you.
> I am **coming** to your house tomorrow.
> We **came** to your party last week.
> Is your family going to **come** to visit?

come = movement to where the speaker is
> Please **come** see me.
> Are you **coming** to my house tomorrow?
> You **came** to my party, didn't you?
> I wish my family could **come** to visit.

take and *bring* = to have with you
Use *take* with *go*.
> **Go** home and **take** your things.
> We're **going** to Janet's party, and we're **taking** a gift.
> He **went** to school and **took** his lunch.

Use *bring* with *come*.
> I'm **coming** to your house, and I'm **bringing** a pizza.
> Did your husband **come** home from his trip? What did he **bring** you?
> I hope your children **came** home from school, and **brought** their books.

> **Come** home, dear daughter, and **bring** your things.
> If you **come** to my party, will you **bring** some cookies?
> Betty **came** over and **brought** her new boyfriend.

7. *Say* and *tell*
say = put into words
Do not use an indirect object with *say*. Use *to* + **direct object**.
> Please **say** what you think. Please **say to me** what you think.
> What did your friend **say**? What did he **say to you**?
> He **said** he wanted to go home. He **said to me** that he wanted to go home.

tell + **indirect object**

> (a) to put into words:
>> Please **tell me** what you think.
>> What did your friend **tell you**?
>> He **told me** he wanted to go home.

> (b) to relate a story or event:
>> He **told us** the story of his life.
>> Please **tell me** what happened.

   (c) to inform:
> He is going to **tell** the police.
> I hope nobody **tells** her parents.
> She **told him** her secret.

   (d) with *the truth*:
> Always **tell the truth**.

8. *Do* and *make*

do = to act or perform
Use *do* before nouns that imply "work" or "effort."
> **do work**
> **do exercises**
> **do homework**
> **do housework**
> **do laundry**
> **do dishes**

make = to create, fabricate, or build
> **make a cake, pie, sandwich**
> **make a dress, suit**
> **make a paper airplane**

make **+ direct object + basic verb** = to force somebody or something to do something
> Don't **make me go**.
> He **made her do** that.
> You can't **make them study**.

Use *make* in many special expressions. For example:

	Meaning
make a bed	arrange the bedding
make a mess	spoil
make an appointment	arrange a meeting
make arrangements	plan
make a mistake	err
make a fuss	complain
make money	earn money

9. *Hope* and *wish*

Hope expresses a desire for something possible.

Present desire for future:
> I **hope** he wins, or I **hope** he will win.
> I **hope** I get a promotion, or I **hope** I will get a promotion.

Present desire when past action is unknown:
> I **hope** he won.
> I **hope** I got a promotion.

Past desire about past:
> I **hoped** he would win.
> I **hoped** I would get a promotion.

Wish expresses a desire for an opposite situation.

Statement	Meaning
Present	
I **wish** he were here.	I am sorry that he isn't here.
He **wishes** I lived there.	He is sorry that I don't live there.
Past	
I **wish** he had been here.	I am sorry that he wasn't here.
She **wishes** we had had a car.	She is sorry that we didn't have a car
Future	
I **wish** I could travel.	I am sorry that I won't be able to travel.
She **wishes** she could go home.	She is sorry that she can't go home.

10. *Watch* and *look at*

You **watch** something that moves, and **look at** something that is still.
> He **watches** TV a lot.
> They **are watching** a baseball game.
> She **looks at** magazines.
> She **is looking at** some photographs.

Watch can mean "to take care of."
> Her sister **is watching** the baby.

11. *Look, look alike*, and *look like*

look + adjective = to seem
> She **looks** tired.
> He **looks** unhappy.
> They **don't look** interested.

alike = the same
> They are **alike**. They are the same.
> They **look alike**. They seem the same physically.

look like + noun = to be similar to, to resemble
> She **looks like** her mother. They **look alike**.
> He doesn't **look like** his brother. They don't **look alike**.
> They **look like** movie stars.

It + *looks like* + subject + verb = to be apparent
  It **looks like** she is tired.
  It **looks like** he is unhappy.
  It **looks like** they are not interested.

It + *looks like* + subject + future verb = a prediction
  It **looks like** it is going to rain.
  It **looks like** they're going to get married.
  It **looks like** he will win.

12. *Belong to* has two meanings:

   (a) be a part of, or a member of something:
       I **belong** to the Garden Club.
       She **belongs** to the Rock Spring Church.

   (b) be owned by someone:
       That book **belongs** to me.
       Those dogs **belong** to our neighbors.

13. *Depend on* has two meanings:

   (a) expect support from someone:
       They **depend** on their parents for everything.

   (b) based on:
       Whether we go on a picnic **depends on** the weather.
       It **depends on** the weather.

§14.

Verbs—Passive Voice

The verb tenses outlined in the previous sections have been in the *active voice.* They give importance to the person who *does* the action. The person is the subject of the sentence.

EXAMPLES

My husband painted the house.
Thomas Edison invented the light bulb.
Shakespeare wrote *Twelfth Night.*
Jeremy loves me.

The *passive voice* is used to shift the emphasis from subject to object. The person who does the action is not the important focus of the sentence.

To form the *passive voice*, use a form of *be* + a **past participle**.

Present Tense	I **am**	misunderstood.
Modals	I can **be**	misunderstood.
Present Progressive	I **am being**	misunderstood.
Future	I **am** going to **be**	misunderstood.
	I will **be**	misunderstood.
Present Perfect	I have **been**	misunderstood.
Past	I **was**	misunderstood.
	I used to **be**	misunderstood.
Past Progressive	I **was being**	misunderstood.
Past Perfect	I had **been**	misunderstood.

To use the passive voice with a modal auxiliary, use the **modal** + *be* + **past participle**.

Present	I **can be**	misunderstood.
Future	I **could be**	misunderstood.
Past	I **could have been**	misunderstood.
Present	I **may be**	misunderstood.
Future	I **might be**	misunderstood.
Past	I **might have been**	misunderstood.
Present/Future	He **must be**	understood.
	He **has to be**	understood.
Past	He **had to be**	understood.

Passive voice sentences give importance to the thing or person that *receives* the action. The receiver of the action is now the subject of the sentence.

EXAMPLES
The house **was painted** (last month).
The light bulb **was invented** (a long time ago).
Twelfth Night **was written** (in Old English).
I **am loved** (and I am happy).

The *passive voice* allows the speaker to avoid identifying the "doer" of the action.

EXAMPLES

She **is spoiled**.	("Somebody" spoils her.)
She **is being punished**.	("Somebody" is punishing her.)
I **am** going to **be promoted**.	("Somebody" is going to promote me.)
We will **be helped**.	("Somebody" will help us.)
We have **been robbed**!	("Somebody" robbed us.)
He **was told** the truth.	("Somebody" told him the truth.)
He **was being helped**.	("Somebody" was helping him.)
They **have been sent** away.	("Somebody" has sent them away.)

§15.

Verbs—Imperative Mood

§15.1
INSTRUCTIONS, SUGGESTIONS, OR COMMANDS

To give instructions, suggestions, or commands, use the *imperative mood*. To make the imperative, use a basic verb with no subject.

Use *please* before the verb or at the end of the phrase.

Please **come** here!
   Come here, *please*!

Please **write** soon.
   Sign your name, *please*.

To make a negative suggestion or command, use *don't* + *basic verb*.

Please **don't come** back!
   Don't come back, *please!*

Please **don't drive** fast.
   Don't be late.
   Don't forget to call me.

EXAMPLES

Giving Directions

To get to my house,
   Get on Route 66, going west.
   Take Exit 67 E.
   Go straight for three miles.
   Turn right on Spring Street.
   Pass three traffic lights.
   Turn left at the fourth light, onto Maple Avenue.
   Look for my house on the right. It is the red brick colonial with the dogwood tree in front.
   Don't park on the street.
   Turn into my driveway, and **park** there.

Giving Instructions

To use the microwave,

> **Put** the food on a paper, plastic, or glass plate.
> **Do not use** a plate with any metal parts.
> **Cover** the food loosely with a paper towel.
> **Pull** the door open.
> **Put** the plate in the center of the oven.
> **Close** the oven door.
> **Press** the timer button.
> **Indicate** the number of minutes needed for the dish.
> **Press** the start button.
> **Wait** the required time.
> **Listen** for the beep.
> **Pull** the door open, and **remove** your warmed food.

§15.1-1 Suggestions That Include the Speaker

To make suggestions that include the speaker, use
let's (not) + *basic verb.*

EXAMPLES

Please **let's go** home.	**Let's not stay** late, *please*!
Let's go home, *please!*	**Let's not argue**.
Let's eat out.	**Let's not spend** too much money.

§15.1-2 More Formal Suggestions

To make more formal suggestions that include the speaker,
use **Shall we** + *basic verb* + **?**

Shall we dance?
Shall we eat at 8 o'clock?

§15.2 *YOU* TO MEAN "ANYBODY"

To ask for or give instructions in conversation, use the
pronoun *you* to mean "anybody"—see **§6.1-1**.

Question	Answer
How **do you** start the machine?	**You** push the button.
How **do you** get to the airport from here?	**You** cross the bridge and go straight ahead.

§15.3 INDIRECT COMMANDS

If you want another person to do something, instead of a command you can use: *want* + name of person (or direct object pronoun) + infinitive—see **§12.1-2**.

EXAMPLES

I want Liz to call me.	I want her to call me.
They want Barry to go home.	They want him to go home.
She wants Helena to stay a little longer.	She wants her to stay a little longer.
He wants his friends to lend him the money.	He wants them to lend him the money.
We wanted Max to finish college.	We wanted him to finish college.
Do you want me to help you?	Yes, I want you to help me.

§16.

Verbs—Subjunctive Mood

The *subjunctive mood* is used
• after certain verbs that express suggestions or demands for future actions.
• after certain expressions that indicate necessity.
• after *wish*, and after *if* to express untrue situations.

§16.1 PRESENT SUBJUNCTIVE

Use the **basic verb** for all persons to form the **present subjunctive**.

1. *Be*

Singular		Plural	
I	**be**	we	**be**
you	**be**	you	**be**
he	**be**	they	**be**
she	**be**		
it	**be**		

2. All Other Verbs

Singular		Plural	
I	**work**	we	**work**
you	**work**	you	**work**
he	**work**	they	**work**
she	**work**		
it	**work**		

EXAMPLES

I suggest that you **be** quiet.

I suggested that you **be** quiet.

He recommends that we **be** on time.

He will recommend that we **be** on time.

She asks that they **be** responsible.

She asked that they **be** responsible.

We demand that you **be** honest.

We will demand that you **be** honest.

They insist that we **be** patient.

They are insisting that we **be** patient.

It is necessary that you **be** careful.

It was necessary that you **be** careful.

It is important that I **be** strong.

It has been important that I **be** strong.

We suggest that he **study** more.

We suggested that he **study** more.

They recommend that we **try** again.

She recommended that we **try** again.

She asks that he **return** next week.

She has asked that he **return** next week.

It is necessary that he **come** home.

It was necessary that he **come** home.

It is important that she **bring** the paper tomorrow.

It was important that she **bring** the paper tomorrow.

§16.2 PAST SUBJUNCTIVE

Regular **past subjunctive** forms are the same as indicative past tense forms:

worked	played	had	did	went	thought

There is one irregular form:

the verb *be* used with *I, he, she,* and *it* is **were**, not *was.*

EXAMPLES

I wish I **were**	If I **were**
I wish he **were**	If he **were**
She wishes she **were**	If she **were**
We wish it **were**	If it **were**

1. Use the past subjunctive after *wish* to express regret that something is not true.

Regret	Subjunctive Sentence
I regret that I am not thin.	I wish I **were** thin.
He regrets that she is not here.	He wishes she **were** here.
She regrets that Kathy does not live nearer.	She wishes Kathy **lived** nearer.
We regret that we do not have a car.	We wish we **had** a car.
They regret that John doesn't work harder.	They wish John **worked** harder.

2. Use the past subjunctive after *if* to express your probable reaction to an untrue situation.

If + subject + **subjunctive**   + subject + **would** + **basic verb**

If   I   **wanted** that dress,   I   **would**   **buy** it.
Meaning: I don't want that dress, and I am not going to buy it.

If   I   **were** you,   I   **would**   **call** her.
Meaning: I think you should call her.

If   you **worked** here,   you   **would**   **understand**.
Meaning: You do not understand because you do not work here.

§16.3 PERFECT SUBJUNCTIVE

Perfect subjunctive forms are the same as indicative past perfect forms.

1. Use the perfect subjunctive after *wish* to express regret that something was not true in the past.

Regret	Subjunctive Sentence
I regret that I was not thin in my youth.	I wish I **had been** thin in my youth.
He regrets that she was not here last night.	He wishes she **had been** here last night.
She regrets that Kathy didn't stay with her when she was sick.	She wishes Kathy **had stayed** with her when she was sick.
We regret that we did not have a car when we were in Los Angeles.	We wish we **had had** a car when we were in Los Angeles.
They regret that John didn't work harder.	They wish John **had worked** harder.

2. Use the perfect subjunctive after *if* to express your probable reaction to a past untrue situation.

If + subject + **past subjunctive**   + subject + **would** + **present perfect verb**

If   I   **had wanted** that dress,   I   **would have bought** it.
Meaning: I didn't buy that dress because I didn't want it.

If   I   **had been** you,   I   **would have called** her.
Meaning: I think you should have called her.

If you **had worked** here, you **would have understood**.
Meaning: You didn't understand because you did not work here.

§16.4
SUBJUNCTIVE
VS. INDICATIVE
AFTER *IF*

1. Use the **indicative** after *if* to predict:

(a) possible action and certain result.
If + subject + **present verb**, (*then*) subject + **present verb**

If I **eat** too much, I **get** sick.
Meaning: Every time I eat too much, I get sick.

If he **is** tired, he **is** grouchy.
Meaning: Whenever he is tired, he is grouchy.

(b) probable action and certain result.
If + subject + **present verb**, (*then*) subject + **future verb**

If I **work** tomorrow, the boss **will be happy**.
Meaning: I expect to work; there is more than a 50 percent possibility that I will work.

If we **go** to South America, we **will go** to Bolivia.
Meaning: We expect to go to South America; there is more than a 50 percent possibility.

2. Use the **subjunctive** after *if*:

(a) to indicate improbable action and conditional result.
If + subject + **subjunctive**, (*then*) subject + *would* + **basic verb**

If I **worked** tomorrow, the boss **would be** happy.
Meaning: I don't expect to work; there is less than a 50 percent possibility.

If we **went** to South America, we **would go** to Bolivia.
Meaning: We don't expect to go to South America; there is less than a 50 percent possibility.

(b) to very politely ask permission to do something.
Would + subject + *mind* + *if* + subject + **subjunctive**

Would you **mind** if I **opened** the window?
Meaning: May I please open the window?

Would Mr. Smith **mind** if we **borrowed** his ladder?
Meaning: May we borrow Mr. Smith's ladder?

§17.

Prepositions

A *preposition* is a word that relates its noun or pronoun object with another word in a sentence.

A preposition + (article) + noun or object pronoun =
a prepositional phrase

for the people
for them

---

§17.1 PREPOSITIONS THAT INDICATE PLACE

over	The white box is **over** the black box.
above	The white box is **above** the black box.
below	The black box is **below** the white box
beneath	The black box is **beneath** the white box
under	The black box is **under** the white box.
underneath	The black box is **underneath** the white box.

A   B   C

behind	Chair A is **behind** chair B.
in back of	Chair A is **in back of** chair B.
in front of	Chair B is **in front of** chair A.
ahead of	Chair B is **ahead of** chair A.
across from	Chair C is **across from** chair B.
opposite	Chair C is **opposite** chair B.

A B   C

against	Chair A is **against** chair B.
by	Chair B is **by** chair C.
beside	Chair B is **beside** chair C.
next to	Chair B is **next to** chair C.

1   2   3

between	Chair 2 is **between** chair 1 and chair 3.

among	The black spot is **among** the white spots.

141

near	Chair A is **near** chair B.
close to	Chair A is **close to** chair B.
far from	Chair C is **far from** chair B.
beyond	Chair D is **beyond** chair C.

on	The white lamp is **on** the table.
upon	The white lamp is **upon** the table.
off	The black lamp is **off** the table.

in	Apple A is **in** the box.
inside	Apple A is **inside** the box.
within	Apple A is **within** the box.
out of	Apple B is **out of** the box.
outside of	Apple B is **outside of** the box.

Use *in, on,* and *at* with addresses and geographical locations.

in	a continent, a country, a state, a city, a town, an inside corner
	in South America
	in Ecuador
	in Quito
on	a coast, a beach, a side, a street, a floor, an outside corner
	on the Atlantic coast
	on the south side
	on Maple Avenue
	on the 10th floor
at	a building (inside, outside, or near), a number
	at the market
	at my friend's house
	at home
	at 2345 Maple Avenue
in	a specific place inside a building
	in her office
	in the kitchen
	in the corner

§17.2 PREPOSITIONS THAT INDICATE DIRECTION

	across	The line goes **across** the box.
	along **by**	The line goes **along** the box. The line goes **by** the box.
	past	The line goes **past** the box.
	through	The line goes **through** the box.
	around	The line goes **around** the box.
	down **up**	The black line goes **down** the hill. The red line goes **up** the hill.
	to **toward** **from**	The black line goes **to** the box. The dotted line is going **toward** the box. The red line goes **from** the box.
	back to	The black line goes **back to** the box.
	into **out of**	The black line goes **into** the box. The red line goes **out of** the box.

| | onto | | The black line goes **onto** the table. |
| | off | | The red line goes **off** the table. |

§17.3 PREPOSITIONS THAT INDICATE TIME

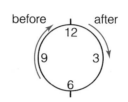

	before		The team practiced **before** the game.
	after		They celebrated **after** the game.
	during	a limited period	The spectators cheered **during** the game.
	since	from then until now	She hasn't eaten **since** last night.
	until, up to	between now and a time	I will stay **until** noon.
	around, about	an approximate time	We will be there **around** 9:30.
	by	no later than a time	Please call me **by** four o'clock.
	for	a length of time	She waited **for** 30 minutes.
	through	past a time or an event	He slept **through** the game.

Use *in, on,* and *at* with certain time expressions.

in	a century, a decade, a year, a season, a month, a period of the day

> **in** the 1800s
> **in** the 1950s
> **in** 1991
> **in** the spring
> **in** February
> **in** the morning
> **in** the afternoon
> **in** the evening

in time	not too late
	He arrived **in time** to see the whole show.

on	a day, a date, a holiday, certain days
	on Monday
	on the 15th
	on St. Patrick's Day
	on her birthday
	on weekends

on time	at the expected time
	Mary is always **on time** for class.

at	night, a specific time
	at night
	at 4 o'clock
	at midnight
	at noon

at present	now
	At present we are studying grammar.

at the moment	now
	I am busy **at the moment**.

§17.4
PREPOSITIONS THAT INDICATE OTHER RELATIONSHIPS

by	forms of communication (mail, phone, fax)	He sent the memo **by** fax.
	forms of transportation (car, bus, train, plane, boat)	They went to town **by** bus.
	people who do things	The dress was made **by** my mother.
		The song was recorded **by** Elvis Presley.
	methods	She made it **by** hand and **by** machine.
with	tools and instruments	He fixed the shelf **with** a hammer.
		I opened the door **with** my key.
in	types of composition (ink, pencil, color)	She wrote the letter **in** ink.

of	materials (wool, glass, metal), belonging	The table is made **of** glass. He is a friend **of** mine. Quito is the capital **of** Ecuador.
from	places people	The bowl is **from** India. The present is **from** Lynn.
with	including other people including things	I went **with** Stephen. I went **with** my suitcase.
without	not including other people not including things	They left **without** me. He is **without** money.
by *one's* self	without another person	She made the cake **by** herself.
instead of	including one person or thing, but not another	Bill came **instead of** Bob.
except	including some things or people, but not particular ones	Everybody was happy **except** Kathy.
as	in the role of	She works **as** a secretary.
for	purposes beneficiaries destinations	We marched **for** peace. He had potatoes **for** dinner. The gift is **for** you. I left **for** Mexico.

§17.5 ASKING QUESTIONS WITH PREPOSITIONS

When the object of the preposition answers a question, the pattern for the question is:

Question Word +	*Be* or Auxiliary Verb +	Subject +	Verb +	Preposition
Where	are	you		from?
Who	are	they		with?
What	are	you	thinking	about?
Who	does	he	work	for?
Whom	did	they	talk	to?
Who	is	she	going	with?
What	are	you	waiting	for?
What	did	he	do that	for?
Who	do	you	sit	next to?
Which street	do	you	live	on?
What city	were	you	born	in?

§17.6
PREPOSITIONS COMBINED WITH NOUNS, ADJECTIVES, AND VERBS

Prepositions are often unpredictable. Learn these combinations as whole units.

EXAMPLES

(a) **Preposition** + (article) + **noun** combinations

in English, **in** Spanish, **in** Arabic	The letter is **in** English.
in the rain, **in** good weather, **in** bad weather	Let's walk **in** the rain.
in a good mood, **in** a bad mood	Mark is always **in** a good mood.
in style	Flat shoes are **in** style this season.
in good / bad shape, **in** good condition, **in** good health	Your mother is **in** good health.
in a hurry	Let's go. We are **in** a hurry.
in charge	You're the boss; you're **in** charge.
in a car, a small boat, a small plane, a helicopter (vehicles in which you cannot walk around)	He's going **in** the car.
in a book, **in** a newspaper, **in** a magazine	I read that story **in** a magazine.
in a low voice, **in** a whisper, **in** a loud voice	She speaks **in** a low, mysterious voice.
in a suit, **in** blue jeans, **in** high heels	He arrived **in** blue jeans and a red shirt.

on	
on a bus, a train, a large plane, a ship (vehicles in which you can walk around)	They're riding **on** the bus.
on a bicycle, motorcycle, skates	We came **on** the motorcycle.
on foot (walking)	I went **on** foot.
on fire	Look out! The pan is **on** fire!
on television, **on** the radio	He's going to be **on** television today. I heard the news **on** the radio.
on paper	Please write it down **on** paper.

| on a nice day | I always take a walk **on** a nice day. |
| **on** strike | They didn't get their benefits, so they went **on** strike. |

at

at home	I've been **at** home all day.
at school	The children are **at** school now.
at work	I left my papers **at** work.

by

| **by** chance | We met **by** chance. |

with

| **with** luck | **With** luck, we will meet again. |

(b) **Adjective + preposition** combinations

about

angry **about** (a thing)	I am **angry about** the strike.
anxious **about**	They are **anxious about** her poor health.
concerned **about**	We are **concerned about** your grades.
crazy **about**	I am **crazy about** my new dress.
excited **about**	She is **excited about** her date.
happy **about**	We are all **happy about** the good news.
honest **about**	He is **honest about** his motives.
nervous **about**	They are really **nervous about** the exam.
sad **about**	She is so **sad about** her father's death.
sorry **about**	I am **sorry about** not calling you.
worried **about**	The mothers are all **worried about** their children.

at

amazed **at**	I am **amazed at** the news of your wedding.
amused **at**	She was **amused at** the idea.
angry **at** (a person)	Everybody was **angry at** the teacher.
annoyed **at**	The teacher was **annoyed at** me.
good **at** (skilled)	Mary is **good at** tennis.
mad **at** (a person)	Now they are **mad at** me.
surprised **at**	I'm **surprised at** you. I didn't think you would do that!

by

amazed **by**	She was **amazed by** the events.
amused **by**	The children were **amused by** the clown.
annoyed **by**	I can't help being **annoyed by** the traffic.
bewildered **by**	We are **bewildered by** their silence.
bored **by**	He was so **bored by** his father's jokes.
confused **by**	I am **confused by** so many rules.
disgusted **by**	The teachers were **disgusted by** the children's behavior.
embarrassed **by**	She was **embarrassed by** her brother's bad manners.
fascinated **by**	He was **fascinated by** her beautiful manners.
frustrated **by**	They are **frustrated by** so many delays.
irritated **by**	Are you **irritated by** the noise?
shocked **by**	We were **shocked by** their foul language.

for

bad **for** (destructive)	Too much fat is **bad for** your health.
difficult **for**	It is **difficult for** me to hear you.
eager **for**	We are **eager for** our vacation.

easy **for**	It is **easy for** her to stand on her head.
good **for** (beneficial)	Walking is **good for** you.
grateful **for** (a thing)	She is so **grateful for** your help.
hard **for**	It is **hard for** us to understand you.
hungry **for**	I am **hungry for** a steak and french fries.
known **for**	She is **known for** her dirty tricks.
prepared **for**	We are not **prepared for** the exam.
qualified **for**	He is very well **qualified for** that job.
ready **for**	She is **ready for** her performance.
remembered **for**	She will be **remembered for** her kindness.
responsible **for** (a thing)	You are **responsible for** buying the food.
sorry **for**	I am **sorry for** disturbing you.
suitable **for**	Those casual clothes are not **suitable for** the office.
thirsty **for**	Are you **thirsty for** a soda? I am!

from

absent **from**	She was **absent from** class today.
different **from**	Your shoes are **different from** mine.
divorced **from**	Her mom is **divorced from** her dad.
exhausted **from**	They were **exhausted from** working.
gone **from**	They have been **gone from** here for weeks.
safe **from**	At home he feels **safe from** all harm.

in

disappointed **in**	Her mother was **disappointed in** her.

interested **in**	They are **interested in** the history of the city.
involved **in**	He is **involved in** that situation.
dressed **in**	She arrived **dressed in** an evening gown.

of

afraid **of**	No wonder she is **afraid of** mice.
ashamed **of**	His family is **ashamed of** his problems.
aware **of**	We were not **aware of** the problem.
capable **of**	She is **capable of** doing better work.
composed **of**	The ocean is **composed of** salt water.
convinced **of**	I am **convinced of** his innocence.
envious **of**	She is so **envious of** my friend.
fond **of**	He is very **fond of** her.
frightened **of**	Are you **frightened of** animals?
full **of**	This glass is **full of** cider.
guilty **of**	They found him **guilty of** the crime.
in charge **of**	We are **in charge of** the party arrangements.
in favor **of**	He is **in favor of** the new law.
in danger **of**	You are **in danger of** being robbed.
innocent **of**	She is **innocent of** any wrongdoing.
jealous **of**	You are just **jealous of** her.
kind **of**	It was so **kind of** you to help us.
made **of**	This bread is **made of** all natural ingredients.
proud **of**	I am very **proud of** you for graduating.
rid **of**	They got **rid of** that old car.
scared **of**	He is **scared of** heights.
sure **of**	Are you absolutely **sure of** that?

terrified **of**	My friend is **terrified of** fire.
tired **of**	We are **tired of** playing games.

on

dependent **on**	She is completely **dependent on** her father.

to

accustomed **to**	We are not **accustomed to** driving in traffic.
addicted **to**	Unfortunately, he is **addicted to** drugs.
bad **to** (a person); abusive	They are **bad to** their mother.
clear **to**	It is **clear to** everyone that you are lying.
committed **to**	We are **committed to** finishing on time.
compared **to**	**Compared to** her, you are lucky!
connected **to**	This street is not **connected to** that street.
courteous **to**	You should be **courteous to** others.
dedicated **to**	He is **dedicated to** his boss.
devoted **to**	She is **devoted to** her job, too.
engaged **to**	Her brother is **engaged to** my sister.
equal **to**	Her act is **equal to** treason.
exposed **to**	At the beach you are **exposed to** the sun.
faithful **to**	She is **faithful to** her husband.
friendly **to**	They are **friendly to** all newcomers.
good **to** (a person); caring	Those children are very **good to** their mother.
grateful **to** (a person)	She is **grateful to** them for their kindness.
inferior **to**	These products are **inferior to** the old ones.
kind **to**	He is always **kind to** strangers.

limited **to**	With that license, you are **limited to** driving during the day; you cannot drive at night.
married **to**	She was **married to** him once.
nice **to**	Thank you for being **nice to** me.
opposed **to**	Our senator is **opposed to** that proposal.
polite **to**	Your son is always **polite to** me.
related **to**	How are you **related to** him? Is he your cousin?
relevant **to**	Please speak later; your ideas are not **relevant to** our discussion.
responsible **to** (a person)	I am **responsible to** the department chairman.
similar **to**	Your new car is **similar to** mine.
superior **to**	His new car was more expensive than yours, but it isn't **superior to** yours.

with

acquainted **with**	Are you **acquainted with** your classmates?
annoyed **with**	I think my friend is **annoyed with** me.
associated **with**	He is **associated with** a new company.
blessed **with**	You are **blessed with** many talents.
bored **with**	They seem to be **bored with** school.
careless **with**	Don't be **careless with** your ATM card.
cluttered **with**	The floor was **cluttered with** dirty clothes.
content **with**	I am really **content with** my situation.
coordinated **with**	Our program is **coordinated with** yours.

crowded **with**	The airport is **crowded with** stranded travelers.
disappointed **with**	He was **disappointed with** the teachers.
disgusted **with**	I am **disgusted with** this dirty place.
equipped **with**	The car is **equipped with** power steering.
familiar **with**	Are you **familiar with** this computer?
fascinated **with**	The baby is **fascinated with** his new toy.
filled **with**	The tank is **filled with** gas.
finished **with**	We are finally **finished with** the painting.
friendly **with**	He is **friendly with** all the newcomers.
furnished **with**	The apartments are **furnished with** extra beds.
honest **with**	Thank you for being **honest with** me.
irritated **with**	The players are **irritated with** their coach for making them practice so much.
patient **with**	The nurses were very **patient with** us.
pleased **with**	I am **pleased with** the results of the test.
satisfied **with**	They were not **satisfied with** the outcome.
upset **with**	The coach was **upset with** the referee.

(c) **Verb + preposition** combinations

about

argue **about**	They **argued about** the new rule all night.
ask **about**	She was **asking about** the homework.
complain **about**	He **complains about** his chores.
dream **about**	I **dream about** you every night.

forget **about**	Don't **forget about** the party you promised.
know **about**	We don't **know** anything **about** this place.
laugh **about**	You will **laugh about** this later on.
talk **about**	Don't **talk about** me when I'm not here.
tell **about**	They **told** us **about** your accident.
think **about**	Who are you **thinking about**?
	They are **thinking about** moving.
worry **about**	Try not to **worry about** this problem.

at

arrive **at** (a building)	She will **arrive at** the airport at 6:10.
laugh **at** (ridicule)	Please don't **laugh at** me when you see my haircut.
stare **at**	The child **stared at** the strange-looking man.
succeed **at**	To **succeed at** this job, you need to work hard.

for

apologize **for**	She **apologized for** being late.
blame **for**	She **blamed** him **for** upsetting her.
care **for**	He **cares for** her a lot.
excuse **for**	Please **excuse** me **for** interrupting.
fight **for**	Sometimes you have to **fight for** your rights.
forgive **for**	He **forgave** her **for** telling a lie.
hope **for**	We are **hoping for** better weather.
pay **for**	You can **pay for** that at the cash register.
pray **for**	He **prayed for** peace.

substitute **for**	Ms. Smith is **substituting for** the teacher today.
thank **for**	I want to **thank** you **for** all your help.
vote **for**	Please don't **vote for** him!

from

borrow **from**	She **borrowed** the sweater **from** Sally.
distinguish **from**	I can't **distinguish** X from Y on the chart.
escape **from**	They managed to **escape from** the building.
graduate **from**	When are you going to **graduate from** college?
hear **from** (get news)	I got a letter today. I finally **heard from** him.
hide **from**	She is trying to **hide from** her old boyfriend.
prevent **from**	She can't **prevent** him **from** calling her.
prohibit **from**	The law **prohibits** you **from** parking here.
protect **from**	The cream will **protect** you **from** sunburn.
recover **from**	She is **recovering from** the flu.
rescue **from**	He **rescued** her **from** the burning building.
rest **from**	You need to **rest from** studying so much.
separate **from**	Try to **separate** the yolks **from** the whites.
stop **from**	You can't **stop** them **from** trying.
subtract **from**	To get the balance, **subtract** the debits **from** the credits.

in

arrive **in** (a city, a country)	When did you **arrive in** this country?
believe **in**	Do you **believe in** love at first sight?

excel **in**	Your son **excels in** mathematics.
participate **in**	I hope you will **participate in** this activity.
succeed **in**	I hope he **succeeds in** getting them to come.

of

accuse **of**	They **accused** us **of** stealing the money.
approve **of**	Her mother doesn't **approve of** her friends.
consist **of**	This mixture **consists of** flour and water.
dream **of**	They are **dreaming of** better times.
take advantage **of**	Try to **take advantage of** this opportunity. Don't let other people **take advantage of** you.
take care **of**	She **takes care of** her sick aunt. If your faucet leaks, the plumber will **take care of** it.

on

concentrate **on**	I can't **concentrate on** my lesson.
count **on**	I know I can **count on** my friends.
decide **on**	They can't **decide on** a date for the wedding.
depend **on**	My friends **depend on** me, too.
insist **on**	He **insisted on** staying here.
plan **on**	When do you **plan on** coming?
rely **on**	I was sure I could **rely on** you to help me.

to

add **to**	Now **add** water **to** this mixture.

admit **to**	He **admitted to** being late three times.
apologize **to** (a person)	She had to **apologize to** the whole family.
apply **to** (a place)	I am **applying to** the state university.
belong **to**	Do you **belong to** a club? Does this car **belong to** you?
compare **to**	**Compare** your schedule **to** mine.
complain **to** (a person)	Don't **complain to** me; **complain to** the boss.
contribute **to**	Your ideas **contribute to** the solution.
lend **to**	Will you **lend** some money **to** her?
listen **to**	She **listens to** the radio in the car.
look forward **to**	We **look forward to** seeing you in October.
object **to**	He **objected to** her attitude.
respond **to**	I hope he **responds to** my letter.
subscribe **to**	Which magazines do you **subscribe to**?
talk **to** (a person)	I need to **talk to** you today.

with

agree **with**	I don't **agree with** you about that.
argue **with**	They **argue with** each other all the time.
compare **with**	You can't **compare** apples **with** oranges.
cover **with**	Be sure to **cover** the food **with** plastic wrap.
disagree **with**	She **disagrees with** all his ideas.
discuss **with**	Can we **discuss** our plan **with** you?
help **with**	I need **help with** the cleaning.
provide **with**	The hotel **provides** you **with** room service.

§17.7 PREPOSITIONS FOLLOWING VERBS

A **preposition** can follow a **verb** and change its meaning.

§17.7-1 Intransitive Verb-Preposition Combinations

Some verb-preposition combinations are *intransitive;* they have no object.

EXAMPLES

Verb + Preposition	Meaning	Sample Sentence
get along	live in harmony	She **gets along** with her roommates.
get around	be knowledgeable	Teenagers really **get around**.
hang around	do nothing	Sometimes they just **hang around**.
get away	escape	Please help me **get away**.
pass away	die	His father **passed away** last night.
drop by	visit without notice	My sister **dropped by** this afternoon.
check in	register	We have to **check in** at the hotel.
drop in	visit	Will you **drop in** later?
get in	enter	Please unlock the door; I can't **get in**.
turn in	go to bed	It's time to **turn in**.
drop off	fall asleep	I **dropped off** when I was reading.
take off	leave/not go to work	What time does the plane **take off**? I'm going to **take off** tomorrow.
drop out	stop attending school	It's too bad he **dropped out**.
check out	end a hotel stay	We have to **check out** before noon.
find out	discover the answer	Try to **find out** where she lives.
get out	leave a session	They **get out** at three.
keep out	not enter	You're not welcome; **keep out**.
look out	be careful	**Look out**! A car is coming!
pass out	lose consciousness	She **passed out** in the hall.
try out	audition	The auditions are tomorrow; are you going to **try out**?

turn out	end	How did the auditions **turn out**?
watch out	be careful	This is a dangerous corner; you have to **watch out**.
start over	begin again	I made a mistake; I want to **start over**.
take over	become boss	Don't invite him; he always **takes over**.
cheer up	be happier	I sure hope he **cheers up**.
get up	arise/stand	What time do you **get up**?
give up	stop trying/ surrender	Keep trying; never **give up**.
grow up	become an adult	Where did you **grow up**?
keep up	achieve the same as others	It is hard to **keep up** when you have two jobs.
make up	stop fighting	I'm glad they finally **made up**.
show up	appear unexpectedly	What time did he **show up**?
throw up	vomit	The sick child **threw up** at school.
turn up	appear unexpectedly	Look who just **turned up**!
wake up	stop sleeping	I **woke up** three times last night.
get through	finish/make contact	When are you going to **get through**? I'm calling, but I can't **get through**.

§17.7-2 Transitive Verb-Preposition Combinations

Transitive verb-preposition combinations have an object. These combinations are either *separable* or *non-separable*.

§17.7-2.1 SEPARABLE VERB-PREPOSITION COMBINATION

With *separable combinations,*
- if the object is a *pronoun,* it must separate the verb and the preposition.
- if the object is a *noun,* it may be placed either before or after the preposition.

Patterns:

Subject	Verb	Noun Object	Preposition
He	**put**	*the hammer*	**down.**

Subject	Verb	Pronoun Object	Preposition
He	**put**	*it*	**down.**

Subject	Verb	Preposition	Noun Object
He	**put**	**down**	*the hammer.*

Do Not Use:

Subject	Verb	Preposition	Pronoun Object
He	put	down	it.

EXAMPLES

Verb	+ Object	+ Preposition	Meaning	
bring	it	about	make it happen	We are trying to bring about a solution.
name	him	after	give him the name of	They named the baby after me.
put	it	away	store it	Please put the picture away.
throw	it	away	put it in the trash	Please throw that ball away.
call	me	back	telephone me again	Call me back at eight.
get	it	back	receive it again	I hope I get my book back.
give	it	back	return it	She will have to give it back.
pay	him	back	return the money	We will pay him back soon.
put	it	back	return it to its place	Please put that chair back where it was.
cut	it	down	make it smaller	The report is too long; cut it down.
put	it	down	release it	That's my money; put it down.
put	her	down	criticize her	He always puts her down.
tear	it	down	destroy it	They tore that building down.
turn	it	down	refuse an offer/ reduce the volume	She turned down the job offer. I had to turn my radio down.
turn	him	down	refuse his request	He wanted to marry her; she turned him down.
write	it	down	note it on paper	Write down my phone number.
fill	it	in	complete it	You have to fill in this form.
hand	it	in	give it to the leader	Students, hand in your papers!
turn	it	in	give it to the leader	I forgot to turn in my paper.
bring	it	on	cause it	The weather brought on my cold.
have	it	on	be wearing it	She has on a new sweater.
keep	it	on	continue wearing	Be sure to keep your ring on.
put	it	on	begin wearing	I can't wait to put my new dress on.
put	me	on	tell me a lie	He says he's a lawyer; I think he's putting me on.

Verb	+ Object	+ Preposition	Meaning	
try	it	on	put it on to test it	Did you try it on at the store?
turn	it	on	make it begin functioning	Turn on the TV.
call	it	off	cancel it	We called off the wedding.
drop	it	off	leave it	Drop the package off tonight.
put	it	off	postpone it	They put the picnic off until Friday.
put	him	off	repel him	That perfume really put him off.
shut	it	off	make it stop functioning	Please shut off the alarm clock!
take	it	off	remove it	Can you take the pan off the stove?
tear	it	off	remove it quickly	He tore off his shirt and made a bandage.
turn	it	off	make it stop functioning	She was glad to turn off the computer.
ask	you	out	invite you	He wants to ask you out.
check	it	out	inspect it	My heater isn't working. Will you check it out?
cut	it	out	stop doing it	That habit is so annoying; please cut it out.
			remove it with scissors	I cut out the article about you.
cross	it	out	delete it	Please cross out the mistake.
figure	it	out	solve it	I can't figure out the riddle.
figure	her	out	understand her	They will never figure her out.
fill	it	out	complete it	Please fill out this form.
find	him	out	discover his secret	Do you think they will find him out?
get	it	out	remove it	Can you get this splinter out?
hand	them	out	give them to a group	The teacher handed the papers out to the class.
kick	them	out	make them leave	The principal kicked them out.
leave	it	out	not include it	Please leave that part out.
pass	it	out	distribute it	Can you pass this information out?
pick	it	out	choose it	My boyfriend picked it out.
point	it	out	indicate it	She pointed out her house on the way.
put	it	out	extinguish it	He was able to put out the fire.
put	us	out	make us leave/ annoy us	She put us out at midnight. That really put us out.
take	it	out	remove it from within	Take the key out.
take	her	out	escort her	She wants you to take her out.

Verb	+ Object +	Preposition	Meaning	
tear	it	out	remove it quickly	He tore the paper out of his notebook.
throw	it	out	put it in the trash	I'm glad you threw that T-shirt out.
try	it	out	use it as a test	Let's try this bike out.
turn	it	out	make a light stop functioning	I'm sleepy; turn out the light.
do	it	over	repeat it	I had to do the test over.
look	it	over	check it	Will you look it over for me?
pick	them	over	choose carefully	Some of these cherries are not ripe; you will have to pick them over.
start	it	over	begin it again	I love that song; please start it over.
take	it	over	do it again	He failed the course and had to take it over.
think	it	over	consider it	Please think over our offer.
turn	it	over	move it other side up	Turn the pot over and see where it was made.
call	us	up	telephone us	He called us up from Hawaii.
bring	it	up	mention it	Don't bring up his accident.
cheer	me	up	make me feel better	The sun cheers me up.
clean	it	up	put it in order	She cleaned up her room.
fill	it	up	fill it completely	I got my tank filled up.
hang	it	up	put it on a hanger/	You have to hang up your coat.
			put the phone down	Please don't hang it up.
keep	it	up	don't stop doing it	The dancing is great. Keep it up!
look	it	up	research it	I'll look it up in the dictionary.
make	it	up	do missed work/	He can make up the test he missed.
			invent it	He made up a crazy story.
pick	it	up	put it in your hands	The bag is there; pick it up.
show	her	up	surpass her publicly	The new singer showed her up.
stand	him	up	not meet him as promised	She stood him up last night.
take	it	up	discuss it/	They took it up with the boss.
			make it smaller, shorter	The seamstress took up my skirt.
tear	it	up	destroy it	I'm glad you tore up that photograph.
think	it	up	invent it	He thought up a wonderful idea.
turn	it	up	make it louder or stronger	That song is great; turn it up!
wake	him	up	make him stop sleeping	He's late for work; wake him up!
follow	it	through	make sure it is completed	It's a good project; make sure you follow it through.

§17.7-2.2 NON-SEPARABLE VERB-PREPOSITION COMBINATIONS

With *non-separable verb-preposition combinations*, the object—noun or pronoun—must follow the preposition.

Pattern:

Subject	Verb	Preposition	Object
She	**cares**	for	*John.*
She	**cares**	for	*him.*

Do Not Use:
She cares John for.
She cares him for.

EXAMPLES

Verb	+ Preposition + Object		Meaning	
come	across	it	find it unexpectedly	I came across these old photographs.
run	across	it	find it unexpectedly	He ran across his old report cards.
come	after	me	pursue me	The reporters are coming after me.
look	after	him	be responsible for him	His mom looks after him.
take	after	me	have my characteristics	My son takes after me.
ask	for	it	request it	You have to ask for the medicine.
care	for	her	love her	She really cares for her husband.
get back	from	it	return from it	When did you get back from your vacation?
hear	from	them	receive communication	Have you heard from your children?
get	in	it	enter it	I can't wait to get in the pool.
check	into	it	investigate it	I'm going to check into that situation.
run	into	it	crash with it	He ran into a tree!
run	into	him	see him unexpectedly	We ran into him at the mall.
look	into	it	investigate it	Please look into this problem.
hear	of	it	have some knowledge of it	I have never heard of that language.
get	out of	it	leave a small vehicle/ be excused from it	Help me get out of the canoe. She promised to babysit; now she wants to get out of it.
keep	out of	it	not become involved with it	You should keep out of their fight.

Verb	+ Preposition	+ Object	Meaning	
run	out of	it	use all of it	I ran out of laundry detergent.
stay	out of	it	not become involved with it	He tried to stay out of their argument.
drop	out of	it	stop participating in it	She dropped out of that organization.
get	off	it	leave a vehicle you ride *on*	He had to get off the bus.
call	on	him	ask him for help	You can call on him any time.
drop in	on	us	visit us unexpectedly	Please drop in on us when you can.
get	on	it	enter a vehicle you ride *on*	They got on the train at the station.
look	out for	it	be prepared for danger	Look out for the potholes in the street.
go	over	it	review it	She went over her paper last night.
get	over	it	recover from it	He finally got over the flu.
run	over	it	destroy it with a vehicle	My hat blew off and a car ran over it.
catch up	with	him	reach him	The police chased him and finally caught up with him.
			learn his news	I haven't seen him in a long time; I want to catch up with him.
fool around	with	it	play with it	Stop fooling around with your pencil and get to work.
get along	with	them	not fight with them	She is trying to get along with her neighbors.
get away	with	it	not be punished for doing it	He cheated and got away with it.
get through	with	it	finish something difficult	She finally got through with her thesis.
keep up	with	her	be equal to her	She is really good, but I'm trying to keep up with her.
put up	with	her	tolerate her	She irritates me, but I'm trying to put up with her.

Preposition combinations are tricky. They are often illogical, they sometimes have more than one meaning, and they sometimes change in meaning. Learn them as you *come across* them.

COMMON VERB-PREPOSITION COMBINATIONS WITH SPECIAL MEANINGS

blow up	explode	The house caught on fire when the furnace blew up.
blow up	get angry	He blew up when he saw the credit card bill.
blow down	destroy by wind	The hurricane could blow the house down.
blow over	be forgotten	The scandal will blow over shortly.
blow out	burst	I sure hope my tire doesn't blow out.

break in	force open	The thief broke in and took our computer.
break out	erupt	Her skin broke out in a rash.
break up	end a relationship	The couple broke up after a year of marriage.
break down	stop functioning	Her car broke down on the highway.
bring on	cause	Her hospital stay brought on pneumonia.
bring about	cause	They hope to bring about peace in that area.
bring up	begin to talk about	She always brings up irrelevant subjects.
bring up	raise children	I was brought up in a strict home.
bring down	cause to fail	That behavior brought down the government.
care for	take charge of	The nurses cared for him during the day.
care for	love	We all care for him.
care about	have interest in	She doesn't care about anybody but herself.
carry on	continue	We must carry on after he retires.
carry on	misbehave	She carries on at that bar every night.
carry out	follow plans	We must carry out this project properly.
carry through	finish	We will carry through with his plans.
catch on	understand	I don't think he catches on.
catch up	reach the others	It is hard to catch up when you have been away.
close up	end the business day	That shop closes up at eight o'clock.
close down	end the business	That store closed down two years ago.
close in	surround	The police are closing in on the escapee.
close out	stop selling an item	The store closed out of those fans.
come out	join society	Come out and join the fun!
come down on	punish	The judge really came down on him.
come through	be reliable	A good friend always comes through.
come about	happen	How did all this come about?
come over	affect	Something strange has come over him.
do in	beat up	Don't let them do you in.
do up	improve	The make-up artist really did her up.
do over	remodel	We want to do over the basement.
drop in	visit without notice	Please drop in to see me.
drop by	visit without notice	Please drop by to see me.
drop out	stop going to school	She dropped out last year.
fall out	shed	Her hair is falling out because of the operation.
fall out	end a friendship	They fell out after that argument.
fall off	fall from a height	The man fell off the ladder.
fall down	fall to the ground	He was running too fast, and he fell down.
fall through	not happen as planned	Our vacation plans fell through.
fall for	accept naively	Don't fall for his charm; it's an act.
fall in	associate with an undesirable group	He fell in with a gang downtown.
fall over	faint	She fell over in the middle of the concert.
get over	recover	I hope you get over your bad cold soon.
get around	avoid	He's trying to get around that regulation.
get through	finish	Try to get through early.
get by	survive	We're not rich, but we get by.
get on	get older	Her father is getting on, but he's lively.
get with	be aware	Don't just hang around; get with it!

get about	move	It's hard for him to get about with crutches.
get in	enter	I was getting in the car when I fell down.
get out	be dismissed	They get out of school before I get out of work.
get out	remove	I hope the dry cleaners can get this spot out.
give in	surrender to pressure	Mom gave in and let me have a party.
give up	stop making an effort	Don't give up; keep on practicing.
give out	distribute	They asked us to give out these brochures.
go on	happen	What's going on? There's so much noise!
go for	like a lot	I really go for the new styles.
go with	look good with	Does this blouse go with this skirt?
go with	date steadily	My friend goes with my brother.
go out	socialize	You need to go out more.
go in for	take interest in	He doesn't go in for museums.
go out for	compete for a team	Her nephew is going out for the baseball team.
go through	suffer	It's hard to imagine what you are going through.
go through	sort	I spent all morning going through my bills.
go by	pass	Did you see that car go by?
go about	wander	He just goes about happily.
go around	wander	She always goes around with a smile on her face.
hand in	give to an authority	You have to hand this in to the teacher.
hand out	distribute	The teacher handed it out to us.
hand over	give under duress	She had to hand the letter over to the judge.
hang out	relax	They come home from school and hang out.
hang around	linger idly	I wish he didn't hang around here so much.
hang up	put clothing up	He doesn't have time to hang up his clothes.
hang up	end a phone call	Please don't hang up! We need to talk.
have on	be wearing	What do you have on?
have to	must	We have to learn this.
have over	invite to one's home	I would love to have you over.
hear of	know about	I've never heard of him. Who is he?
hear from	get news of	Did you hear from your friends in Phoenix?
keep on	continue	Keep on trying! You'll make it.
keep away	not get close	Keep away from that fence.
keep off	not tread on	They told us to keep off their property.
keep out	not enter	I have to keep out of my brother's room.
keep in	not allow out	His mother keeps him in all afternoon.
keep up	stay apace	I'm trying to keep up, but I'm tired.
keep at	not stop	Keep at it; you'll make it.
keep for	guard	My friend kept my watch for me while I played.
kick around	abuse	I wish he didn't kick his dog around so much.
kick out	dismiss	The principal kicked them out of school.
kick in	add help	When the weather gets cold, the heater kicks in.
kick over	think about	Kick this idea over, and let me know what you decide.
live for	love	She lives for her job.
live to	enjoy	They live to dance.
live on	continue living	Our ancestors live on in our memories.
live on	depend on for life	They live on bread and water.
live through	suffer	You will have to live through this period.

look for	search	I'm looking for my glasses.
look at	observe	She's looking at my magazine.
look through	examine and search	We looked through our files, and found this.
look over	scan	They're looking over the new books.
look into	investigate	The police are looking into this incident.
look around	observe, relaxed	They're having fun looking around the city.
look over	observe for selection	The teachers are looking over the textbooks.
look in	check	I'll look in this afternoon, to see how you are.
look out	be careful	Look out! There's a car coming.
look up	search for information	Look those words up in the dictionary.
look after	take care of	A nice woman looks after my children.
look down on	feel superior to	Never look down on anyone.
look up to	respect	I always looked up to my Latin teacher.
pass on	tell others	Please don't pass that information on.
pass by	ignore	He passed us by when he came to town.
pass for	be accepted falsely	She's only sixteen, but she passes for twenty-one.
pass in	give to an authority	We had to pass our tests in to the teacher.
pass over	not promote	They passed him over; he will not be a director.
pass through	visit on the way	Don't fall for him; he's only passing through.
pass out	lose consciousness	He passed out from the heat.
pass up	miss an opportunity	Don't pass up these bargains.
pick up	put in your hands	Pick up your pencil and write.
pick up	collect	Help me pick up the trash.
pick up	give a ride to	My mother is coming to pick me up.
pick out	select	Help us pick out the prizes.
pick over	choose carefully	You have to pick over these cherries carefully.
pick on	selectively mistreat	I think the coach picks on your daughter.
pick at	scratch	Try not to pick at your sore.
put on	begin to wear	Put on your coat and go home.
put off	postpone	It rained, so they put off the picnic.
put out	extinguish	The rain put out the fire.
put down	release	Put your bags down and rest.
put through	allow contact	The secretary put us through to the chief.
run around	socialize indiscriminately	I think he runs around with a wild group.
run into	meet by accident	We ran into an old friend at the mall.
run for	seek election	Are you running for office this term?
run out of	exhaust a supply of	We ran out of gas, and had to walk.
run up	spend a lot	He ran up a huge bill at the restaurant.
run by	tell something	Let me run this by you to see what you think.
run over	go over with a vehicle	He ran over my hat with his motorcycle.
run down	not take care of	They really ran that house down.
see to	take responsibility	They will behave; I'll see to that myself.
see through	detect	Can you see my scar through these stockings?
see through	not abandon	I'll stay with you; I'll see you through.
show up	appear	Her brother showed up two hours late.
show through	be visible	Yes, your scar shows through your stockings.
show around	take on a tour	Please show us around your new house.
stand up	be erect on your feet	Stand up when he comes in the room.
stand for	mean	What do your initials stand for?
stand for	believe in	What does your club stand for?
stand for	allow	I will not stand for cheating in my class.

stand out	look different	That bright color stands out from the rest.
stand in	substitute	Cecily is standing in for the main singer tonight.
stand by	wait	Please stand by; we'll have news in a minute.
stand by	give support	He stands by his wife despite her bad behavior.
take in	make smaller	The seamstress took my dress in for me.
take in	give shelter to	She takes in anybody who needs help.
take off	remove	Please take off your shoes.
take off	leave	What time did the plane take off?
take off	not go to work	Do you think you can take off tomorrow?
take for	believe to be	He takes me for a weakling.
take on	accept responsibility for	Are you going to take that project on?
take up	pursue an interest	He took up gardening recently.
take up	make shorter	I took my skirt up three inches.
take down	write an account of	Be sure to take this information down.
take out	invite to go out	I'd like to take you out sometime.
take over	assume responsibility	That bully always takes over.
take around	give a tour	Will you take us around the mall?
tear up	destroy	She tore up the paper.
tear down	destroy	They tore down the building.
tear out	remove	I tore the check out of the checkbook.
think of	have in one's mind	I'm thinking of you.
think about	have in one's mind	Are you thinking about me?
think through	consider carefully	We need to think this problem through.
think over	consider carefully	Before we buy the house, we have to think it over.
think up	invent	He thought up a wonderful solution.
throw out	discard	Throw out those tennis shoes.
throw away	discard	Throw away those tennis shoes.
throw over	remove from power	We will throw that bully over.
throw up	vomit	I am sorry you threw up your dinner.
tie in	relate	Your report ties in with our new project.
tie on	attach with a cord	Tie a bow on the package.
tie up	immobilize	They tied up all the telephone lines.
tie up	put a cord around	Help me tie up this box.
try to	make an effort	Try to finish on time.
try on	put on to test	May I try this dress on?
try out	use to test	May I try this bicycle out?
try out	audition	She is trying out for the school play.
turn on	start a machine or light	You can turn on the light now.
turn out	end	Everything turned out all right.
turn out	extinguish a light	You can turn out the light now.
turn off	extinguish a light or machine	You can turn off the machine now.
turn to	ask for help from	I always turn to you when I have a problem.
turn up	appear unexpectedly	He turned up after three years of absence.
turn in	go to bed	I'm tired. I'm going to turn in.
turn down	refuse an offer	He turned down that job.
turn over	move halfway around	Turn over and go to sleep.
turn away	face a different direction	She turned away when he said hello.
wear off	disappear	The tread wore off my tires after six months.
wear out	become useless	My tires wear out in six months.

§18.

Adverbs

The question words **"Where?" "When?"** and **"How?"** and individual words that answer these questions are *adverbs*.

§18.1 ADVERBS OF LOCATION

An adverb can tell the place of the subject after the verb *be*, or tell the place of the action after other verbs.

Prepositions as Adverbs

Certain prepositions function as adverbs when they are not followed by an object:

> ***in, inside, out, outside***
> ***in front, in back, behind***
> ***over, up***
> ***down, below, under, underneath***
> ***close, near, far***
> ***across, by, past,*** and ***through***

Question	Answer
Where is he?	He is **out**.
Where do they live?	They don't live **far**.

Other Adverbs of Location	Meaning
here	in this place
there	in that place
everywhere	in all places
nowhere	not in any place
not anywhere	not in any place
anywhere	in all possible places
away	in another place
indoors	in a building
inside	in a building
outdoors	not in a building
outside	not in a building
upstairs	on the floor above
downstairs	on the floor below
high	a distance above
low	a distance below
underneath	below

Adverbs of location are usually placed after the verb.

Question	Answer
Where is the airport?	It is **there**.
Where are Alice and Jerry?	They are **away**.
Where are the stores?	They are **nearby**.
Where is Joe?	He is **here**.
Where are you going?	I am not going **far**.
Where does he work?	He works **upstairs**.
Where did she go?	She went **outside**.
Where have they gone?	They have gone **ahead**.
Where will we see you?	We will see you **below**.

To show surprise or excitement, put the adverb before the subject:

      Here he is!   **Up** you go!   **Away** they went!

§18.2 ADVERBS OF TIME

An adverb can tell the time of the subject after *be* or the time of the action after other verbs.

Prepositions as Adverbs

The preposition ***before*** functions as an adverb when it is not followed by an object.

Question	Answer
Was he here?	Yes. He was here **before**.

Other Adverbs of Time	Meaning
now	at the present time
then	at that time, or after that
soon	a short time after now
later	after now, after then
afterwards	after now, after then
early	before the expected time
late	after the expected time
momentarily	very soon
yet	now, as expected
already	before now
recently	a short time before now
lately	a short time before now
still	now, as before
not anymore	not now, as before
ago	a length of time before now
today	the present day
tonight	today at night
yesterday	the day before today
tomorrow	the day after today

Adjective + Noun Combinations as Adverbs of Time

the day before yesterday	two days ago
the day after tomorrow	two days after now
this morning	the morning of today; can be present or past
present	It is 9:00 A.M. The sun is shining this morning.
past	It is 2:00 P.M. It is raining now. The sun was shining this morning.
this afternoon	the afternoon of today; can be present, past, or future
future	It is 9:00 A.M. The sun is shining. It is going to rain this afternoon.
present	It is 2:00 P.M. It is raining this afternoon.
past	It is 10:00 P.M. It is clear now, but it was raining this afternoon.
this evening	the evening of today; can be present, past, or future
future	It is 2:00 P.M. It is going to clear up this evening.
present	It is 7:00 P.M. It is clear this evening.
past	It is 10:00 P.M. It stopped raining this evening at 6:00 P.M.
this week	the present week
this Tuesday	the nearest Tuesday to today; can be past or future
this month	the present month
this February	the nearest February to now; can be past or future
last night	the night before today
last week	the week before this week
the week before last	the week before last week
last Friday	the Friday before now
last month	the month before this month
last May	the May before now
last year	the year before this year
next week	the week after the present week
the week after next	the week after next week

next Friday	the Friday of the present week <u>or</u> the Friday of next week
next month	the month after the present month
next May	the next future May; can be this year or next year
next year	the year after the present year
sometime	an unspecified future time

Adverbs of time are usually placed after the verb.

Question	Answer
What time is it?	It is **early**.
When is your birthday?	It is **this Friday**.
When is the best time?	It is **now**.
When are the parties?	They are **tomorrow**.
When was the wedding?	It was **last week**.
When are you coming?	I'm coming **now**.
When were they studying?	They were studying **then**.
When did she tell you?	She told me **recently**.
When did they move here?	They moved here **five years ago**.

Exceptions:
Already is placed:
- after a form of *be.*

> I am **already** a doctor.

- after an auxiliary verb.

> I have **already** finished medical school.
> He is **already** working on his thesis.
> Is she here **yet**?   Yes, she is **already** here.
>   No, she **isn't** here **yet**.

- before or after other verbs.

> I **already** studied chemistry.
> I studied chemistry **already**.

Still is placed:
- after a form of *be.*

> I am **still** here.
> We are **still** upstairs.

- after an auxiliary verb.

> We are **still** waiting.
> You should **still** try.

- before other verbs.

> He **still** plays golf every day.
> I **still** want to see you.
> Are they **still** talking?   Yes, they are **still** talking.
>   No, they are **not** talking
>   **anymore**.

§18.3
ADVERBS OF INSTANCE

An adverb can tell the number of times an action occurs. These adverbs are placed at the end of the phrase.

once	one time
twice	two times
again	one more time

Adjective + noun combinations as adverbs:

three times	**ten times**	**a hundred times**

Question	Answer
How many times are you going to call?	I'm going to call **once**.
How many times did you see the movie?	I saw it **twice**.
How many times will they come back?	They will come back **again**.
How many times did you go to the store?	We went **four times**.

§18.4
ADVERBS OF FREQUENCY

An adverb can tell the frequency of an action. The adverb comes before the verb.

Question	Answer	Meaning
How often do you study?	I **never** study.	0 percent of the time
	I **hardly ever** study.	almost never
	I **rarely** study.	almost never
	I **seldom** study.	almost never
	I **occasionally** study.	25–50 percent of the time
	I **often** study.	50–75 percent of the time
	I **frequently** study.	50–75 percent of the time
	I **usually** study.	75–90 percent of the time
	I **always** study.	100 percent of the time

Sometimes can be placed after the verb or before the subject.

I study **sometimes**.	25–50 percent of the time
Sometimes I study.	

Once, twice, or *x times a week* is placed after the verb or before the subject.

I study **twice a week**.
Twice a week I study.

§18.5 ADVERBS OF MANNER

An adverb can indicate the way an action is performed. Most adverbs of manner are formed by adding **ly** to an adjective.

slow**ly**	quick**ly**
soft**ly**	loud**ly**
sweet**ly**	sour**ly**
nice**ly**	mean**ly**
careful**ly**	careless**ly**

When the adjective ends in *y*, drop the *y* and add **ily**.

crazy	craz**ily**
noisy	nois**ily**
busy	bus**ily**
happy	happ**ily**

When the adjective ends in *le*, change the *le* to **ly**.

responsible	responsi**bly**
capable	capa**bly**
comparable	compara**bly**

A few adverbs are the same as their corresponding adjectives.

fast	**fast**
hard	**hard**
late	**late**
early	**early**

The adverb that corresponds to the adjective *good* is **well**.

The adverb that corresponds to the adjective *bad* is **badly**.

The adverb is placed after the verb when there is no object.

How do you dance?	I dance **well**.
	I dance **fast**.
	I dance **badly**.
	I dance **slowly**.

When there is a direct object, the adverb is placed after it.

How do you dance?	I dance the waltz **well**.
	I dance the waltz **fast**.
	I dance the waltz **badly**.
	I dance the waltz **slowly**.

Do not place the adverb between the verb and the direct object.

Do Not Use:	I dance well the waltz.

Note: Several words that end in *ly* are adjectives, not adverbs; they do not have corresponding adverb forms.

friendly	lively
ugly	lovely
sickly	lonely
deadly	cowardly
heavenly	

§18.6 COMPARING ADVERBS OF MANNER

(a) Before adverbs that end in *ly*,

use *more* + adverb + *than* for a positive comparison:
> She works **more slowly than** I do.
> Kyung checks his work **more carefully than** Thomas does.

use *not as* + adverb + *as* for a negative comparison:
> I don't work **as slowly as** she does.

The negative superlative is rarely used. Use the adjective instead:
> *Awkward:* Thomas works the least carefully of all.
> *Better:* Thomas is the least careful of all.
> *Even better:* Thomas is not as careful as the others.

(b) With *fast, hard, late,* and *early,*

add *er* for a positive comparison:
> I work **faster than** she does.
> Brenda works **harder than** Thomas does.

Brenda works **later than** Thomas does.
Thomas leaves **earlier than** Brenda does.

use *the* + **adverb** + *est* for the superlative:
She works **the fastest** of all.
Brenda works **the hardest** of all.
Brenda works **the latest** of all.
Thomas leaves **the earliest** of all.

use *not as* + **adverb** + *as* for a negative comparison:
She doesn't work **as fast as** I do.
Thomas doesn't work **as hard as** Brenda does.
Brenda doesn't leave **as early as** Thomas does.

use *not as* + **adverb** + *as* + **the others** for the negative superlative:
He does **not** work **as fast as** the others.
He does **not** work **as hard as** the others.
He does **not** work **as late as** the others.
She does **not** leave **as early as** the others.

(c) With **well**,

use *better than* for a positive comparison or a superlative:
She works **better than** he does.
She works **better than** the others.

use *not as well as* for a negative comparison or a superlative:
She doesn't play **as well as** her friend.
She doesn't play **as well as** the others.

§18.7 ADVERBS THAT INTENSIFY VERBS

An adverb can indicate the intensity of the action of a verb.

almost	not quite
nearly	not quite
hardly	a little, but not enough
scarcely	a little, but not enough
only	in a limited way
just	a little
somewhat	a little
well enough	in a satisfactory way
really	very well

Almost, *nearly*, *hardly*, *scarcely*, *only*, *just*, and *really* are placed before the verb. When used with a progressive tense, they separate the *be* form from the *ing* form— see §9.

A little, very little, somewhat, well enough, and *well* are placed after the verb.

Question	Answer	Meaning
Does the engine run? Is the engine running?	It **almost** runs. It is **almost** running.	It doesn't run but it might run soon.
	It **nearly** runs. It is **nearly** running.	It doesn't run yet.
	It **hardly** runs. It is **hardly** running.	It runs **very little**.
	It **scarcely** runs. It is **scarcely** running.	It runs **very little**.
	It **just** runs. It is **just** running.	It runs **a little bit**.
	It runs **somewhat**.	It runs **a little bit**.
	It **only** runs **a little**.	It **just** runs **somewhat**.
	It runs **well enough**.	It runs in a satisfactory way.
	It **really** runs. It is **really** running.	It runs **well**.

§18.8 ADVERBS THAT INTENSIFY ADJECTIVES AND OTHER ADVERBS

An adverb can indicate the *intensity* of an adjective or of another adverb.

Question	Answer	Meaning
	adverb + adjective	
How good is she?	She is **fairly** good.	She is average.
	She is **pretty** good.	She is better than average.
	She is **rather** good.	She is better than average.
	She is **quite** good.	She is better than average.
	She is **very** good.	She is much better than average.
	She is **extremely** good.	She is excellent.
	She is **unusually** good.	She is outstanding.
	She is **too** good.	She is so good that it is bad.
	She is **not too** good.	She is pretty bad.
	adverb + adverb	
How does she work?	She works **fairly** quickly.	She works faster than average
	She works **pretty** quickly.	She works faster than average.
	She works **rather** quickly.	She works faster than average.
	She works **quite** quickly.	She works faster than average.
	She works **very** quickly.	She works faster than average.
	She works **extremely** quickly.	She works much faster than average.
	She works **unusually** quickly.	She works faster than most people.
	She works **too** quickly.	She works so fast that it is bad.

§19.

Conjunctions

A *conjunction* is a word that connects words, phrases, or clauses. Each conjunction defines a specific relationship between the parts it connects.

§19.1 COORDINATING CONJUNCTIONS

A *coordinating conjunction* joins sentence parts that have the same grammatical form.

(a) **And** indicates similarity.

The *skirt* **and** *blouse* are yellow.	The *skirt* is yellow. The *blouse* is yellow.
Sally was *singing* **and** *dancing*.	Sally was *singing*. Sally was *dancing*.
David worked *slowly* **and** *carefully*.	David worked *slowly*. David worked *carefully*.

(b) **Or** indicates a necessary choice.

I want an *apple* **or** an *orange*.	I want only one piece of fruit.
She is from *Chicago* **or** *New York*.	She is from one of these cities.

(c) **But** indicates difference.
Note: Use a <u>comma</u> before **but**.

Jane went to the movies, **but** I didn't (go).	Jane *went* to the movies. I *didn't go* to the movies.
I like oranges, **but** not grapefruit.	I *like* oranges. I *don't like* grapefruit.
I like oranges, **but** he likes grapefruit.	*I* like oranges. *He* likes grapefruit.

David worked slowly, **but** not carefully.	David *worked* slowly. David *did not work* carefully.

(d) *Yet* indicates difference that is not logical.
Note: Use a <u>comma</u> before *yet*:

Jane was *tired*, **yet** *happy*.	Jane was *tired*. Jane was *happy*.
I *dieted*, **yet** lost no weight.	I *dieted*. I *didn't lose* weight.
David *worked* hard, **yet** he *didn't receive* payment.	David *worked* hard. David *did not receive* payment.

(e) *For* connects a fact with its cause.
Note: Use a <u>comma</u> before *for*:

Mary went home, **for** *she was sick.*	Mary went home. (fact) Mary was sick. (reason)
I am sure Bob was there, **for** *I saw him.*	I am sure Bob was there. (fact) I saw him. (reason)
They are late, **for** *they got lost.*	They are late. (fact) They got lost. (reason)

(f) *So* indicates a result.
Note: Use a <u>comma</u> before *so*:

Mary was sick, **so** *she went home.*	Mary was sick. (fact) Mary went home. (result)
They got lost, **so** *they were late.*	They got lost. (fact) They were late. (result)

§19.1-1 Joining Independent Clauses

(a) A coordinating conjunction can join two independent clauses to make one sentence.

EXAMPLES
John is my brother, **and** Mary is my sister.
I sold my house yesterday, **but** I didn't sell my car.

(b) Use *too, so, either,* and *neither* with coordinating conjunctions for emphasis.

(1) To join two affirmative clauses, use:

and + subject + verb + *too*   or   *and so* + verb + subject

EXAMPLES

John is tall. Bob is tall.

John is tall, **and** Bob is **too**.	or	John is tall, **and so** is Bob.

Mary is singing. Carol is singing.

Mary is singing, **and** Carol is **too**.	or	Mary is singing, **and so** is Carol.

Ted drives to work. Joe drives to work.

Ted drives to work, **and** Joe does **too**.	or	Ted drives to work, **and so** does Joe.

(2) To join two negative clauses, use:

and + subject + verb + *not either*   or   *and neither* + verb + subject

EXAMPLES

John isn't tall. I am not tall.

John isn't tall, **and** I'm **not either**.	John isn't tall, **and neither** am I.

Mary isn't singing. Carol isn't singing.

Mary isn't singing, **and** Carol isn't **either**.	Mary isn't singing, **and neither** is Carol.

Ted didn't drive to work. Joe didn't drive to work.

Ted didn't drive to work, and Joe did**n't either**.	Ted didn't drive to work, **and neither** did Joe.

(3) To join one affirmative clause and one negative clause, use:

but + subject + *be* or auxiliary verb + *not*

EXAMPLES

Mary is short. Donna isn't short.
Mary is short, **but** Donna **isn't**.

He lives here. I don't live here.
He lives here, **but** I **don't**.

Carol was singing. Joe wasn't singing.
Carol was singing, **but** Joe **wasn't**.

Joe drove to work. Ted didn't drive to work.
Joe drove to work, **but** Ted **didn't**.

(4) To join one negative clause and one affirmative
clause, use:

but + subject + *be* or auxiliary verb

EXAMPLES
Donna isn't short. Mary is short.
Donna isn't short, **but** Mary **is**.

I don't live here. He lives here.
I don't live here, **but** he **does**.

Joe wasn't singing. Carol was singing.
Joe wasn't singing, **but** Carol **was**.

Ted didn't drive to work. Joe drove to work.
Ted didn't drive to work, **but** Joe **did**.

§19.2
CORRELATIVE CONJUNCTIONS

Correlative conjunctions are pairs of conjunctions. The first conjunction emphasizes the meaning of the second.

(a) *both. . . and* emphasizes the equality of two items:
She wants **both** ice cream **and** cake.

(b) *not only. . . but also* emphasizes the equal importance
of the second item:
She wants **not only** ice cream, **but also** cake.

(c) *either. . . or* emphasizes the need to choose only <u>one</u>
item:
She wants **either** ice cream **or** cake.

(d) *neither. . . nor* emphasizes that both items are negative:
She wants **neither** ice cream **nor** cake.

(e) *whether. . . or not* emphasizes that the first item is
more important than the second:
She will eat ice cream **whether or not** she eats
cake.
or
She will eat ice cream **whether** she eats cake **or
not**.

§19.3
SUBORDINATING CONJUNCTIONS

A *subordinating conjunction* begins a subordinate clause and shows its relationship with the main clause.

(a) Time relationships:

before	earlier action
after	later action
until	a limited time of action
when	a specific time of action
while	action at the same time

The *subordinate clause* can come first, followed by a comma:

Before we went home**,** we washed the dishes.
After I went to bed, I fell asleep.
Until he gets here, I am going to stay.
When he gets here, I am going to leave.
While she sleeps, he watches the baby.

The *main clause* can come first, and there is no comma:

We washed the dishes **before** we went home.
I fell asleep **after** I went to bed.
I am going to stay **until** he gets here.
I am going to leave **when** he gets here.
He watches the baby **while** she sleeps.

(b) Resulting relationships:

so that	to make action possible

So that she can read, she wears glasses.
She wears glasses **so that** she can read.

(c) Conditional relationships:

if	action dependent on other action
unless	required action to avoid negative action
whether (or not)	action on any condition

If you come early, I will dance with you.
Unless you come early, I won't dance with you.
Whether you come early **or not**, I won't dance with you.
I will dance with you **if** you come early.
I won't dance with you **unless** you come early.
I won't dance with you **whether or not** you come early.

(d) Other relationships:

where	a specific place
as if	in an untrue manner
rather than	preferable action
that	a fact
whether	unknown information

Where you live, there is a lot of traffic.
As if they weren't scared, they got on the plane.
Rather than upset her mother, she stayed home.
That she is a genius is certain.
Whether he went to work I don't know. (awkward)
There is a lot of traffic **where** you live.
They got on the plane **as if** they weren't scared.
She stayed home **rather than** upset her mother.
It is certain **that** she is a genius.
I don't know **whether** he went to work.

§20.

Discourse Markers

Discourse markers are words and expressions that tell the listener or reader how to interpret the words that follow them. Some basic messages and the discourse markers that introduce them are illustrated in this chapter. Discourse markers can be confusing, as they do not have exact equivalents in any two languages.

§20.1 EXPRESSING CHRONOLOGICAL ORDER

The following discourse markers are used to describe the order in which actions happen, as in a story or in giving directions:

(a) To introduce the first action: *First / In the first place*

(b) To introduce the second action: *Second / Next*

(c) To introduce the action that follows the previous action described: *Then / Next / After that*

(d) To introduce an action that occurs at the same time as another action: *Meanwhile / In the meantime*

(e) To introduce the final action: *Finally*

(f) To add an action that happened after the main story is finished: *Subsequently*

The word *then* is not followed by a comma. All of the other expressions in this section are followed by a comma.

EXAMPLES
A story: "Not my favorite day"
> **First, / In the first place**, my car broke down on the highway.
> **Second, / Next**, I realized that my cell phone didn't work.
> **Then / Next,** a policeman came and gave me a ticket.

> **Then / After that,** I waited an hour and a half for a tow truck.
> **Meanwhile, / In the meantime,** since I couldn't find anything to read, I sat there the whole time with nothing to do.
> **Finally,** the tow truck arrived and took my car away. (Fortunately, they took me home too.)
> **Subsequently,** I received a huge bill from the repair shop.

A recipe: "An easy cake"

> **First,** buy a cake mix, a can of frosting, vegetable oil, and eggs.
> **Next,** preheat the oven and grease two cake pans.
> **Then** mix everything together with an electric mixer.
> **After that,** pour the batter into the pans and place them in the oven.
> **After about thirty minutes,** take the cakes out of the oven, remove them from the pans, and let them cool.
> **Finally,** put the cakes on a serving plate and frost them.

§20.2 MAKING AN ARGUMENT MORE CONVINCING

The following discourse markers are used to introduce new information or to make an argument more convincing.

(a) To add the first information:

and / also / as well as

Do not use a comma after *and* or *as well as*.
> We should hire him.
> He is intelligent **and** responsible.
> He is intelligent **as well as** responsible.

Use a comma after *also* when it occurs at the beginning of a clause, but not if it is in the middle of one.
> He is intelligent; **also,** he is responsible.
> He is intelligent; he is **also** responsible.

(b) To add the next information:

in addition / plus

We should hire him.
He is intelligent and responsible; **in addition**, he
has a lot of experience.
He is intelligent and responsible, **plus,** he has a lot
of experience.

(c) To add information to defend a negative position:

besides

I don't want to hire him.
He is lazy and irresponsible. **Besides**, he has no
experience in this field.

(d) To add still more information:

furthermore

We should hire him.
He is intelligent and responsible; **in addition**, he
has a lot of experience.
Furthermore, he is cheerful and great to work with.

(e) To add more surprising information:

on top of that / to top it all off

We should hire him.
He is intelligent and responsible; in addition, he has
a lot of experience.
Furthermore, he is cheerful and great to work with.
On top of that, he works at night and on weekends.
To top it all off, he works at night and on weekends.

(f) To add the final and most important information:

moreover

We should hire him.
He is intelligent and responsible; in addition, he has
a lot of experience.

Furthermore, he is cheerful and great to work with. On top of that, he works at night and on weekends. **Moreover**, he has already been approved for the position by the committee.

Use a comma after *in addition, plus, besides, furthermore, on top of that, to top it all off,* and *moreover.*

§20.3 ILLUSTRATING PREVIOUS INFORMATION

The following discourse markers can be used to introduce information that reinforces a previously stated comment. Use a comma after these expressions.

in fact / as a matter of fact / indeed / actually

EXAMPLES

Yes, I know Washington quite well; **in fact / as a matter of fact, / indeed, / actually,** I lived there for ten years.

Sure, I know where Park Street is; **in fact, / as a matter of fact, / indeed, / actually,** I'm on my way there now.

She's a very smart girl; **in fact, / as a matter of fact, / indeed, / actually,** she's the best student in the class.

He's a good man; **in fact, / as a matter of fact, / indeed, / actually,** he's one of the nicest people I know.

No, she doesn't work here. **In fact, / As a matter of fact, / Indeed, / Actually,** I've never seen her before.

§20.4 CONTRADICTING PREVIOUS INFORMATION

The following discourse markers can be used to contradict a previous statement.

(a) To introduce information that contrasts with the previous information:

but / however

Use a comma before *but.* Do not use a comma after *but.*
He's intelligent, **but** he's irresponsible.

Use a period or a semi-colon or a comma before *however.*
Use a comma after *however*:
He's intelligent; **however**, he's irresponsible.

(b) To introduce an opposing statement:

on the other hand / in contrast

Use a comma after these expressions.

He's lazy and irresponsible. His brother, **on the other hand, / in contrast,** is a very hard worker.

(c) To introduce a statement that is not logical or expected in view of the previous information:

nevertheless / still

Use a comma after these expressions.

He's lazy and irresponsible; **nevertheless, / still,** I think we should give him a chance.

(d) To introduce a replacement for an item in the previous statement:

instead

Use a comma after *instead* when it occurs at the beginning of a sentence. Do not use a comma before *instead* when it occurs at the end of a sentence.

I don't want to hire him; **instead**, we should hire his brother.

I don't want to hire him; we should hire his brother **instead**.

(e) To introduce an opposite result if a condition is not met:

otherwise

Use a comma after *otherwise* when it occurs at the beginning of a sentence. Do not use a comma before *otherwise* when it occurs at the end of a sentence.

He will get a promotion; **otherwise,** he will move to another company.

He will get a promotion; he will move to another company **otherwise**.

§20.5 CORRECTING PREVIOUS INFORMATION

The following discourse markers can be used to introduce information that corrects a previous statement.

in fact / as a matter of fact / actually / (a pause)

Use a comma after *in fact, as a matter of fact,* or *actually.*

No, he isn't short; **in fact, / as a matter of fact, / actually, / (a pause)** he's quite tall.

No, I'm not her boss; **in fact, / as a matter of fact, / actually, / (a pause)** she's <u>my</u> boss.

He isn't an architect; **(pause)** he's an <u>engineer</u>.

§20.6 INDICATING THE CONSEQUENCES OF AN ACTION

The following discourse markers may be used to add information that describes the consequences of an action.

so / consequently / therefore / thus / as a result

Do not use a comma after *so* or *then.*

Use a comma after *consequently, therefore, thus,* and *as a result.*

We went to Mia's house, but she wasn't there, **so** we came back.

We went to Mia's house, but she wasn't there; **so / consequently, / therefore,** she doesn't know the news.

We were unable to contact her. **Thus, / As a result,** she doesn't know the news.

§20.7 EXPLAINING PREVIOUS INFORMATION

The following discourse markers can introduce statements that clarify or elaborate on previous information.

(a) To introduce another way of saying something:

in other words / that is / I mean

Use a comma after these expressions.

I think we should look at other programs; **in other words,** this one is unworkable.

She lives pretty far out of town, **that is,** beyond the beltway.

I want to go on a vacation. **I mean,** I really need a rest.

(b) To suggest an example of several choices:

for example / for instance

Use a comma before or after these expressions.
> You need a rest. Take a week off and go to the beach,
> **for example. / for instance**.
> You need a rest. **For example, / for instance,** take a
> week off and go to the beach.

(c) To give a specific example:

specifically

Use a comma after *specifically*.
> I want to take some time off, **specifically,** the month of
> July, so I can attend a wedding in my country.

§20.8 REDUCING THE IMPORTANCE OF THE PREVIOUS INFORMATION

The following discourse markers may be used to change the perspective of a previous statement.

(a) To add information that becomes more important than the previous information:

anyway / anyhow / at any rate / in any case

Use a comma after these expressions, but not before them.
> I don't want that job, but I'm sending them my résumé
> **anyway. / anyhow**.
> It's too bad she lost her job. **At any rate / In any case**,
> she doesn't have to worry, because her husband
> earns good money.

(b) To add a comment that explains why the previous information is not important:

after all

> I don't like the new car he bought, but **after all**, it's his
> car, not mine.

§20.9 VERIFYING PREVIOUS INFORMATION

The following expressions can be used to emphasize the validity of your comments.

Use a comma after these discourse markers.

(a) To emphasize that the previous statement is true:

really / indeed

I want to thank you all for coming to this graduation ceremony; **really, / indeed,** it is wonderful to see you all.

(b) To indicate that your audience already knows that the previous information is true:

naturally / of course / certainly

Naturally, / Of course, / Certainly, all of the students are happy that this day has finally arrived.

§20.10 EXPRESSING REASONS FOR AN ACTION

The following discourse markers can explain the motive of an action.

(a) To inform someone of the reason for an action:

because

Do not use a comma before or after *because*.
She invited you to her party **because** she likes you.

(b) To refer to the already known motive of an action:

since

Use a comma after the clause introduced by *since*:
Since she likes you, she invited you to her party.
Since she invited you, you should tell her whether you are going or not.

(c) To express "considering the fact that":

since

Since she got here early, I asked her to help me set the table.
Since we're going to the same hotel, let's share a taxi.
Since you didn't sleep last night, you should take a nap.
Since I don't have any money, he bought my ticket.

Do not confuse these meanings of *since* with that of the preposition *since* (see §17.3).

§20.11 EXPRESSING CONCESSION OR CONDITION

The following discourse markers can be used to explain one's reason for an action.

Use a comma before these expressions, but not after them.

(a) To introduce an illogical fact in view of the information in the accompanying clause:

although / even though / in spite of the fact that

She worked all day, **although / even though / in spite of the fact that** she was sick.
Although / Even though / In spite of the fact that she was sick, she worked all day.

(b) To indicate an extreme example that illogically does not change the accompanying information:

even if

She won't accept the job, **even if** we triple her present salary.
Even if we triple her present salary, she won't accept the job.

(c) To indicate something that is not true and that if it were true it would not change the accompanying information:

even if + subjunctive + *would*

Even if he were the last man on earth, I wouldn't marry him.

I wouldn't marry him **even if** he were the last man on earth.

See §16 for more information on subjunctives and §16.4 for details on *would.*

§20.12 SUMMARIZING

The following expressions express a conclusion to a series of events. Use a comma after these discourse markers.

(a) To give the last detail of a story:

so / in the end

So, / In the end, they solved all their problems and lived happily ever after.

(b) To sum up what was previously said:

in short / in summary

In short, / In summary, we have made a lot of progress, but we still have a lot to do.

(c) To end a presentation of ideas:

in conclusion

In conclusion, I would like to thank all of you who have worked so hard on this project.

Special Topics

§21.

Numbers

§21.1
WHOLE
NUMBERS

Read and say aloud the numbers between 0 and 99 as they are written below:

1	one	26	twenty-six	51	fifty-one	76	seventy-six
2	two	27	twenty-seven	52	fifty-two	77	seventy-seven
3	three	28	twenty-eight	53	fifty-three	78	seventy-eight
4	four	29	twenty-nine	54	fifty-four	79	seventy-nine
5	five	30	thirty	55	fifty-five	80	eighty
6	six	31	thirty-one	56	fifty-six	81	eighty-one
7	seven	32	thirty-two	57	fifty-seven	82	eighty-two
8	eight	33	thirty-three	58	fifty-eight	83	eighty-three
9	nine	34	thirty-four	59	fifty-nine	84	eighty-four
10	ten	35	thirty-five	60	sixty	85	eighty-five
11	eleven	36	thirty-six	61	sixty-one	86	eighty-six
12	twelve	37	thirty-seven	62	sixty-two	87	eighty-seven
13	thirteen	38	thirty-eight	63	sixty-three	88	eighty-eight
14	fourteen	39	thirty-nine	64	sixty-four	89	eighty-nine
15	fifteen	40	forty	65	sixty-five	90	ninety
16	sixteen	41	forty-one	66	sixty-six	91	ninety-one
17	seventeen	42	forty-two	67	sixty-seven	92	ninety-two
18	eighteen	43	forty-three	68	sixty-eight	93	ninety-three
19	nineteen	44	forty-four	69	sixty-nine	94	ninety-four
20	twenty	45	forty-five	70	seventy	95	ninety-five
21	twenty-one	46	forty-six	71	seventy-one	96	ninety-six
22	twenty-two	47	forty-seven	72	seventy-two	97	ninety-seven
23	twenty-three	48	forty-eight	73	seventy-three	98	ninety-eight
24	twenty-four	49	forty-nine	74	seventy-four	99	ninety-nine
25	twenty-five	50	fifty	75	seventy-five		

For the number 100 say one hundred   or   a hundred
              200   two hundred
              300   three hundred
              400   four hundred
              500   five hundred
              600   six hundred
              700   seven hundred
              800   eight hundred
              900   nine hundred

For numbers between the hundreds, say:

     256   two hundred and fifty-six
     649   six hundred and forty-nine
     706   seven hundred and six

For the
number   1,000   say   one thousand   or   a
                                                 thousand
     20,000   twenty thousand
     36,000   thirty-six thousand
   400,000   four hundred thousand
   512,000   five hundred and twelve
                     thousand
   603,000   six hundred and three
                     thousand

For numbers between the thousands, say:

    1,637   one thousand, six hundred and
              thirty-seven
  15,742   fifteen thousand, seven hundred and
              forty-two
  59,825   fifty-nine thousand, eight hundred and
              twenty-five
500,032   five hundred thousand and thirty two
999,999   nine hundred and ninety-nine thousand,
              nine hundred and ninety-nine

For 1,000,000   say   one million   or   a million
  46,000,000   forty-six million
792,000,000   seven hundred and
                   ninety-two million

For numbers between the millions, say:

    2,364,572   two million, three hundred and sixty-four thousand, five hundred and seventy-two

Higher numbers are usually estimated and written in words.

1,000,000,000		one billion	or	a billion
	or	about a billion		
		around a billion		
		almost a billion		
		more than a billion		
1,000,000,000,000		a trillion		

That company is worth billions of dollars.
The country is trillions of dollars in debt.

§21.2
FRACTIONS

To read or say fractions of numbers, say:

½	one-half	or	a half
3½	three and a half		
⅔	two-thirds		
6⅔	six and two-thirds		
¾	three-fourths	or	three quarters
4¾	four and three-quarters		
⅗	three-fifths		
2⅗	two and three-fifths		
⅝	five-eighths		
5⅝	five and five-eighths		

To say fractions with measurements (see Measurement Table in appendix), say:

½ cup	half a cup	or	a half-cup	or	one half-cup
½ mile	half a mile		a half-mile		one half-mile
⅔ teaspoon	two-thirds of a teaspoon				
¾ yard	three-quarters of a yard				
⅝ inch	five-eighths of an inch				
1½ cups	one and a half cups		or		a cup and a half
3½ cups	three and a half cups				
2⅔ tea-spoons	two and two-thirds teaspoons				
3⅝ yards	three and five-eighths yards				

§21.3
DECIMALS

To read or say decimal numbers, say:

3.5	three point five	or	three and five-tenths
4.9	four point nine		four and nine-tenths
6.75	six point seven five		six and seventy-five hundredths
8.32	eight point three two		eight and thirty-two hundredths

To talk about money, say:

a penny	or	one cent	or	a cent
a nickel		five cents		
a dime		ten cents		
a quarter		twenty-five cents		
a dollar bill		a one	or	a single
a five-dollar bill		a five		
a ten-dollar bill		a ten		
three twenty-dollar bills		three twenties		

Amounts of money are expressed as follows:

$5.63	five dollars and sixty-three cents
$10.72	ten dollars and seventy-two cents
$564.03	five hundred and sixty-four dollars and three cents
$3,729.17	three thousand, seven hundred and twenty-nine dollars and seventeen cents

§22.

Days and Dates

What day is it?

The names of the days of the week are:

Sunday
Monday
Tuesday
Wednesday
Thursday
Friday
Saturday

Saturday and Sunday are *the weekend*.

To tell the day of an event, use **on**:

When does your vacation start?	It starts **on** Monday.
When are you leaving?	I'm leaving **on** Tuesday.

What month is it?

The months of the year are:

January
February
March
April
May
June
July
August
September
October
November
December

To tell the month of an event, use **in**:

When does your vacation start?	It starts **in** August.
When are you leaving?	I'm leaving **in** September.

What's the date?

To write the date, use **month + cardinal number + comma + year**:

November 23, 1974

To say the date aloud, use an <u>ordinal number</u> — see **§7.1-2**.

> *the* + ordinal number + *of* + month
> or
> month + ordinal number

It's the 29th of March.	It's March 29th.
It's the 1st of May.	It's May 1st.
It's the 4th of July.	It's July 4th.
It's the 31st of December.	It's December 31st.

To tell the date of an event, use *on*:

When does your vacation start?	It starts **on** the 28th of August.
When are you leaving?	I'm leaving **on** September 3rd.

For a year, say:

1776	seventeen seventy-six
1852	eighteen fifty-two
1965	nineteen sixty-five
1999	nineteen ninety-nine

To tell the year of an event, use *in*:

When does your vacation start?	It starts **in** 2007.
When are you leaving?	I'm leaving **in** 2008.

§23.

Telling Time

To give the present time, when the time is exactly on the hour, use:

> *It is* + the hour + *o'clock*
> or
> *It is* + the hour + A.M. or P.M.

A.M. = in the morning
P.M. = in the afternoon, evening, or at night

What time is it?

It is one o'clock.	or	It is one A.M.
It is two o'clock.		It is two P.M.
It is seven o'clock.		It is seven A.M.
It is eleven o'clock.		It's eleven P.M.
It is noon.		It's twelve P.M.
It is midnight.		It's twelve A.M.

When the time is before or after the hour, use:

> the digital form: *It is* + the hour + the number of minutes past the hour
> or
> the traditional form: *It is* + the number of minutes after the hour or the number of minutes before the hour

What time is it?

Digital Form	Traditional Forms	
It's one-oh-five.	It's five after one.	It's five past one.
It's two-ten.	It's ten after two.	It's ten past two.
It's three-fifteen.	It's fifteen after three.	It's fifteen past three.
	It's a quarter after three.	It's a quarter past three.
It's four-twenty.	It's twenty after four.	It's twenty past four.
It's five-twenty-five.	It's twenty-five after five.	It's twenty-five past five.
It's six-thirty.	It's six-thirty.	It's half past six.
It's seven-thirty-five.	It's twenty-five to eight.	It's twenty-five of eight.
It's eight-forty.	It's twenty to nine.	It's twenty of nine.
It's nine-forty-five.	It's fifteen to ten.	It's fifteen of ten.
	It's a quarter to ten.	It's a quarter of ten.
It's ten-fifty.	It's ten to eleven.	It's ten of eleven.
It's eleven-fifty-five.	It's five to twelve.	It's five of twelve.

To give the time of a future event, use **at + the time**:

What time is the concert?	It's at eight o'clock. It's at 8:00 P.M.
What time is the party?	It's at seven-thirty.
What time does the class start?	It starts at five-fifteen.
What time are we leaving?	We're leaving at 6:00 A.M.

To emphasize an exact time, use **on the dot** or **sharp**:

What time does the class start?	It starts at five-fifteen on the dot.
What time are we leaving?	We're leaving at 6:00 A.M. sharp.

§24.

Talking About the Weather

To tell present weather conditions, use:

It's + adjective

How's the weather?

It's nice.
It's pleasant.
It's dreary.
It's sunny.
It's cloudy.
It's rainy.
It's foggy.
It's hot. (See temperature chart in appendix)
It's warm.
It's cool.
It's chilly.
It's cold.
It's freezing.
It's windy.
It's humid.

When there is precipitation at the moment, use

It's + present participle

It's raining.
It's snowing.
It's sleeting.
It's hailing.

Extreme weather events include the following:

What is happening?

There is lightning.	(a flash of electricity in the sky)
There is thunder.	(the loud noise after lightning)
It's a storm.	(a strong wind with rain, snow, or hail, or thunder and lightning)
It's a gale.	(a strong wind)
It's a hurricane.	(violent winds over 75 miles per hour)

It's a cyclone.	(a violent storm moving around a center of low pressure, which also moves)
It's a tornado.	(a violent, destructive wind)
It's a flood.	(a flow of water over land that is usually dry)
It's an earthquake.	(a shaking or sliding of the ground caused by changes underneath)

LET'S REVIEW

Test Yourself

§1.

Letters and Words

1. Fill in the blanks to identify the following items:
   a. *Today, fast, happily,* and *here* are examples of _____.
   b. *Tall, new, red,* and *pretty* are _____.
   c. *Mon., Sept., ch., Mr.,* and *Mrs.* are _____.
   d. *I, he, him, them, us,* and *her* are _____.
   e. *a, e, i, o,* and *u* are _____.
   f. *went, gone, have,* and *sing,* are _____.
   g. *for, out, by,* and *to* are _____.
   h. *I, m, t,* and *s* are _____.
   i. *but, so, and,* and *however* are _____.
   j. *nurse, town,* and *books* are _____.

2. Write the abbreviations for the following:
   a. medical doctor _____.
   b. the title of a married woman _____.
   c. and so forth _____.
   d. the degree of a dentist _____.
   e. that is _____.
   f. doctor of laws _____.
   g. Robert Runyon, whose father has the same name _____.
   h. in the morning _____.
   i. for example _____.
   j. the business title of a woman _____.

§2.

Capitalization

3. Write capital letters where necessary:
   a. mr. jones is from canada.
      _____

   b. do you think i am john's brother?
      _____

   c. he was born on tuesday, the 5th of february.
      _____

   d. my good friend carol is from new york, but she lives in washington, d. c.
      _____

   e. california, michigan, and texas are all states of the united states of america.
      _____

§3.

Punctuation

4. Punctuate the following sentences, and write capital letters where necessary:
   a. here comes miss phillips our new secretary

   _____

   b. where are the computer discs

   _____

   c. soo young bought three tables a sofa and two chairs

   _____

   d. i need the following things paper pencils a stapler and some staples

   _____

   e. mrs johnson doesn't have a book so she is using marys

   _____

§4.

Sentences

5. Underline the subject in the following sentences:
   a. John and James are here.
   b. My friends play tennis.
   c. Her brother likes swimming and diving.
   d. Swimming and diving are fun.
   e. It is nice to see you.

6. Underline the predicate in the following sentences:
   a. John and James are here.
   b. My friends play tennis.
   c. Her brother likes swimming and diving.
   d. He swims and dives every day.
   e. Swimming is fun.

7. Underline the complement in the following sentences:
   a. Mary is my sister.
   b. She seems tired today.
   c. The tests look difficult.
   d. Are you sure?
   e. I don't want to get sick.

8. Underline the direct object in the following sentences:
   a. Susan called Mary yesterday.
   b. I love candy and flowers.
   c. We need money.
   d. Do you have friends here?
   e. He bought three tickets.

9. Underline the indirect object in the following sentences:
   a. He gave her the money.
   b. Did you tell us to go home?
   c. We are going to show you the presents tomorrow.
   d. David sent Mary a letter.
   e. I told them the secret.

§5.

Nouns

10. Write the plural forms of the following nouns:
    a. girl   _____
    b. series   _____
    c. tomato   _____
    d. person   _____
    e. city   _____
    f. leaf   _____
    g. box   _____
    h. piano   _____
    i. child   _____
    j. man   _____

11. Write the names of the non-count nouns:
    a. tables, chairs, and beds _____
    b. letters and postcards _____
    c. tools and supplies _____
    d. nickels, dimes, and quarters _____
    e. necklaces, bracelets, and rings _____
    f. facts of interest _____
    g. notes, sounds, and songs _____
    h. cleaning and dusting _____
    i. assignments for after school _____
    j. suggestions of help _____

12. Choose the correct noun to fill in the blank:
    a. I need a _____.
            ring   rings   jewelry
    b. She wants three _____.
            ring   rings   jewelry
    c. They need a few _____.
            money   dollars   dollar
    d. I made a little _____.
            money   dollars   dollar
    e. He spoke to each _____.
            children   girls   child
    f. We have some _____.
            friend   friends   neighbor
    g. Both _____ are nice.
            sisters   brother   daughter

h. They made an _____.
   car   appointments   appointment
i. He doesn't have any _____.
   friend   sister   brothers
j. She has many _____.
   friends   sister   family
k. Give them every _____.
   box   boxes
l. They have too much _____.
   chairs   tables   furniture
m. We have too many _____.
   chairs   table   furniture

13. In each sentence, rewrite the noun in parentheses, and make it plural if necessary:
   a. I drank two (coffee) _____ before lunch.
   b. They grow a lot of (coffee) _____ in Colombia.
   c. She served (chicken) _____ and french fries for dinner.
   d. She raises (chicken) _____ on her farm.
   e. He wears (glass) _____ for reading.
   f. I would love a (glass) _____ of water.
   g. Are these cups made of (glass) _____?
   h. I used a lot of (paper) _____ when I wrote that (paper) _____ on the economy.

14. Identify and capitalize the proper nouns:
   a. They left in july.
   b. We are going next friday.
   c. Her birthday party is at her sister charlotte's new house.
   d. Do you want to vist the white house when you are in washington?
   e. Mr. and mrs. harrison live in new york city.
   f. They lived in the state of louisiana before.
   g. You have to cross an old bridge to get across old creek.

15. Combine each pair of sentences into one, using an appositive:

a. Mary is John's wife. She is a doctor.

_____.

b. I like Barbara. She is my new neighbor.

_____.

c. You should call Jack. He is the computer expert.

_____.

d. The market has fresh vegetables. The market is our favorite place to shop.

_____.

e. Carolyn is the best singer in the choir. She is my sister.

_____.

16. Write the possessive form of the noun in the following sentences:

a. A house that the Harrises own is the _____ house.

b. Dresses that Sally has are _____ dresses.

c. The cars that my friends have are _____ cars.

d. The money that the people have is _____ money.

e. A book that James has is _____ book.

17. Rewrite the following to show possession:

a. My friend has a mother.

_____.

b. The book has a name.

_____.

c. The school has an address.

_____.

d. My friend has an address.

_____.

e. The team has a captain.

_____.

f. The country has a president.

_____.

g. The suit has a color.

_____.

h. The teacher has a name.

_____.

    i. The cat has a leg.

_____.

    j. The table has a leg.

_____.

    k. Sayed has a leg.

_____.

18. Use *more, less*, or *fewer* to combine each pair of sentences into one:

    a. I have five books. You have three books.

_____.

    b. She has four rings. Her friend has two rings.

_____.

    c. I have a lot of information. He has a little information.

_____.

    d. They have little money. We have some money.

_____.

19. Use *the same* to combine each pair of sentences into one:

    a. He has three pencils. She has three pencils.

_____.

    b. My shoes are size six. Your shoes are size six.

_____.

    c. This turkey weighs twenty pounds. That turkey weighs twenty pounds.

_____.

    d. Your husband is six feet tall. My husband is six feet tall.

_____.

    e. This fabric is four yards long. That fabric is four yards long.

_____.

    f. A man is here to see you. He was here before.

_____.

§6.

Pronouns

20. Change the underlined nouns to subject pronouns:
     a. <u>Angela</u> was here yesterday.

     _____.

     b. <u>Ken and Sharon</u> walked home.

     _____.

     c. <u>Amy and Tracy</u> told us about the movie.

     _____.

     d. <u>Tom</u> really liked it.

     _____.

     e. <u>Tom and I</u> are going out tomorrow night.

     _____.

21. Fill in the blanks with the correct impersonal
     pronouns:
     a. I am new in town. Where do _____
         buy school supplies here?
     b. Oh, _____ sell them at the drugstore.
     c. At the drugstore? Do _____ sell
         hardware there, too?
     d. Yes, _____ do.
         _____ can buy sewing supplies
         there, too!
     e. _____ can buy a lot of things at
         the drugstore!

22. Change the underlined nouns to object pronouns:
     a. We are buying the basket for <u>Marilyn</u>.

     _____.

     b. She told <u>Sally and me</u> that she liked <u>the basket</u>.

     _____.

     c. I'm not sending <u>David</u> the pictures.

     _____.

     d. I'd rather send <u>the pictures</u> to <u>his mother</u>.

     _____.

     e. She always calls <u>me and my husband</u> when
         she's here.

     _____.

23. Change the underlined nouns to pronouns:
    a. Janice and Cheryl liked Doug's car.

    _____.

    b. Please give the tickets to Joel.

    _____.

    c. Tony wanted to buy the ring for Patricia.

    _____.

    d. These hats are Bonnie's and Judy's.

    _____.

    e. Joe hurt Joe on Joe's way to Christina's house.

    _____.

24. Use reciprocal pronouns to combine each pair of sentences into one sentence:
    a. Jim likes Ellie. Ellie likes Jim.

    _____.

    b. Matt helps Paul. Paul helps Matt.

    _____.

    c. Lisa called William. William called Lisa.

    _____.

    d. Brian promised Miriam. Miriam promised Brian.

    _____.

25. Write the correct pronouns in the blanks:
    a. (My friend and I) _____ are tired. Please give _____ a drink of water.
    b. Thank you for helping my friend and _____.
    c. I saw (James and Judy) _____ at the football game.
    d. (James) _____ was watching the game, but (Judy) _____ wasn't.
    e. (Judy) _____ and I began to talk.
    f. Later, I told _____ goodbye, and I waved to _____, too. _____ both waved back to _____.
    g. (David) _____ called me last night and told _____ that _____ was coming to study with _____.
    h. I told _____ that _____ could come to my house at 8 o'clock, and that he should bring _____ book.

    i. (Sandra and Cheryl) Sandra and _____ are sisters.

    j. They don't live near _____, but they talk to _____ on the phone every day.

    k. Cheryl said that _____ had talked to _____ sister for two hours yesterday.

26. Write in the correct reflexive or intensive pronouns:

    a. Who made your dress?

          I did. I made it _____.

    b. Who went with Julie?

          Nobody. She went _____.

    c. Nobody can help him; he needs to help _____.

    d. I can't get back in the store because the door locked _____ behind me.

    e. If you want a birthday party, why don't you plan it _____?

27. Write in the correct possessive pronouns:

    a. This dish belongs to Pat and Sam. It is _____.

    b. That pizza is Joe's. It is _____.

    c. Those sandwiches are Patricia's. They are _____.

    d. You brought the cake. It is _____.

    e. Peter and I made the apple pie. It is _____.

    f. Cecil gave me this plate. It is _____.

28. Rewrite the sentences using "belong to":

    a. That's Jan's purse.

        _____.

    b. This is our car.

        _____.

    c. Those are the neighbors' flowers.

        _____.

    d. Which coat is yours?

        _____.

29. Complete the following with the correct relative pronouns:
    a. She is a girl. She sold us the cookies.
       Who is she? She is the girl _____
       sold us the cookies.
    b. I bought the cookies. They had chocolate icing.
       Which cookies did you buy? I bought the ones
       _____ had chocolate icing.
    c. I paid the man. He is standing over there.
       Who(m) did you pay? The man _____
       I paid is standing over there.
    d. He is a man. His daughter sold us the cookies.
       Who is he? He is the man _____
       daughter sold us the cookies.

30. Match each pronoun with its meaning:
too many	_____	a. a small amount
neither	_____	b. not one or the other
another	_____	c. a large number
few	_____	d. more than is good
either	_____	e. not one person
someone	_____	f. a small number
somewhere	_____	g. one place
not anyone	_____	h. one person
a few	_____	i. one or the other
a lot	_____	j. not enough
a little	_____	k. one more

31. Choose *another, the other, others,* or *the others* to complete the following:
    a. New York is a big city. There are many _____.
    b. New York is a city in the east. Washington is

       _____.
    c. Do you know any of _____?
    d. There are two New Yorks. One is a city, and
       _____ is a state.

32. Fill in the blanks with the correct pronoun from the list on the right:

a. There are no people here. There isn't _____ in the store.

b. I hear a voice. _____ is in the store.

c. I can't find my watch _____.

d. I hope I find it _____.

e. We can't find _____ to eat.

f. I need to eat _____.

g. The box is empty. There is _____ in it.

h. She is a doctor, and I am _____, too.

i. He ate two cookies. Now he wants _____.

j. We gave tickets to all the participants. _____ has a ticket.

another
something
anybody
one
anywhere
nothing
each
someone
anything
somewhere

§7.

Adjectives

33. Choose *a, an, the,* or *no article (0)* for the following:
    a. She is _____ artist.
    b. We are _____ friends.
    c. That is _____ book I sent you.
    d. Those are not _____ flowers I sent you.
    e. New York is _____ big city.
    f. That is _____ interesting question.
    g. That is _____ interesting information.
    h. He sends me _____ flowers every day.
    i. Can you give me _____ advice?
    j. He is _____ big boy now.

34. Choose *0* or *the* before the following proper nouns:
    a. _____ Joann   g. _____ Chile
    b. _____ September   h. _____ Clarks
    c. _____ Philippines   i. _____ Atlantic Ocean
    d. _____ India   j. _____ University of
    e. _____ United States   Michigan
    f. _____ Wednesday   k. _____ Mrs. Martin
                             l. _____ Western
                                     Hemisphere

35. Choose *0* or *the* to fill in the blanks correctly:
    a. The student is on his way to _____ school now.
    b. Peter is going to _____ jail to visit his friend.
    c. I didn't go to _____ work today.
    d. I stayed at _____ home.
    e. I always eat _____ dinner by myself.
    f. She had _____ dinner at that restaurant
       _____ last night.
    g. _____ last week was _____ last week of our
       vacation.

36. Express the following ordinal numbers in words:
    a. 1st   _____
    b. 3rd   _____
    c. 8th   _____
    d. 12th _____
    e. 16th _____
    f. 22nd _____
    g. 34th _____
    h. 45th _____
    i. 67th _____
    j. 99th _____

37. Fill in the blanks with the correct possessive adjectives:
    a. That's my brother's book. It's _____ book.
    b. Mary says it's hers. She says it's _____ book.
    c. No, it isn't hers; it's ours. I say it's _____ book.
    d. Maybe it belongs to Mark and Patty. Maybe it's _____ book.
    e. You are all wrong. It's mine. See, it has _____ name inside the front cover.

38. Choose the correct noun determiner in the following sentences:
    a. I need _____ jewelry.
          a   a little   a few
    b. She wants _____ bracelets.
          a   a little   a few
    c. They need _____ money.
          a lot   a lot of   a few
    d. I made _____ dollars.
          another   a few   any
    e. He spoke to _____ children.
          all of the   every   each
    f. We have _____ neighbor.
          some   a few   one
    g. He doesn't have _____ neighbors.
          a few   any   one
    h. She bought _____ new chairs.
          another   any   three
    i. He has _____ friends.
          many   too many   too much
    j. I have _____ homework.
          many   too many   too much

39. Choose *this, that, these,* or *those* to fill in the blanks correctly:
    a. _____ ring I am wearing was my mother's.
    b. I gave him _____ shirt he has on.
    c. Are _____ dresses over there on sale?
    d. I can't find _____ information you sent me.
    e. My feet hurt. I need to take _____ shoes off.
    f. I came here because _____ shop is my favorite.

40. Write in the correct proper adjectives:
    a. He is a citizen of the United States. He is an _____ citizen.
    b. She is from Italy. She is _____.
    c. That is the flag of Mexico. It is the _____ flag.
    d. This wine is from France. It is _____ wine.
    e. Her shoes were made in Spain. They are _____ shoes.

41. Choose the correct adjective in the following sentences:
    a. I bought a _____ box.
       jewelry   earring   earrings
    b. My sister works at a _____ store.
       dresses   curtains   shoe
    c. The book was so _____ that I got _____ and fell asleep.
       boring   bored
    d. We were _____ because the show was _____.
       fascinating   fascinated
    e. The dress was expensive; it was a _____ dress.
       three-hundred-dollar   three-hundred-dollars
    f. Her husband is big; he is a _____ athlete.
       six-foot, two-hundred-pound
       six-feet, two-hundred pounds

42. Provide the correct adjective form in each sentence:
    a. This hat is (elegant) _____ of all.
    b. Those are (nice) _____ houses in the neighborhood.
    c. You have an (easy) _____ assignment than I.
    d. Your teacher is (patient) _____ than mine.
    e. The weather is much (hot) _____ than last month's.
    f. She is a (good) _____ player than her sister.
    g. Her dishes are (same) _____ mine.
    h. Her furniture is (different) _____ mine.
    i. The weather is getting (warm, gradually) _____.
    j. That movie is (bad) _____ than the one we saw last week.

43. Provide the correct form of the adjectives *cheap* or *expensive:*

    My shoes cost $20. Your shoes cost $30. Bob's shoes cost $30. Jane's shoes cost $60.

    a. My shoes are _____ yours.
    b. Your shoes are _____ mine.
    c. Bob's shoes are _____ yours.
    d. Jane's shoes are _____ ours.
    e. Jane's shoes are _____ of all.
    f. My shoes are _____ of all.

44. Write in the correct form of the adjectives *light* or *heavy:*

    Bobby weighs fifty pounds. Billy weighs fifty-five pounds. Jimmy weighs fifty-five pounds. John weighs sixty pounds.

    a. Bobby is _____ Jimmy.
    b. Jimmy is _____ Billy.
    c. John is _____ Jimmy.
    d. John is _____ of all.
    e. Bobby is _____ of all.

45. Put the adjectives in the correct order:
    a. _____ skirt.
       yellow / long / beautiful / her
    b. _____ blouse
       ugly / red / old / my
    c. _____ tie
       lovely / his / silk / blue
    d. _____ coat
       your / wool / new / nice
    e. _____ shoes
       dirty / leather / old / those

46. Use *else* to express the following:
    a. I don't see another person.

    _____.

    b. We don't need another thing.

    _____.

    c. We want to go to another place.

    _____.

    d. I think he is looking for another thing.

    _____.

    e. No other place will please him.

    _____.

    f. I can't live with a different person.

    _____.

§8.

Verbs—Introduction

47. Circle the correct word in the following definitions:
   a. To indicate the time of the action of a sentence, use the correct _____.

      tense   mood   voice

   b. To emphasize the subject of a sentence, use the _____.

      subjunctive mood
      active voice
      passive voice

   c. To emphasize the object of the action, use the _____.

      subjunctive mood
      active voice
      passive voice

   d. An infinitive is _____.

      the basic form + *ed*
      the basic form + *ing*
      to + the basic form

   e. To find a verb in the dictionary, look for the _____.

      infinitive   present tense   basic form

48. Write the present participle form of each of the following verbs:

   a. cry _____   f. sleep _____
   b. freeze _____   g. whip _____
   c. bring _____   h. choose _____
   d. die _____   i. study _____
   e. shop _____   j. occur _____

49. Write the past participle form of each of the following verbs:

   a. try _____   f. dance _____
   b. permit _____   g. sew _____
   c. agree _____   h. clean _____
   d. fold _____   i. play _____
   e. ship _____   j. study _____

§9.

Verbs—Present Time

50. Fill in the blanks with the correct present tense form of *be:*
    a. They _____ fine.
    b. She _____ beautiful.
    c. No. There (not) _____ any spoons.
    d. I _____ from New York.
    e. It _____ Mary's book.
    f. We _____ the secretaries.
    g. The car _____ in the parking lot.
    h. Their parties _____ on Sundays.
    i. Her new dress _____ purple.
    j. No, John (not) _____ my brother.

51. Write a question for each of the previous statements.
    a. _____.
    b. _____.
    c. _____.
    d. _____.
    e. _____.
    f. _____.
    g. _____.
    h. _____.
    i. _____.
    j. _____.

52. Answer the following questions with a positive short form:
    a. Are you well?

    _____.

    b. Is he happy?

    _____.

    c. Are they here?

    _____.

    d. Is she alone?

    _____.

    e. Are we late?

    _____.

    f. Is it O.K.?

    _____.

g. Am I your friend?

_____.

h. Is there a telephone here?

_____.

i. Are there any good restaurants near here?

_____.

j. Is it cold?

_____.

53. Answer the following questions with a negative short answer:

a. Are you well?

_____.

b. Is he happy?

_____.

c. Are they here?

_____.

d. Is she alone?

_____.

e. Are we late?

_____.

f. Is it O.K.?

_____.

g. Am I your assistant?

_____.

h. Is there a telephone here?

_____.

i. Are there any good restaurants near here?

_____.

j. Is it hot?

_____.

54. For each of the following statements, write a response that shows you are surprised:

a. We are sisters.

_____.

b. He isn't hungry.

_____.

c. She is asleep.

_____.

d. They aren't at home.

_____.

e. I'm not tired.

_____.

f. You are beautiful.

_____.

g. He is my boyfriend.

_____.

h. She isn't married.

_____.

§9.1-2
The Present Tense— Other Verbs

55. Write the *he / she / it* form of the following verbs:
    a. have   He _____
    b. go   Mr. Jones _____
    c. laugh   He _____
    d. come   It _____
    e. cry   Billy _____
    f. take   She _____
    g. sing   Miss Ortiz _____
    h. do   Jessica _____
    i. work   it _____
    j. love   He _____

56. Write the negative forms for the following:
    a. have   Kim _____
    b. go   Larry _____
    c. laugh   Lisa _____
    d. come   It _____
    e. cry   She _____
    f. take   He _____
    g. do   Ms. Martin _____
    h. work   he _____
    i. exercise   she _____

57. Write a surprised response to the following statements:
    a. I don't have a car.

    _____.

    b. She doesn't like me.

    _____.

    c. We love it here.

    _____.

    d. He needs help.

    _____.

    e. They don't live here anymore.

    _____.

58. Rewrite the following sentences, putting the time words in the correct place:

a. We go to the movies on Saturdays. (usually)

_____.

b. We eat dinner. (at eight o'clock)

_____.

c. He helps us. (often)

_____.

d. He helps us. (sometimes)

_____.

e. He helps us. (on the weekends)

_____.

f. She takes trips. (occasionally)

_____.

g. I wear a bathing suit. (in the summer)

_____.

h. They visit me. (rarely)

_____.

i. I call them. (always, at night)

_____.

j. She studies. (never, in the afternoon)

_____.

k. He exercises. (every day, at six o'clock)

_____.

l. We exercise. (often, in the morning)

_____.

59. Write a question that is answered by the underlined word in each of the following sentences:

a. We like Peggy.

_____?

b. We call Peggy.

_____?

c. Peggy is our friend.

_____?

d. We take her to the zoo.

_____?

e. We take her to the zoo.

_____?

f. We see animals.

_____?

g. They smell bad.

_____?

60. Write a question that is answered by the underlined word in each of the following sentences:
    a. I have <u>six</u> cousins.

    _____?

    b. They live <u>here</u> now.

    _____?

    c. <u>They</u> eat a lot.

    _____?

    d. My aunt cooks <u>chicken</u>.

    _____?

    e. <u>My aunt</u> cooks chicken.

    _____?

    f. My cousins eat <u>a lot</u> of chicken.

    _____?

    g. My aunt buys the chicken <u>at the market</u>.

    _____?

    h. She usually shops <u>on Saturdays</u>.

    _____?

61. Fill in the blanks with the correct verb form:
    a. They (go) _____ to the movies on Saturdays.
    b. We (like) _____ chocolate ice cream.
    c. No, he (live/not) _____ here.
    d. No, I (have/not) _____ a car.
    e. She (work) _____ at the bank.
    f. My friend and I usually (meet) _____ in the library.
    g. Sylvia (leave) _____ home at 6 o'clock.
    h. She (watch) _____ television every evening.

62. Write a question for each of the previous statements.
    a. _____?
    b. _____?
    c. _____?
    d. _____?
    e. _____?
    f. _____?
    g. _____?
    h. _____?

§9.1-3
Present Tense
Modals

63. Express the following, using modals:

   a. You are able to sing.

   _____.

   b. You don't know if your friend is at home.

   _____.

   c. You give your employee permission to go home.

   _____.

   d. You ask someone to help you carry a package.

   _____.

   e. You ask for advice about calling a doctor.

   _____.

   f. You advise a friend to go to the doctor.

   _____.

   g. You are required to work.

   _____.

   h. Your friend does not need to work.

   _____.

   i. You warn your friend not to make noise.

   _____.

   j. You prefer to live in the city.

   _____.

64. Fill in the blanks to complete the following:

   a. Can you dance?
      Yes, I _____.
   b. Can your sister play the piano?
      Yes, she _____.
   c. Can your brothers sing?
      No, they _____.
   d. Where is Mike?
      I don't know. He _____ sick.
   e. Where are Debbie and Scott?
      I don't know. _____ they are lost.
   f. May we go home now, Miss Gibbs?
      Yes, you _____.
   g. May Johnnie go home, too?
      No, he _____.
   h. You look sick. I think you _____ stay home.
      You _____ work when you are sick.
      It is very important for me to work. I
      _____ work today.
   i. No, you _____ . Your boss says you
      _____ work today.
      Yes, but my boss _____ pay my bills.

j. You are very sick. The doctor says you
    _____ work when you are sick.
k. Geoff isn't here yet. He is usually on time. He
    _____ in a traffic jam.
l. I want to order a salad. What _____ you
    _____ to eat?
    I never eat salad. I _____ _____ have
    a sandwich than a salad.

§9.2 PRESENT PROGRESSIVE TENSE

65. Write in the present progressive form of each verb in
     the following sentences:
     a. He (sleep) _____ at present.
     b. She (study) _____ at the moment.
     c. We (paint) _____ the living room this week.
     d. They (drive) _____ home now.
     e. I (relax) _____ this month because I am on
         vacation.
     f. _____ you (enjoy) _____ your vacation?

66. Make the sentences negative:
     a. He (sleep) _____ at present.
     b. She (study) _____ at the moment.
     c. We (paint) _____ the living room this week.
     d. They (drive) _____ home now.
     e. I (relax) _____ this month because I am not
         on vacation.

67. Rewrite the sentences using the present progressive
     tense:
     a. Mark continues to be asleep.

         _____.

     b. Joe calls me a lot and I am annoyed.

         _____.

     c. Heather doesn't work now, as before.

         _____.

     d. George doesn't study here now, as before.

         _____.

     e. Sam studies here now, as before.

         _____.

68. Choose between the present tense and the present
     progressive tense in the following expressions:
     a. He (like) _____ movies.
     b. We (eat) _____ at 6:30 every night.
     c. They (watch) _____ TV right now.
     d. She always (wash) _____ the dishes after
         dinner.
     e. I (write) _____ this exercise.
     f. My mother can't help you; she (talk) _____
         on the telephone.
     g. I (want) _____ my dinner now.
     h. They (have) _____ a party in that room.
     i. They (have) _____ a lot of money now.
     j. My sister isn't here; she (study) _____ at
         the library.
     k. I (think) _____ he's nice.
     l. I (think) _____ about him now.

69. Choose the present tense or the present progressive
     tense to fill in the blanks in the following paragraph:

     I am a kindergarten teacher, and I would like to tell
     you about my class. The children always (come)
     a. _____ to school ready for fun and games.
     Cindy, for example, (enjoy) b. _____ the toys in
     the corner right now. At the moment, she and Mary
     (play) c. _____ with the blocks. They (talk)
     d. _____ about their favorite colors. Cindy (like)
     e. _____ blue, and Mary (like) f. _____
     red. Cindy (stay) g. _____ with a babysitter this
     year, and she rarely (play) h. _____ with other
     children. At home she (be) i. _____ quiet, and
     she never (invite) j. _____ friends to her house.
     Another child is Bobby. He (paint) k. _____ a
     picture this morning. He (use) l. _____ all
     the colors in the box, and (make) m. _____
     a beautiful present for his mother. At home, he
     always (watch) n. _____ TV. Look! There (be)
     o. _____ Jennifer. She (jump) p. _____
     rope with her friend, Kathy. They (have) q. _____
     a good time.

§9.4 PRESENT PERFECT TENSE

70. Write the present perfect form of each verb:
    a. We live. _____
    b. They eat. _____
    c. He sleeps. _____
    d. She cries. _____
    e. You come. _____
    f. We go. _____
    g. I work. _____
    h. We write. _____
    i. You study. _____
    j. She reads. _____

71. Change the following present tense verbs to the present perfect:
    a. I don't change. _____
    b. He doesn't break anything. _____
    c. She doesn't win. _____
    d. You don't promise, do you? _____
    e. He doesn't help, does he? _____

72. Choose *since* or *for* to fill in the blanks in the following sentences:
    a. I have lived here _____ 1988.
    b. They have been our neighbors _____ twelve years.
    c. He has worked there _____ a long time.
    d. I have been waiting _____ five o'clock.
    e. They have been talking _____ midnight.

73. Write a question for each of the statements in the preceding question.
    a. _____?
    b. _____?
    c. _____?
    d. _____?
    e. _____?

74. Write a sentence using the present perfect tense to give a reason for each of the following facts:

    a. She knows how to drive this car.

    _____.

    b. I know where your house is.

    _____.

    c. We know every scene in that movie.

    _____.

    d. They are not hungry.

    _____.

    e. He is very hungry.

    _____.

75. Use the present perfect tense to express the following:

    a. My goal is to walk six miles. I need to walk two more miles.

    _____.

    b. My plan is to lose twenty pounds in total. I need to lose ten more pounds.

    _____.

    c. My budget allows me to spend $100 in total. I have $25 left.

    _____.

    d. My assignment is to write three papers. I need to write one more.

    _____.

76. Fill in the blanks with the correct present perfect verb form:

    a. We (work) _____ here for two years.
    b. They (help) _____ him for a long time.
    c. I (eat/not) _____ dinner yet.
    d. She (be) _____ in Alaska twice.
    e. He (play/never) _____ football before.
    f. I (answer) _____ 20 questions today so far.
    g. She is walking in the door right now. She (arrive)

    _____ .

77. Write a question for each of the previous statements.

    a. _____?
    b. _____?
    c. _____?
    d. _____?
    e. _____?
    f. _____?
    g. _____?

§10.

Verbs—Past Time

78. Fill in the blanks with a past form of *be:*
    a. I _____ sick.
    b. We _____ in Las Vegas.
    c. No, they (not) _____ late.
    d. She _____ my favorite teacher.
    e. It _____ 5:30 P.M.

79. Write a question for each of the previous statements.
    a. _____?
    b. _____?
    c. _____?
    d. _____?
    e. _____?

80. Write the past tense forms of the following verbs:

    a. stand   _____   k. bend   _____
    b. try   _____   l. fold   _____
    c. work   _____   m. hold   _____
    d. study   _____   n. know   _____
    e. see   _____   o. show   _____
    f. agree   _____   p. hear   _____
    g. teach   _____   q. wear   _____
    h. buy   _____   r. sell   _____
    i. bring   _____   s. tell   _____
    j. go   _____   t. do   _____

81. Fill in the blanks with the correct past tense verb form:
    a. We (begin) _____ this morning at ten o'clock.
    b. I (stop) _____ at six o'clock.
    c. Mary (help) _____ me yesterday.
    d. No, he (go/not) _____ to Spain last summer.
    e. They (go) _____ home two hours ago.
    f. No, we (eat/not) _____ at my friend's house last night.
    g. My brother and I (leave) _____ home at seven o'clock.
    h. No, Vicki and Joan (call/not) _____ me today.

    i. Yes, I (have) _____ a good time at the party.
    j. She (cry) _____ when he left.

82. Write a question for each of the previous statements.
    a. _____?
    b. _____?
    c. _____?
    d. _____?
    e. _____?
    f. _____?
    g. _____?
    h. _____?
    i. _____?
    j. _____?

83. Choose the correct tense—the present perfect or the past—to complete the following sentences:
    a. I am studying. I (start) _____ to study fifteen minutes ago. I (study) _____ for fifteen minutes.
    b. We live in this house. We (move) _____ here in 2004. We (live) _____ since 2004.
    c. Nancy (meet) _____ Sharon in college. They (know) _____ each other for twelve years.
    d. When they were in college, they (do) _____ a lot of things together.
    e. They (work) _____ at the bookstore, they (take) _____ the same classes, and they (live) _____ in the same dormitory.
    f. Now, they live in different cities, and they (not, see) _____ each other for a long time.

84. Change the following sentences from the present to the past:
    a. I can work.

    _____.

    b. Should we go?

    _____.

    c. They may take a vacation. (They have permission.)

    _____.

    d. He may be sick. (It is possible that he is sick.)

    _____.

    e. He must work there. (He probably works there.)

    _____.

    f. She has to study.

    _____.

85. Express the following using past tense modal auxiliaries:
    a. I wasn't able to go.

    _____.

    b. They probably played all day.

    _____.

    c. He was required to be there.

    _____.

    d. I advised you to do it.

    _____.

    e. Maybe she went.

    _____.

§10.2
PAST
PROGRESSIVE
TENSE

86. Fill in the blanks with the past progressive verb form:
    a. I went to bed at 10:00 P.M. and woke up at 6:00 A.M. At 2:00 A.M. I (sleep) _____.
    b. Margaret sat down to eat at 6:00 P.M. The door-bell rang at 6:05, when Margaret (eat) _____ dinner.
    c. Jason rode his bike yesterday afternoon; Adam watched TV yesterday afternoon. While Jason (ride) _____ his bike, Adam (watch) _____ TV.
    d. My sister called her friend on the telephone this morning and they talked all day. I tried to call at noon, but the line was busy. My sister (talk) _____ to her friend.

87. Choose the past tense or the past progressive tense to fill in the blanks:
    a. While you were watching TV, I (sew) _____ in my room.
    b. While I (sew) _____ , I (think) _____ about our argument.
    c. I (be) _____ upset, because you (seem) _____ to be so angry.
    d. I (want) _____ to scream, but I (begin) _____ to cry instead.
    e. When you (come) _____ in my room, I (cry) _____ because I (think) _____ you (love, not) _____ me anymore.

88. Choose the correct tense—the past progressive or the past—to complete the following paragraph:

Last week, while I (drive) a. _____ to work,
I (see) b. _____ an accident. A woman (wait)
c. _____ at a traffic light. When the light (turn)
d. _____ green, her car (stall) e. _____.
The driver in back of her (not, pay attention)
f. _____ , and his car (run) g. _____ into
the back of hers. It (make) h. _____ a loud
crash. The woman (get) i. _____ out of her car
and (start) j. _____ to yell at the man. She (still,
yell) k. _____ at him when I (drive) l. _____
away.

89. Choose the correct tense—the past progressive or the past—to complete the following paragraph:

Last night, while I (cook) a. _____ dinner, I
(burn) b. _____ my finger. I (be) c. _____
scared, so I (go) d. _____ to the emergency
room at the hospital. The nurse (tell) e. _____
me to wait. I (wait) f. _____ for two hours.
Finally, they (call) g. _____ my name and I (go)
h. _____ to a small room. I (wait) i. _____
there another hour. While I (sit) j. _____ there I
(hear) k. _____ a lot of noises from other
rooms, and I (see) l. _____ several people on
stretchers. One patient (get) m. _____ medicine throught an IV tube. I (be) n. _____ tired
and I (fall) o. _____ asleep. When the doctor
(come) p. _____ in, I (sleep) q. _____ . He
(wake) r. _____ me up. Then he (look) s.
_____ at my finger. He (put) t. _____
some cream on it and (say) u. _____ it was
O.K. Then the nurse (give) v. _____ me a bill
and (tell) w. _____ me to go home.

90. Use the past progressive to express the following:
    a. I planned to go to the circus; I didn't go because I didn't have enough time.

    _____.

    b. We planned to call you; we didn't call you because we didn't have a quarter.

    _____.

    c. They planned to have a party; they didn't have the party because the teacher disapproved.

    _____.

    d. She planned to stay at home; she didn't stay at home because her friend invited her to the movies.

    _____.

§10.3
USED TO . . .

91. Use *used to* to express the following:
    a. I was fat before; I am not fat now.

    _____.

    b. We lived there before; we do not live there now.

    _____.

    c. He smoked before; he does not smoke now.

    _____.

    d. He was married before; he is not married now.

    _____.

    e. She was nice before; she is not nice now.

    _____.

    f. They were happy before; they are not happy now.

    _____.

    g. He laughed before; he does not laugh now.

    _____.

    h. We ate dinner together before; we do not eat dinner together now.

§10.4
WOULD IN THE
PAST TENSE

92. Use *would* to express the following:
    a. She always told jokes.

    _____.

    b. She always made my favorite food.

    _____.

    c. He always helped me with my homework.

    _____.

    d. We always had lots of fun.

    _____.

    e. They never fought.

    _____.

§10.5 PAST PERFECT TENSE

93. Write the past perfect forms of the verbs to complete the following sentences:
   a. I (help) _____ before.
   b. She (not / be) _____ there before.
   c. We (sing) _____ that song many times before.
   d. He (go) _____ to bed early that night.
   e. They (eat) _____ too much.
   f. He (not / see) _____ our new house yet.

94. Use the past perfect tense to give a reason for each of the following statements:
   a. She wasn't hungry.

      _____.

   b. I was very hungry.

      _____.

   c. Joe knew how to drive that car.

      _____.

   d. Jeremy and his friends knew every scene in that movie.

      _____.

95. Combine each pair of sentences into one sentence. Choose the past tense or the past perfect tense to put the events in the correct order:
   a. First, I didn't read the newspaper. Second, I left for the office.
      When _____

   b. At six o'clock, Sue ate dinner. At seven o'clock, Joel invited her to go out.
      When Joel _____

   c. First, we called the gas station for help. Then my dad saw us.
      When _____

   d. The dance started at eight o'clock. I arrived at ten o'clock.
      When _____

96. Choose the correct tense—the present perfect or the past perfect—to complete the following sentences:
    a. I am hungry because I (not/eat) _____ dinner.
       I was hungry because I (not/eat) _____ dinner.
    b. Barbara is tired because she (work) _____ all day.
       Barbara was tired because she (work) _____ all day.
    c. James cooked a big dinner because he (invite) _____ his friends to eat.
       James is cooking a big dinner because he (invite) _____ his friends to eat.
    d. We are staying an extra week in the city because we (not/see) _____ all the sights.
       We stayed an extra week in the city because we (not/see) _____ all the sights.
    e. Alison and David were worried about the exam yesterday because they (not/study) _____ .
       Alison and David are worried about the exam today because they (not/study) _____ .

§10.6 PAST PERFECT PROGRESSIVE TENSE

97. Change the past tense forms of the verbs to the past perfect progressive forms:
    a. She (wrote) _____ a diary for a long time.
    b. He (lived) _____ here for a long time.
    c. She (hoped) _____ to get married for a long time.
    d. We (thought) _____ about that for a long time.
    e. Henry and Roxanne (wanted) _____ to have a baby for a long time.

98. Use the past perfect progressive to express the following:
    a. We worked hard all day; we were exhausted.

       _____.
    b. They danced all night; they slept until noon.

       _____.
    c. She ate potato chips all day; she didn't eat her dinner.

       _____.
    d. He studied for six years; he was happy to get his degree.

       _____

§11.

Verbs—Future Time

99. Write the present progressive form of the verbs in the blanks:
   a. I (leave) _____ tomorrow.
   b. She (come) _____ next week.
   c. He (study) _____ at the university next year.
   d. We (watch) _____ TV at eight o'clock.
   e. They (not / go) _____ home until later.

100. Write the *going to* form of the verbs in the blanks:
   a. I (leave) _____ tomorrow.
   b. She (come) _____ next week.
   c. He (study) _____ at the university next year.
   d. We (watch) _____ TV at eight o'clock.
   e. They (not/go) _____ until later.

101. Indicate a 50 percent possibility of the following events:
   a. He (work) _____ .
   b. She (not / come) _____ .
   c. They (bring) _____ their daughter.
   d. We (take) _____ that course.
   e. You (not /need) _____ a coat.

102. Indicate a 99 percent possibility of the following events:
   a. I (arrive) _____ by morning.
   b. They (finish) _____ by May.
   c. He (call) _____ at ten o'clock.
   d. The party (be over) _____ by midnight.

103. Indicate a 90 percent possibility of the following events:
   a. He (graduate) _____ in June.
   b. They (get married) _____ next fall.
   c. She (stop working) _____ soon.
   d. The project (be finished) _____ by next year.

104. Indicate a 10 percent possibility of the following events:
    a. I (call) _____ you tomorrow.
    b. We (be) _____ home until late.
    c. They (tell) _____ us their plans.
    d. She (get married) _____ again.

105. Promise the following:
    a. I (call) _____ .
    b. We (bring) _____ cookies.
    c. He (be) _____ on time.
    d. I (write) _____ you a letter.

106. Predict the following:
    a. Your son (pass) _____ the course.
    b. It (rain) _____ tomorrow.
    c. It (not / snow) _____ tomorrow.
    d. My mother (worry) _____ about me.
    e. She (win) _____ the election.
    f. They (get angry) _____ .
    g. He (change) _____ everything.

107. a. Accept the following requests with a short answer:
    Will you help me?

    _____

    Will you all pay attention, please?

    _____

    b. Refuse the following requests with a short answer:
    Will you help me?

    _____

    Will you give me your telephone number?

    _____

108. Supply the verb for the following scheduled events:
    a. The movie (start) _____ at seven o'clock.
    b. The train (leave) _____ at 4:30.
    c. The class (end) _____ at 7:15.
    d. The games (begin) _____ tomorrow.

109. Use future modal auxiliaries to express the following:
      a. I cannot drive yet. I _____ soon.
      b. He doesn't have to study now, but he _____ in the future.
      c. We can't help you today, but we _____ tomorrow.
      d. You may leave the room now, but you _____ after the test begins.
      e. I want to travel to South America now, and I _____ in the future, too.

110. Fill in the blanks with the correct form of the verbs in the following sentences:
      a. He will get here before I (leave) _____.
      b. I will leave after he (get here) _____.
      c. She will leave before he (get here) _____.
      d. He will get here after she (leave) _____.
      e. I will be happy as soon as they (arrive) _____.
      f. I might cry when they (say) _____ goodbye.

111. Rewrite the following sentences using a future expression to show the indicated meanings:
      a. John is sick; there is only a 10 percent possibility that he will go to work tomorrow.

          _____

      b. I plan to study tomorrow.

          _____

      c. I promise to help you next week.

          _____

      d. We are almost home. There is a 99 percent possibility that we will arrive at 3:00 P.M.

          _____

      e. Teresa is scheduled to travel next week.

          _____

      f. There is a 50 percent possibility that Ann will take a vacation in August.

          _____

      g. Arthur refuses to work in that place.

          _____

      h. You predict rain for tomorrow.

          _____

      i. There will be no need for her to return tonight.

          _____

      j. After three months you are going to have the ability to swim.

          _____

§11.5
FUTURE
PROGRESSIVE
TENSE

112.   Fill in the blanks with the future progressive forms of the verbs:
  a. I (play) _____ tennis at four o'clock.
  b. He (prepare) _____ his speech then.
  c. She (run) _____ the marathon that day.
  d. We (make) _____ a cake this afternoon.
  e. They (practice) _____ tomorrow evening.

113.   Write a question for each of the statements in the preceding question.
  a. _____?
  b. _____?
  c. _____?
  d. _____?
  e. _____?

§11.6
FUTURE
PERFECT
TENSE

114.   Fill in the blanks with the future perfect forms of the verbs:
  a. She (finish) _____ the project by September.
  b. I (send) _____ my tax forms by April 15th.
  c. We (do) _____ all our work before 6:30.
  d. They (call) _____ us by then.
  e. He (move) _____ to his new house before November.

§12.

Verbs—Additional Patterns

115. Write the subjects or objects of the following sentences as gerunds:
    a. (Sing) _____ is a lot of fun.
    b. My cousin loves (travel) _____ .
    c. She is not afraid of (get lost) _____ .
    d. (Travel) _____ makes her very happy.
    e. I do not enjoy (drive) _____ in traffic.
    f. (Wait) _____ makes me nervous.
    g. I'll have to quit (go) _____ to work during rush hour.
    h. We can finish (talk) _____ about this later.

116. Fill in the blanks with the correct verb form:
    a. We will consider (go) _____ to the beach.
    b. They discussed (take) _____ a trip to Argentina.
    c. I hope we finish (work) _____ on that project soon.
    d. She admitted (tell) _____ him my telephone number.
    e. He finally quit (smoke) _____ .

117. Express the following using a gerund expression:
    a. We want to bowl.

    _____

    b. They like to fish.

    _____

    c. He has to shop.

    _____

    d. She hates to camp.

    _____

    e. She wants to dance.

    _____

118. Use *feel like* to express the following:
    a. What do you *want to do* now?

    _____

    b. Do you *want to go swimming*?

    _____

    c. No. I *wanted to go swimming* yesterday.

    _____

    d. Today I *want to dance.*

    _____

119. Use the gerund form to *very politely* ask the following:
    a. Take off your hat.

    _____

    b. Save my seat.

    _____

    c. Help us.

    _____

    d. Lend me $100.

    _____

    e. Take me home after the meeting.

    _____

120. Fill in the blanks with the correct form of the verb:
    a. These rags are good for (clean) _____ .
    b. I am so tired of (drive) _____ in traffic.
    c. My new friend is crazy about (dance) _____ .
    d. She never gives up; she keeps on (try) _____ .
    e. Those boys are in (train) _____ for the race.
    f. They get in shape by (run) _____ ten miles
       a day.

121. Rewrite the sentences, changing the possessive
    nouns to pronouns (**§6.5**):
    a. They appreciated Susan's coming.

    _____

    b. She regrets Tim's resigning.

    _____

    c. She loves Steve's dancing.

    _____

    d. They don't like their mother's singing.

    _____

    e. Jim's cooking is pretty good.

    _____

122. Write the subjects or objects of the following
     sentences as infinitives:
     a. They can't afford (lose) _____ that money.
     b. I need (learn) _____ how to use the
        computer.
     c. (Manage) _____ that would be great.
     d. (Forget) _____ my appointment would be a
        mistake.
     e. I didn't mean (hurt) _____ your feelings.
     f. Allan promised (help) _____ his co-workers.
     g. We finally learned (use) _____ the
        computer.
     h. Your friends appear (be) _____ comfortable.
     i. Brandon decided (study) _____ at the
        college.

123. Fill in the blanks with the correct form of the verb:
     a. He says he can't afford (buy) _____ a
        house.
     b. I guess they decided (play) _____ football.
     c. Has she promised (marry) _____ you?
     d. We intend (finish) _____ studying first.
     e. The children are begging (stay) _____ home
        today.
     f. I planned (save) _____ a little money this year.

124. Rewrite the sentences using the infinitive form of the
     verb:
     a. I need milk; I'm going to the store.

        _____

     b. They are going to Aisha's house; they want to
        see her.

        _____

     c. Melissa cannot lift that box; she is not strong
        enough.

        _____

     d. Danny can get his driver's license; he is old
        enough.

        _____

     e. I drive home; the drive lasts twenty minutes.

        _____

     f. Jackie cleans her room; she needs two hours.

        _____

g. I heard your good news; I am glad.

_____

h. I heard your bad news; I am sorry.

_____

125. Choose the correct form of the verb—the gerund, the infinitive, or the basic verb—to express the following:
    a. Please stop (drive) _____ so fast.
    b. Please take a break; stop (talk) _____ to me for a minute.
    c. Please help me (take) _____ out the trash.
    d. June tried (sleep) _____ , but couldn't.
    e. She tried (take) _____ pills to help her sleep.
    f. The boss let her (go) _____ home early.
    g. Mike's mother makes him (get up) _____ early.
    h. He used (wake up) _____ every day at eight; now he wakes up at six.
    i. Now he is used to (wake up) _____ at six.

126. Choose the gerund, the infinitive, or the basic verb to complete the following sentences:
    a. I hope you don't mind (help) _____ us.
    b. They decided (postpone) _____ the picnic.
    c. Please help your brother (wash) _____ the car.
    d. He claims (have) _____ found the treasure.
    e. He was sorry (learn) _____ the truth.
    f. She will deny (see) _____ them.
    g. They tried to make him (go) _____ home.
    h. She will refuse (talk) _____ to us.
    i. It took ten minutes (drive) _____ here.
    j. Her mother made her (clean) _____ the room.
    k. How did you manage (find) _____ this?
    l. We really appreciate (hear) _____ about your trip.
    m. Don't forget (tape) _____ the program.
    n. Can you imagine (live) _____ in that cold climate?
    o. We want to go (shop) _____ .
    p. What do you feel like (do) _____ ?
    q. He wants to keep on (work) _____ .
    r. I regret your (lose) _____ the election.

127. Fill in the blanks with the correct form of the verb—
the gerund or the infinitive:
a. I enjoy (dance) _____ with you.
b. He always forgets (call) _____ me.
c. Al and Harry promised (write) _____ letters.
d. She goes (shop) _____ every day.
e. Let's keep on (work) _____ until midnight.
f. I intend (earn) _____ more money.
g. Lynn and I need (find) _____ a new
apartment.
h. Ask Martin (help) _____ you.
i. I want my nephew (graduate) _____ from
high school.
j. The students used (wear) _____ jeans to
school.
k. The students are used (wear) _____ jeans
to school.
l. Andy likes (listen) _____ to music.

128. Punctuate the following sentences:
a. Molly asked   Are you coming with us
b. Sam said   I'm not going anywhere
c. I will wait here   he told her
d. Then he added   Don't worry about me

129. Change the verbs from present to past to report the
following:
a. Molly said, "I am going to the store."
Molly said she _____ to the store.
b. Peter answered, "I want to go with you."
Peter answered that he _____ to go with
her.
c. She told him, "No, you can't go this time."
She told him that he _____ go that time.
d. He cried, "I don't want to stay here."
He cried that he _____ to stay there.
e. "Do you want anything from the store?" she
asked.
She asked if he _____ anything from the
store.
f. He said, "Will you bring me a new toy?"
He asked if she _____ him a new toy.

130. Change the verbs from the past to the past perfect to report the following:
    a. Molly said, "I went to the store."
       Molly said that she _____ to the store.
    b. Peter said, "I wanted to go with you."
       Peter said that he _____ to go with her.
    c. "What did you do while I was gone?" she asked.
       She asked him what he _____ while she was gone.
    d. He told her, "I played with my toys while you were gone."
       He told her that he _____ with his toys while she was gone.
    e. "What did you bring me?" he asked.
       He asked her what she _____ him.

131. Change the following direct quotes to reported speech:
    a. "Martha is clever," said Steve.
       _____

    b. "Jessica wants ice cream," said Mrs. Adams.
       _____

    c. "We can't swim," yelled the children.
       _____

    d. "They didn't do it right," reported the lady.
       _____

    e. "I'm not going to drive," said Jerry.
       _____

    f. "Is Sam going to work?" asked Joan.
       _____

    g. "Have they finished yet?" asked the reporter.
       _____

    h. "When are they going to finish?" he asked later.
       _____

    i. "Where did she go?" asked Dad.
       _____

132. Change the following reports to direct quotes:
    a. Ralph said he was going home.
       _____

    b. Judy asked him if he was tired.
       _____

    c. Ralph told her that he was exhausted because he had been working all day.
       _____

    d. Judy replied that he deserved a rest.

    _____

    e. Ralph asked how many hours she had worked.

    _____

    f. Judy replied that she had worked eight hours.

    _____

    g. She said she thought she would go home, too.

    _____

133. Rewrite the following questions beginning with _Do you know. . .:_
    a. Where is her house?

    _____

    b. Why is she leaving?

    _____

    c. Where does Monica live?

    _____

    d. Where did Freddy buy that hat?

    _____

134. Answer the following questions with _I don't know +_ the included question:
    a. Who is that lady?

    _____

    b. When is the party?

    _____

    c. Where are the buses?

    _____

    d. What does Katrina do?

    _____

    e. Why did they go home?

    _____

135. Restate the following questions beginning with _Can you tell me +_ the included question:
    a. Where is the president's office?

    _____

    b. Who is her boyfriend?

    _____

    c. Where Main Street is?

    _____

    d. What time is it?

    _____

    e. When did they get here?

    _____

f. Why did they leave?

_____

g. When are you going to begin?

_____

136. Use the infinitive form to answer the included question in the following sentences:
   a. Do you know where we should go?
      No, I don't know _____.
   b. Can you tell me how I can get to the station?
      Yes, I can tell you _____.
   c. Will you find out who(m) we should call for information?
      Yes, I will find out _____.
   d. Do you know when I should leave for the airport?
      No, I don't know _____.

137. Add a tag question to each of the following sentences:
   a. He is adorable.

   _____

   b. We aren't finished.

   _____

   c. She is afraid.

   _____

   d. They are cold.

   _____

   e. You like ice cream.

   _____

   f. He wants a drink.

   _____

   g. I haven't been there.

   _____

   h. You have performed already.

   _____

   i. He hasn't called us.

   _____

   j. He was there.

   _____

   k. You went to the game.

   _____

   l. He tried to help you.

   _____

   m. They didn't like the dessert.

   _____

n. He hadn't seen the movie.

_____

o. She had been working all day.

_____

138. Arrange the following words into sentences, using object pronouns wherever possible:

Subject	Verb	Indirect Object	Direct Object
a. David	gives	Helen	money
b. Helen	draws	David	pictures
c. Sandra	mentioned	Larry	party
d. Robin	asked	Sally	question
e. Paul	explains	the students	lessons
f. Richard	built	his wife	house

a. _____.

b. _____.

c. _____.

d. _____.

e. _____.

f. _____.

§13.

Verbs—Special Usage

139. Use *get + an adjective* to express "become" in the following sentences. Be sure to put *get* in the correct tense:
    a. If I am late, my father will _____ angry.
    b. I don't want my mother to _____ worried.
    c. She is not old, but she is _____ gray.
    d. My father isn't old either, but he is _____ bald.
    e. If you run around in circles, you will _____ dizzy.
    f. Don't _____ excited, but I think we are _____ a new car.
    g. Ann _____ cold, so I brought her home.
    h. Brenda and Pete _____ married last July.

140. Use *have + a past participle* to express the following:
    a. Somebody else is going to cut my hair.

    _____

    b. Somebody else cuts our grass every week.

    _____

    c. Somebody else changes his oil regularly.

    _____

    d. Somebody else irons his shirts for him.

    _____

    e. Somebody else cleaned her house last week.

    _____

    f. Somebody else repaired the damage last year for us.

    _____

    g. Somebody else is going to paint our house next week.

    _____

141. Write in the correct verb to complete each of the
      following sentences:
      a. Please _____ Barbara if she is coming home.
             ask   ask for
      b. Please _____ three tickets.
             ask   ask for
      c. Will you _____ me some money?
             borrow   lend
      d. How much do you want to _____ from me?
             borrow   lend
      e. I'm _____ you to _____ me $100.
             asking   asking for   borrow   lend

142. Write in the correct verb to complete each of the
      following sentences:
      a. I _____ to my mother every day.
             speak   talk
      b. She _____ only Russian.
             speaks   talks
      c. The president is going to _____ on
         television tonight.
             speak   talk
      d. He _____ to his friends at the reception last
         night.
             spoke   talked

143. Write in the correct verb:
      a. The meeting is here at my house. Please
         (go/come) _____ to my house at two o'clock
         and (take/bring) _____ a cake. When you
         leave, be sure to (take/bring) _____ your
         plate.
      b. O.K. I will (go/come) _____ to your house
         and (take/bring) _____ a cake. When I
         leave, I won't forget to (take/bring) _____
         my plate.
      c. The next meeting is at Janet's house. I'm not
         (going/coming) _____ , are you?
      d. Yes, I'm (going/coming) _____ , but I'm not
         (taking/bringing) _____ anything. Janet
         never (takes/brings) _____ anything to my
         house.

144. Write in the correct verb:
     a. Don't _____ anything to Mickey.
        say   tell
     b. _____ him that it's a secret.
        Say   Tell
     c. Mickey always _____ our secrets to everybody.
        says   tells
     d. He _____ it's very important to _____
        says   tells   say   tell
        the truth.

145. Write in the correct verb:
     a. We have to _____ our homework.
        do   make
     b. My brother will _____ some exercises with you.
        do   make
     c. He never _____ mistakes.
        does   makes
     d. While he helps you _____ your homework,
        do   make
        I will _____ you a sandwich.
        do   make

146. Write in the correct verb:
     a. I _____ you were here now.
        hope   wish
     b. I _____ you can come tomorrow.
        hope   wish
     c. I _____ you could come tomorrow.
        hope   wish
     d. I _____ you would win yesterday.
        hoped   wished
     e. I _____ you had won yesterday.
        hope   wish

147. Write in the correct verb:
     a. The girls are _____ some old family photographs.
        looking at   watching
     b. Our cousins are _____ some old family movies.
        looking at   watching
     c. Beth _____ beautiful today.
        looks like   looks
     d. She certainly _____ her mother.
        looks like   looks
     e. They really _____ .
        look like   look alike

§14.

Verbs—Passive Voice

148. Change the following sentences from the active
     voice to the passive voice:
     a. Nobody understands me.

     _____

     b. Everybody loves that teacher.

     _____

     c. They make these rugs in Iran.

     _____

     d. They care for her.

     _____

     e. People call him a lot.

     _____

     f. Somebody is helping them.

     _____

149. Change the following sentences from the active
     voice to the passive voice:
     a. Nobody understood me.

     _____

     b. Everybody loved that teacher.

     _____

     c. They made these rugs in Iran.

     _____

     d. They cared for her.

     _____

     e. People called him a lot.

     _____

     f. Somebody was helping them.

     _____

     g. Somebody wrote this poem in 1865.

     _____

150. Change the following sentences from the active voice to the passive voice:
    a. Nobody has understood me.

    _____

    b. They have cared for her.

    _____

    c. People have called him a lot.

    _____

    d. Somebody has helped them.

    _____

    e. Somebody has robbed the bank on the corner.

    _____

§15.

Verbs—Imperative Mood

151. Express the following using the command form:
   a. Tell someone to call you.

   _____

   b. Tell John to send you a letter.

   _____

   c. Tell your mother not to leave.

   _____

   d. Tell Erin not to drive fast.

   _____

   e. Suggest dancing with you to Pat.

   _____

   f. Suggest going to a movie with you to a friend.

   _____

   g. Tell your friend you don't want to argue with him.

   _____

   h. Suggest to your friend that you and he not play tennis today.

   _____

152. Use the impersonal *you* to ask for the following information:
   a. You want to know how to start a machine.

   _____

   b. You want to know how to get to Center Street.

   _____

   c. You want to know where people park.

   _____

   d. You want to know how much people have to pay to ride on the metro.

   _____

   e. You want to know where people can mail letters.

   _____

153. Change the following commands to the impersonal *you* forms:
    a. Put your money in the slot. Push the start button.
    _____

    b. Go straight ahead. Turn left.
    _____

    c. Park on the street.
    _____

    d. Mail letters at the post office.
    _____

154. A teacher needs help in cleaning up her classroom. Express what she wants from her students:
    a. "Adam, erase the blackboard."
       She wants _____.
    b. "Jessica, pick up the toys."
       She wants _____.
    c. "Amy and Lisa, put away the crayons."
       She wants _____.
    d. "David and Brian, put the chairs in place."
       She wants _____.
    e. "Reza, put the trash in the wastebasket."
       She wants _____.

155. What did the teacher want her students to do in the preceding question? Use object pronouns in your answers:
    a. What help did she want from *Adam?*
    _____

    b. What help did she want from *Jessica*?
    _____

    c. What help did she want from *Amy and Lisa?*
    _____

    d. What help did she want from *David and Brian?*
    _____

    e. What help did she want from *John?*
    _____

§16.

Verbs—Subjunctive Mood

156. Express the following using subjunctive forms:
   a. I want him to be quiet.
      I suggest _____.
   b. She wants us to be responsible.
      She insists _____.
   c. He wants her to be careful.
      He demands _____.
   d. I want you to come home.
      I insist _____.
   e. She wants him to get a tutor.
      She recommends _____.

157. Combine each pair of sentences into one sentence, beginning with *I wish:*
   a. I don't have a ticket. I want a ticket.

      _____

   b. He doesn't go to school. I want him to go to school.

      _____

   c. She works on weekends. I don't want her to work on weekends.

      _____

   d. We don't have any money. We want money.

      _____

   e. They leave their dirty dishes in the sink. I don't want them to do that.

      _____

158. Combine each pair of sentences into one sentence, beginning with *I wish:*
   a. They went home early. I regret that.

      _____

   b. You called me at 6:00 A.M. I regret that.

      _____

   c. She quit her job. I regret that.

      _____

   d. He found out the truth. I regret that.

      _____

   e. We didn't tell him in time. I regret that.

      _____

159. Combine each pair of sentences into one sentence, beginning with *If:*
    a. I don't have a lot of money. I want to take a trip to Europe.

    _____

    b. She isn't here. I want to dance with her.

    _____

    c. He doesn't have a diploma. He can't get a job.

    _____

    d. We are not lucky. We want to win the lottery.

    _____

160. Combine each pair of sentences into one sentence, beginning with *If:*
    a. I didn't have a lot of money. I wanted to take a trip to Europe.

    _____

    b. She wasn't here. I wanted to dance with her.

    _____

    c. He didn't have a diploma. He couldn't get a job.

    _____

    d. We were not lucky. We wanted to win the lottery.

    _____

161. Use the indicative after *if* to restate the following sentences:
    a. Every time I walk, I get tired.
    If _____.
    b. Whenever he reads, he falls asleep.
    If _____.
    c. When she drinks milk, she gets a stomachache.
    If _____.
    d. Whenever he is awake, he watches TV.
    If _____.

162. Use the indicative after *if* to restate the following sentences, showing probable action and certain result:
    a. I expect to go home early; my wife will be happy.
    If _____.
    b. I will probably get a vacation in August; I will go to Asia.
    If _____.

c. He will probably marry her; he will move to California.

If _____.

d. They will probably buy that house; they will make a beautiful garden.

If _____.

e. We expect to move in February; we will give you our furniture.

If _____.

163. Rewrite the following sentences, changing the probable action to improbable action:

a. If I go to the beach, I will buy a bathing suit. I don't think I'm going to the beach.

If _____.

b. If she buys that dress, she will have to lose ten pounds. I don't think she is going to buy that dress.

If _____.

c. If he wins the lottery, he will buy a fabulous new car. I don't think he is going to win the lottery.

If _____.

d. If we take a trip around the world, we will visit you. I don't think we are going to take a trip around the world.

If _____.

e. If they get married, they will have a lot of problems. I don't think they are going to get married.

If _____.

§17.

Prepositions

164. Write in the correct prepositions:

Where is the star?

a. _____ the box

b. _____ the box

c. _____ the box

d. _____ the box

e. _____ the box

f. _____ the box

165. Write in the correct prepositions:
   a. Washington, D.C. is _____ the United States.
   b. It is the capital _____ the United States.
   c. Our house is _____ Springfield.
   d. It is _____ Oak Street.
   e. It is _____ number 1432.

166.   Write in the correct prepositions.

Where is the dotted line going?

a. _____ the box

b. _____ the box

c. _____ the box

d. _____ the box

167.   Write in the correct prepositions:
   a. Her son was born _____ 1995, _____ April,
      _____ the 15th, _____ three o'clock
      _____ the morning.
   b. Betty hasn't been here _____ January 14th.
   c. We haven't seen her _____ three weeks.
   d. We are leaving _____ 4:00 on the dot, so be
      here _____ 3:55.
   e. Frances is going to stay _____ June 15th. She
      will stay _____ ten days.
   f. We always go to a restaurant _____ my birthday.
   g. Do you ever go out _____ night?

168.   Write in the correct prepositions:
   a. Why are you _____ a hurry?
      I want to be _____ time for work.
   b. Do you want to come _____ my car?
      Thanks. I usually ride _____ the bus.
      Now I will get to work _____ time to have a
      cup of coffee.

169. Write in the correct prepositions:
    a. What are you looking _____?
       I'm trying to find my glasses so I can look _____ these photographs.
       Then I need to look _____ some telephone numbers.
    b. Have you looked _____ top of your desk?
    c. Look _____ the drawer. Maybe they are _____ there.

170. Write in the correct prepositions:
    a. My mother made the dress; it was made _____ her.
    b. It is my dress; she made it _____ me.
    c. She made it _____ her sewing machine, but she did the embroidery _____ hand.
    d. John gave me a present; the present is _____ John.
    e. He bought the jewelry _____ Colombia; the jewelry is _____ Colombia.
    f. It was made _____ Colombia. It is made _____ gold.
    g. They went to Hawaii _____ plane.
    h. I didn't go with them; they left _____ me.
    i. They left _____ National Airport.

171. Complete the questions that the following statements answer:
    a. I went to the movies with Marty. Who/m _____ ?
    b. She is thinking about her trip. What _____ ?
    c. They live on Maple Street. What street _____ ?
    d. He lives in Chicago. What city _____ ?
    e. We talked to everybody there. Who/m _____ ?

172. Write in the correct preposition:
    a. She is very good _____ tennis.
    b. Fruit is very good _____ your health.
    c. Her husband is very good _____ her.
    d. She is very good _____ young children.

173. Fill in the blanks with the correct prepositions:
    a. I am _____ good shape.
    b. We met _____ chance.
    c. He is going to be _____ television.
    d. She is always _____ a bad mood.
    e. They love to walk _____ the rain.

f. _____ a little luck, we will meet.
g. The fire truck came because the woods were _____ fire.
h. I rode _____ the bus.
i. He rode _____ the car.
j. Jeans are always _____ style.
k. Do you do your homework _____ home, or _____ school?

174. Fill in the blanks with the correct prepositions:
    a. She is excited _____ her vacation.
    b. Are you prepared _____ the test?
    c. They are really involved _____ their business.
    d. You have been absent _____ class three times.
    e. I think she is capable _____ better work.
    f. She is finally finished _____ her assignment.
    g. Are you scared _____ wild animals?
    h. We were very grateful _____ them for helping us.
    i. We were very grateful _____ the help.
    j. I am sorry _____ that.
    k. They were very disappointed _____ him.
    l. He was absent _____ school for six days.

175. Fill in the blanks with the correct prepositions:
    a. I dreamed _____ you last night.
    b. Let me tell you _____ my family.
    c. Stop staring _____ me!
    d. He always takes advantage _____ others.
    e. Do you agree _____ me?
    f. She has applied _____ six colleges.
    g. We can count _____ him.
    h. He is devoted _____ her.
    i. Are you finished _____ this table?
    j. I want to thank you _____ all your help.
    k. Is she participating _____ this election?

176. Replace the words in parentheses with a verb + preposition combination:
    a. Please (be careful) _____.
    b. I (went to sleep) _____.
    c. I hope they (escaped) _____.
    d. Maybe he will (appear unexpectedly) _____.
    e. He (does nothing) _____ all day.
    f. (Do not enter) _____ !

g. She will have to (begin again) _____.

h. You can (register) _____ at the desk.

i. They (live in harmony) _____.

j. Please (discover the answer) _____.

k. What time do you (arise) _____ in the morning?

l. Please don't (stop trying) _____.

177. Change the underlined objects to pronouns and write each complete sentence in the correct order:

a. Please throw the trash away.

_____

b. Are you going to pay Jim back?

_____

c. I wrote down your telephone number.

_____

d. We will look into the problem.

_____

e. You need to hand in the reports.

_____

f. May I try on the dress?

_____

g. I had to ask for the number.

_____

h. She had to clean up the mess.

_____

i. He tried to do the work over.

_____

j. She likes to pick out her own clothes.

_____

k. They ran out of staples.

_____

l. We will have to call our customers back.

_____

m. Try to get over your anger.

_____

n. They called off the picnic.

_____

o. Do you think you can catch up with Tom and Ed?

_____

§18.

Adverbs

178. Replace the words in parentheses with an adverb:
 a. Please come (to this place) _____ .
 b. He is not at home. He is (in another place)
  _____ on business.
 c. I can't find my glasses (in any place) _____.
 d. Have you looked (on the next floor up) _____ ?
 e. Yes. I have looked (in that place) _____ and
  (on the floor below) _____ , too. I have looked
  (a distance above) _____ and (a distance
  below) _____ . I have looked (in all places)
  _____ .

 f. They are probably (below) _____ something.

179. Replace the words in parentheses with an adverb:
 a. Please don't come (after the expected time)

  _____.

 b. I saw him three years (before now)

  _____.

 c. He's going to come (the week after the present week)

  _____.

 d. I hope he calls me (a short time after now)

  _____.

 e. I haven't seen him (a short time before now)

  _____.

 f. He doesn't come to class (now, as before)

  _____.

 g. Is he (now, as before) _____ studying?

180. Replace the words in parentheses with an adverb:
 a. What are you going to do (today at night)

  _____.

 b. I'm going to the library (after now)

  _____.

 c. (After that) _____ I'm going to get
  something to eat, and (after that)
  _____ I'm going home.

181. Fill in the blanks with the correct time expressions:
    a. (The present day) _____ is the 18th of May.
    b. _____ was the 17th.
    c. The 16th was_____ .
    d. _____ is the 19th.
    e. The 20th is _____ .

182. Fill in the blanks with the time expression that indi-
    cates the part of the day:
    a. It is 7:00 P.M. The weather has been changing all
       day. _____ at 6:00 A.M. it was sunny.
    b. It began to rain at one o'clock _____ .
       It stopped at 3:00 P.M.
    c. Then it began to rain again at six _____ .
       I sure hope it stops before eleven tonight.

183. Write in the correct time expressions:
    a. It is June. My co-workers and I are planning our
       vacations. Joe already took his vacation
       _____ month. (in May)
    b. Cara is away _____ week, and Melissa
       plans to go away _____ month. (in July)
    c. I guess I will take off _____ Friday (the day
       after tomorrow) and all of _____ week.
    d. I didn't get a vacation _____ year.

184. Fill in the blanks to indicate the number of times:
    a. The phone only rang (one time)

       _____ .

    b. Maybe the caller will try (one more time)

       _____ .

    c. People usually let the phone ring at least six

       _____ .

    d. I always try to pick it up after it rings (two times)

       _____ .

185. Match the following adverbs with their meanings:
    a. sometimes   0 percent of the time
    b. always   5 percent of the time
    c. hardly ever   25 percent of the time
    d. never   60 percent of the time
    e. usually   80 percent of the time
    f. frequently   100 percent of the time

186. Write in the adverbs that correspond to the following adjectives:
    a. good   _____
    b. careful   _____
    c. fast   _____
    d. quick   _____
    e. easy   _____
    f. hard   _____
    g. busy   _____
    h. able   _____
    i. late   _____
    j. responsible   _____
    k. early   _____
    l. bad   _____
    m. slow   _____
    n. better than   _____
    o. slower than   _____
    p. faster than   _____
    q. easier than   _____
    r. worse than   _____
    s. more careful than _____
    t. quieter than   _____
    u. less capable than _____
    v. the most responsible _____
    w. not as easy as   _____
    x. not as good as   _____

187. Fill in the blanks to complete the following ideas:
    a. My air-conditioner only cools the room to 79 degrees. It _____ works.
    b. My neighbor's air-conditioner cools the room to 65 degrees. It _____ works.
    c. Another neighbor's air-conditioner cools the room to 72 degrees. It works _____ .
    d. The engineer is working on mine now. It is almost fixed. He says it _____ works.

188. Match the expressions with their meanings:
    a. fairly good   excellent
    b. not too good   bad
    c. rather good   average
    d. extremely good   better than average

189. Answer the following questions with complete sentences, making sure the adverbs are in the correct position:

a. Where are you going? (outside)

_____

b. When is he going to New York? (tomorrow)

_____

c. Are they sleeping? (Yes, still)

_____

d. Have you finished? (Yes, already)

_____

e. Have you finished? (No, yet)

_____

f. Does she take lessons? (No, not as before)

_____

g. How often does she practice? (seldom)

_____

h. When do they play? (usually, in the afternoon)

_____

i. When does your friend call? (sometimes, in the evening)

_____

j. How does he paint? (very well)

_____

k. How tall is John? (pretty tall)

_____

§19.

Conjunctions

190. Add conjunctions to combine the indicated words:
   a. June _____ Joyce were singing _____
       dancing.
   b. I want one dessert: ice cream _____ cake.
   c. Geoff likes chocolate _____ not vanilla.
   d. Joel was angry _____ calm.
   e. Laura _____ Kevin made two trips; they
       went _____ to Nashville, _____ to
       New Orleans.
   f. We have room for one more thing: a table
       _____ a cabinet.
   g. I want both. I want a table _____ a cabinet.
   h. George was tired, _____ he went home
       early.
   i. George went home early, _____ Josh
       stayed until late.
   j. Josh stayed, _____ he was having a
       wonderful time.

191. Combine each pair of sentences into one sentence,
      using *too* or *either*:
   a. Kathleen is happy. Glenn is happy.
       _____

   b. Jack works hard. Mike works hard.
       _____

   c. Emily left yesterday. Jeremy left yesterday.
       _____

   d. Val was cooking. Renee was cooking.
       _____

   e. Sue isn't tired. Joel isn't tired.
       _____

   f. Kevin didn't come. Scott didn't come.
       _____

   g. Carolyn wasn't driving. Bob wasn't driving.
       _____

   h. We didn't see them. Gayle didn't see them.
       _____

192. Rewrite the sentences you wrote in the preceding questions, using *so* or *neither*:
   a. _____?
   b. _____?
   c. _____?
   d. _____?
   e. _____?
   f. _____?
   g. _____?
   h. _____?

193. Write in the correct conjunction pairs:
   a. I want two desserts. I want _____ cheese-cake _____ apple pie.
   b. He is very talented. He plays _____ the piano _____ the trombone and the saxophone.
   c. She is not very musical. She _____ plays _____ sings.
   d. She made her children take music lessons, _____ they wanted them _____ .
   e. They had to study an instrument: _____ the piano _____ the guitar.

194. Fill in the correct subordinating conjunctions:
   a. We went to the movies at 10:00 P.M. We washed the dishes at 9:00 P.M.
   We washed the dishes _____ we went to the movies.
   b. They left at 6:00 P.M. We got there at 6:30.
   We got there _____ they left.
   They didn't wait _____ we arrived.
   c. She was sleeping from one until three. I was sleeping from one until three.
   _____ she was sleeping, I was sleeping.
   d. He has graduated from college. We are going to celebrate.
   We are going to celebrate _____ he has graduated from college.
   e. She got a driver's license. Now she can drive.
   She got a driver's license _____ she could drive.
   f. They were very hungry. They didn't eat anything.
   _____ they were hungry, they didn't eat anything.

g. He bought a ticket early. He didn't want to risk missing the concert.
He bought a ticket early _____ risk missing the concert.
h. She is nervous. She is singing well.
She is singing well _____ she is nervous.

§20.

Discourse Markers

195. Choose from the following discourse markers to complete the sentences:

   after   after that   then   finally   first
   second   meanwhile

   a. To operate this machine, _____ , put your clothes in.
   b. _____ add the detergent and close the lid.
   c. _____ select the water temperature and wash time.
   d. _____ push the starter knob in, turn it to the right to the cycle you prefer, and pull it to start.
   e. _____ , go do something else.
   f. _____ about thirty minutes, when the washing machine has stopped, remove the clothes from the machine.
   g. _____ , put the clothes in the dryer or hang them on a line.

196. Choose from the following expressions to complete the sentences:

   and   as well as   in addition   plus   besides
   furthermore   on top of that   moreover

   a. I think we should buy this house. It is close to the city _____ the metro.
   b. _____ , the neighborhood is beautiful.
   c. _____ there are a lot of shops within walking distance.
   d. _____ , it is less expensive than some smaller houses we have seen.
   e. _____ , we will have room for our future children.

197. Complete each sentence with a statement that reflects the message of the underlined words:
    a. Yes, I know Carol; <u>as a matter of fact</u>, _____
    _____
    b. This dinner is delicious; <u>indeed</u>, _____
    _____
    c. I enjoyed the party last night; <u>actually</u>, _____
    _____

198. Choose from the following expressions to complete the sentences:

    but　however　on the other hand　in contrast
    nevertheless　still　instead　otherwise

    a. She's a nice girl. Her sister, _____ , is a pain in the neck.
    b. He must like you a lot; _____ , he wouldn't call you so often.
    c. He's always tired when he gets home. _____ , he helps with the housework.
    d. It's an interesting job, _____ , it doesn't pay very much.
    d. She didn't like the blue dress, so she bought the red one _____ .

199. Choose from the following expressions to complete the sentences:

    that is　for example　specifically　I mean
    in other words

    a. He's having a lot of trouble keeping up with the rest of the class; _____ , he should repeat the course.
    b. I need to go out—to the movies, to a concert, or to a restaurant, _____
    c. I need to go out; _____ , to the concert on Saturday night.
    d. The movie was great; _____ , really terrific.
    e. There are 25 prizes; _____ , one for each child.

200. Choose the best expression for each sentence:
    a. They didn't invite him to the party, but he went (anyway / after all) _____ .
    b. I don't always agree with the boss, but I do what he tells me to do; (anyhow / anyway / after all) _____ , he's the boss.
    c. She can paint the kitchen red if she wants to; (anyhow / after all) _____ , it's her kitchen.
    d. We can't decide whether to rent an apartment or buy a house. (In any case / After all) _____ , we don't have to decide until next spring.

201. Choose from the following expressions to complete the sentences:

    although   even though   even if

    a. He can read and write, _____ he's only four years old.
    b. We will play the game tomorrow, _____ it rains.
    c. They played last night, _____ it rained.
    d. He wouldn't accept that job _____ they paid him a million dollars.

202. Choose from the following expressions to complete the sentences:

    in the end   in short   in summary   in conclusion

    a. In spite of all their problems _____ they got married and moved away.
    b. We have to plan, organize, economize, and cooperate in order to do better. _____ , we have to try harder.
    c. They went swimming, they played ball, they made a lot of new friends, and they went to new places. _____ , they had a wonderful time.
    d. It was a good year for the company. _____ , I would like to tell you all how much I enjoyed working with you this year.

§21.

Numbers

203. Write the following numbers as they should be read or said:

a. 64

_____

b. 377

_____

c. 4,541

_____

d. 20,302

_____

e. 400,001

_____

f. 6,000,312

_____

g. 6½ miles

_____

h. 1¾ acres

_____

i. $10.34

_____

j. $5,428.21

_____

k. $10,000,000

_____

§22.

Days and Dates

204. Answer the following questions in complete sentences:
    a. What day is before Friday?

    _____

    b. What day is between Tuesday and Thursday?

    _____

    c. What are Saturday and Sunday?

    _____

    d. What month is before September?

    _____

    e. What month is after March?

    _____

    f. When is Independence Day in the United States?

    _____

§23.

Telling Time

205. Write the times shown on the following clocks:

a.

b.

_____

_____

c.

d.

_____

_____

e.

f.

_____

_____

g.

h.

_____

_____

i.

j.

_____

_____

k.

l.

_____

_____

§24.

Talking About the Weather

206. Match the words in Column A with the meanings in Column B:

Column A	Column B
a. 75 degrees	hot weather
b. lightning	cold weather
c. a flood	pleasant weather
d. 35 degrees	a circular storm
e. thunder	winds over 75 miles per hour
f. hurricane	a flow of water over usually dry land
g. 95 degrees	a loud noise
h. cyclone	electricity in the sky

Review Exercise

207. Answer the following questions in complete
      sentences:
      a. What time is it?

      _____

      b. What are you doing?

      _____

      c. How do you feel?

      _____

      d. Why do you feel that way?

      _____

      e. How many questions have you answered?

      _____

      f. What are you going to do after you finish this
          test?

      _____

      g. What were you doing at 9 o'clock this morning?

      _____

      h. Where were you then?

      _____

      i. What time did you arrive there?

      _____

      j. Who was there when you arrived?

      _____

      k. What was she or he doing?

      _____

      l. How long had she been there?

      _____

      m. What time did you eat lunch yesterday?

      _____

      n. Had you had breakfast?

      _____

      o. How did you feel when you got home yesterday?

      _____

      p. Why did you feel that way?

      _____

      q. Did you finish all the tests?

      _____

      r. Are you proud of yourself? You should be!

      _____

Answers

1. a. adverbs
    b. adjectives
    c. abbreviations
    d. pronouns
    e. vowels
    f. verbs
    g. prepositions
    h. consonants
    i. conjunctions
    j. nouns

2. a. M.D.
    b. Mrs.
    c. etc.
    d. D.D.S.
    e. i.e.
    f. LL.D.
    g. Robert Runyon, Jr.
    h. A.M.
    i. e.g.
    j. Ms.

3. a. Mr. Jones is from Canada.
    b. Do you think I am John's brother?
    c. He was born on Tuesday, the 5th of February.
    d. My good friend, Carol, is from New York, but she lives in Washington, D.C.
    e. California, Michigan, and Texas are all states of the United States of America.

4. a. Here comes Miss Phillips, our new secretary!
    b. Where are the computer discs?
    c. Soo Young bought three tables, a sofa, and two chairs.
    d. I need the following things: paper, pencils, a stapler, and some staples.
    e. Mrs. Johnson doesn't have a book, so she is using Mary's.

5. a. John and James
   b. My friends
   c. Her brother
   d. Swimming and diving
   e. It

6. a. are
   b. play
   c. likes
   d. swims and dives
   e. is

7. a. my sister
   b. tired
   c. difficult
   d. sure
   e. sick

8. a. Mary
   b. candy and flowers
   c. money
   d. friends
   e. three tickets

9. a. her
   b. us
   c. you
   d. Mary
   e. them

10. a. girls
    b. series
    c. tomatoes
    d. people
    e. cities
    f. leaves
    g. boxes
    h. pianos
    i. children
    j. men

11. a. furniture
    b. mail
    c. hardware
    d. change
    e. jewelry

    f. information
    g. music
    h. housework
    i. homework
    j. advice

12. a. ring
    b. rings
    c. dollars
    d. money
    e. child
    f. friends
    g. sisters
    h. appointment
    i. brothers
    j. friends
    k. box
    l. furniture
    m. chairs

13. a. coffees
    b. coffee
    c. chicken
    d. chickens
    e. glasses
    f. glass
    g. glass
    h. paper   paper

14. a. July
    b. Friday
    c. Charlotte's
    d. White House, Washington
    e. Mr. and Mrs. Harrison, New York City
    f. Louisiana
    g. Old Creek

15. a. Mary, John's wife, is a doctor.
    b. I like Barbara, my new neighbor.
    c. You should call Jack, the computer expert.
    d. The market, our favorite place to shop, has fresh
        vegetables.
    e. Carolyn, the best singer in the choir, is my sister.

16. a. Harrises'
    b. Sally's
    c. my friends'
    d. the people's
    e. James's

17. a. my friend's mother
    b. the name of the book
    c. the address of the school
    d. my friend's address
    e. the captain of the team   or   the team's captain
    f. the president of the country
    g. the color of the suit
    h. the teacher's name
    i. the cat's leg or the leg of the cat
    j. the leg of the table
    k. Sayed's leg

18. a. I have more books than you do. / You have fewer books than I do.
    b. She has more rings than her friend does. / Her friend has fewer rings than she does.
    c. I have more information than he does. / He has less information than I do.
    d. They have less money than we do. / We have more money than they do.

19. a. They have the same number of pencils.
    b. Our shoes are the same size.
    c. These turkeys are the same weight.
    d. Our husbands are the same height.
    e. These fabrics are the same length.
    f. The same man is here to see you.

20. a. She
    b. They
    c. They
    d. He
    e. We

21. a. you
    b. they
    c. they
    d. they   You
    e. You

22. a. her
    b. us   it
    c. him
    d. them   her
    e. us

23. a. They his
    b. them   him
    c. He it her
    d. theirs
    e. He   himself   his   her

24. a. Jim and Ellie like each other.
    b. Matt and Paul help each other.
    c. Lisa and William called each other.
    d. Brian and Miriam promised each other.

25. a. We   us
    b. me
    c. them
    d. He   she
    e. She
    f. her   him   They   me
    g. He   me   he   me
    h. him   he   his
    i. she
    j. each other   each other
    k. she   her

26. a. myself
    b. by herself
    c. himself
    d. itself
    e. yourself

27. a. theirs
    b. his
    c. hers
    d. yours
    e. ours
    f. mine

28. a. That purse belongs to Jan.
    b. This car belongs to us.
    c. Those flowers belong to the neighbors.
    d. Which coat belongs to you?

29. a. who
    b. that
    c. who(m)
    d. whose

30. d b k j i h g e f c a

31. a. others
    b. another
    c. the others
    d. the other

32. a. anybody
    b. Someone
    c. anywhere
    d. somewhere
    e. anything
    f. something
    g. nothing
    h. one
    i. another
    j. Each

33. a. an
    b. 0
    c. the
    d. the
    e. a
    f. an
    g. 0
    h. 0
    i. 0
    j. a

34. a. 0
    b. 0
    c. the
    d. 0
    e. the
    f. 0
    g. 0

h. the
i. the
j. the
k. 0
l. the

35. a. 0
b. the
c. 0
d. 0
e. 0
f. 0   0
g. 0   the

36. a. the first
b. the third
c. the eighth
d. the twelfth
e. the sixteenth
f. the twenty-second
g. the thirty-fourth
h. the forty-fifth
i. the sixty-seventh
j. the ninety-ninth

37. a. his
b. her
c. our
d. their
e. my

38. a. a little
b. a few
c. a lot of
d. a few
e. all of the
f. one
g. any
h. three
i. many
j. too much

39. a. This
    b. that
    c. those
    d. that
    e. these
    f. this

40. a. American
    b. Italian
    c. Mexican
    d. French
    e. Spanish

41. a. jewelry
    b. shoe
    c. boring   bored
    d. fascinated   fascinating
    e. three-hundred-dollar
    f. six-foot, two-hundred-pound

42. a. the most elegant
    b. the nicest
    c. easier
    d. more patient
    e. hotter
    f. better
    g. the same as
    h. different from
    i. warmer and warmer
    j. worse

43. a. cheaper than / less expensive than
    b. more expensive than
    c. as expensive as / as cheap as
    d. more expensive than
    e. the most expensive
    f. the cheapest

44. a. lighter than
    b. as light as
    c. heavier than / not as light as
    d. the heaviest
    e. the lightest

45. a. her beautiful long yellow
     b. my ugly old red
     c. his lovely blue silk
     d. your nice new wool
     e. those dirty old leather

46. a. I don't see anyone else.
     b. We don't need anything else.
     c. We want to go someplace else.
     d. I think he is looking for something else.
     e. No place else will please him.
     f. I can't live with anyone / anybody else.

47. a. tense
     b. active voice
     c. passive voice
     d. to + the basic form
     e. basic form

48. a. crying
     b. freezing
     c. bringing
     d. dying
     e. shopping
     f. sleeping
     g. whipping
     h. choosing
     i. studying
     j. occurring

49. a. tried
     b. permitted
     c. agreed
     d. folded
     e. shipped
     f. danced
     g. sewed
     h. cleaned
     i. played
     j. studied

50. a. are
     b. is
     c. aren't / are not
     d. am
     e. is

f. are
g. is
h. are
i. is
j. is not / isn't

51. a. How are they?
b. What is she like?
c. Are there any spoons?
d. Where are you from?
e. Whose book is it?
f. Who are you?
g. Where is the car?
h. When are their parties?
i. What color is her new dress?
j. Is John your brother?

52. a. Yes, I am.
b. Yes, he is.
c. Yes, they are.
d. Yes, she is.
e. Yes, you are.
f. Yes, it is.
g. Yes, you are.
h. Yes, there is.
i. Yes, there are.
j. Yes, it is.

53. a. No, I'm not.
b. No, he isn't / he's not
c. No, they aren't / they're not
d. Not, she isn't / she's not
e. No, you aren't / you're not
f. No, it isn't / it's not
g. No, you aren't / you're not
h. No, there isn't / there's not
i. No, there aren't
j. No, it isn't / it's not

54. a. You are?
b. He isn't?
c. She is?
d. They aren't ?
e. You aren't?
f. I am?
g. He is?
h. She isn't?

55. a. has
    b. goes
    c. laughs
    d. comes
    e. cries
    f. takes
    g. sings
    h. does
    i. works
    j. loves

56. a. doesn't have
    b. doesn't go
    c. doesn't laugh
    d. doesn't come
    e. doesn't cry
    f. doesn't take
    g. doesn't do
    h. doesn't work
    i. doesn't exercise

57. a. You don't?
    b. She doesn't?
    c. You do?
    d. He does?
    e. They don't?

58. a. We usually go to the movies on Saturdays.
    b. We eat dinner at eight o'clock.
    c. He often helps us.
    d. Sometimes he helps us. / He helps us sometimes.
    e. He helps us on the weekends.
    f. She occasionally takes trips.
    g. I wear a bathing suit in the summer.
    h. They rarely visit me.
    i. I always call them at night.
    j. She never studies in the afternoon.
    k. He exercises every day at six o'clock.
    l. We often exercise in the morning.

59. a. Who likes Peggy?
    b. Who(m) do you call?
    c. Who is your friend?
    d. Who takes her to the zoo?
    e. Who(m) do you take to the zoo?
    f. What do you see?
    g. What smells bad?

60. a. How many cousins do you have?
    b. Where do they live now?
    c. Who eats a lot?
    d. What does your aunt cook?
    e. Who cooks chicken?
    f. How much chicken do they eat?
    g. Where does she buy the chicken?
    h. When does she usually shop?

61. a. go
    b. like
    c. doesn't live
    d. don't have
    e. works
    f. meet
    g. leaves
    h. watches

62. a. What do they do on Saturdays? / Where do they go on Saturdays?
    b. What kind of ice cream do you like? / Do you like chocolate ice cream?
    c. Does he live here?
    d. Do you have a car?
    e. Where does she work?
    f. Where do you and your friend meet?
    g. What time does Sylvia leave home?
    h. What does she do every evening? or When does she watch television?

63. a. I can sing.
    b. He may be at home. / He might be at home. / Maybe he is at home.
    c. You may go home.
    d. Will (would, could) you help me carry this package?
    e. Should I call a doctor?
    f. You should go to the doctor.
    g. I have to work.
    h. She (He) doesn't have to work.
    i. You mustn't make noise.
    j. I would rather live in the city.

64. a. can
    b. can
    c. can't / cannot
    d. might / may
    e. Maybe
    f. may
    g. may not
    h. should   shouldn't   have to
    i. don't   don't have to   doesn't have to
    j. mustn't
    k. must be
    l. would   like   would rather

65. a. is sleeping
    b. is studying
    c. are painting
    d. are driving
    e. am relaxing
    f. are   enjoying

66. a. isn't sleeping
    b. isn't studying
    c. aren't painting
    d. aren't driving
    e. I'm not relaxing

67. a. Mark is still sleeping.
    b. Joe is always calling me.
    c. Heather isn't working anymore.
    d. George isn't studying here anymore.
    e. Sam is still studying here.

68. a. likes
    b. eat
    c. are watching
    d. washes
    e. am writing
    f. is talking
    g. want
    h. are having
    i. have
    j. is studying
    k. think
    l. am thinking

69. a. come
b. is enjoying
c. are playing
d. are talking
e. likes
f. likes
g. is staying
h. plays
i. is
j. invites
k. is painting
l. is using
m. making
n. watches
o. is
p. is jumping
q. are having

70. a. have lived
b. have eaten
c. has slept
d. has cried
e. have come
f. have gone
g. have worked
h. have written
i. have studied
j. has read

71. a. haven't changed
b. hasn't broken
c. hasn't won
d. haven't promised, have
e. hasn't helped, has

72. a. since
b. for
c. for
d. since
e. since

73. a. How long have you lived here?
b. How long have they been your neighbors?
c. How long has he worked there?
d. How long have you been waiting?
e. How long have they been talking?

74. a. She has driven this car before.
     b. I have been to your house before.
     c. We have seen that movie before.
     d. They have already eaten.
     e. He hasn't eaten.

75. a. I have (already) walked four miles.
     b. I have lost ten pounds (so far).
     c. I have (already) spent $75.
     d. I have (already) written two papers.

76. a. have worked
     b. have helped (have been helping)
     c. have not eaten
     d. has been
     e. has never played
     f. have answered
     g. has just arrived

77. a. How long have you worked (have you been
         working) here?
     b. How long have they helped (have they been
         helping) him?
     c. Have you eaten dinner yet?
     d. Has she ever been in Alaska? / Has she been in
         Alaska before? / How many times has she been
         in Alaska?
     e. Has he ever played football? / Has he played
         football before?
     f. How many questions have you answered so far?
     g. Has she arrived yet?

78. a. was
     b. were
     c. weren't
     d. was
     e. was

79. a. How were you?
     b. Where were you?
     c. Were they late?
     d. Who was she?
     e. What time was it?

80. a. stood
     b. tried
     c. worked
     d. studied
     e. saw
     f. agreed
     g. taught
     h. bought
     i. brought
     j. went
     k. bent
     l. folded
     m. held
     n. knew
     o. showed
     p. heard
     q. wore
     r. sold
     s. told
     t. did

81. a. began
     b. stopped
     c. helped
     d. didn't go
     e. went
     f. didn't eat
     g. left
     h. did not call
     i. had
     j. cried

82. a. What time did you begin? / When did you begin?
     b. What time did you stop? / When did you stop?
     c. When did Mary help you? / Who helped you? / Who(m) did Mary help?
     d. Did he go to Spain last summer?
     e. What time did they go home?
     f. Did you eat at your friend's house last night?
     g. What time did you leave home?
     h. Did Vicki and Joan call you today?
     i. Did you have a good time at the party?
     j. What did she do when he left?

83. a. started   have studied / have been studying
     b. moved   have lived / have been living
     c. met   have known
     d. did
     e. worked   took   lived
     f. have not seen

84. a. I could work.
     b. Should we have gone?
     c. They were allowed to take a vacation. / They
         could have taken a vacation.
     d. He may have been sick. / He might have been
         sick. / Maybe he was sick.
     e. He must have worked there.
     f. She had to study.

85. a. I couldn't go.
     b. They must have played all day.
     c. He had to be there.
     d. You should have done it.
     e. She might have gone. / She may have gone.

86. a. was sleeping
     b. was eating
     c. was riding   was watching
     d. was still talking

87. a. was sewing
     b. was sewing   was thinking
     c. was   seemed
     d. wanted   began
     e. came   was crying   thought   didn't love

88. a. was driving
     b. saw
     c. was waiting
     d. turned
     e. stalled
     f. was not paying attention
     g. ran
     h. made
     i. got
     j. started
     k. was still yelling
     l. drove

89.
a. was cooking
b. burned
c. was
d. went
e. told
f. waited
g. called
h. went
i. waited
j. was sitting
k. heard
l. saw
m. was getting
n. was
o. fell
p. came
q. was sleeping
r. woke
s. looked
t. put
u. said
v. gave
w. told

90.
a. I was going to go to the circus, but I didn't have enough time.
b. We were going to call you, but we didn't have a quarter.
c. They were going to have a party, but the teacher disapproved.
d. She was going to stay home, but her friend invited her to the movies.

91.
a. I used to be fat.
b. We used to live there.
c. He used to smoke.
d. He used to be married.
e. She used to be nice.
f. They used to be happy.
g. He used to laugh.
h. We used to eat dinner together.

92.
a. She would tell jokes.
b. She would make my favorite food.
c. He would help me with my homework.
d. We would have fun.
e. They would never fight.

93. a. had helped
    b. had not been
    c. had sung
    d. had gone
    e. had eaten
    f. had not seen

94. a. She had (already) eaten.
    b. I hadn't eaten (yet).
    c. He had driven that car before.
    d. They had seen that movie before.

95. a. When I left for the office, I hadn't read the newspaper (yet).
    b. When Joel invited her to go out, Sue had (already) eaten dinner.
    c. When my dad saw us, we had already called the gas station for help.
    d. When I arrived at the dance, it had already started.

96. a. have not   had not
    b. has worked   had worked
    c. had invited   has invited
    d. have not seen   had not seen
    e. had not studied   have not studied

97. a. had been writing
    b. had been living
    c. had been hoping
    d. had been thinking
    e. had been wanting

98. a. We were exhausted because we had been working hard all day.
    b. They slept until noon because they had been dancing all night.
    c. She didn't eat her dinner because she had been eating potato chips all day.
    d. He was happy to get his degree because he had been studying for six years.

99. a. am leaving
    b. is coming
    c. is studying
    d. are watching
    e. aren't going

100. a. am going to leave
     b. is going to come
     c. is going to study
     d. are going to watch
     e. are not going to go

101. a. He may work. / He might work. / Maybe he will work.
     b. She may not come. / She might not come. / Maybe she won't come.
     c. They may bring / They might bring / Maybe they will bring
     d. We may take / We might take / Maybe we will take
     e. You may need / You might need / Maybe you will need

102. a. should arrive
     b. should finish
     c. should call
     d. should be over

103. a. will probably graduate
     b. will probably get married
     c. will probably stop working
     d. will probably be finished

104. a. probably won't call
     b. probably won't be
     c. probably won't tell
     d. probably won't get married

105. a. I will call.
     b. We will bring
     c. He will be
     d. I will write

106. a. will pass
     b. will rain
     c. won't snow
     d. will worry
     e. will win
     f. will get angy
     g. will change

107. a. Yes, I will.   Yes, we will.
    b. No, I won't.   No, I won't.

108. a. starts
    b. leaves
    c. ends
    d. begin

109. a. will be able to (drive)
    b. will have to (study)
    c. will be able to (help you)
    d. will not be allowed to (leave the room)
    e. will want to (travel to South America)

110. a. leave
    b. gets here
    c. gets here
    d. leaves
    e. arrive
    f. say

111. a. John probably won't go to work tomorrow.
    b. I am studying tomorrow. / I am going to study tomorrow.
    c. I will help you next week.
    d. We should arrive at 3:00 P.M.
    e. Teresa is traveling next week.
    f. Ann might take a vacation in August. / Ann may take a vacation in August. / Maybe Ann will take a vacation in August.
    g. Arthur won't work in that place.
    h. It will rain tomorrow.
    i. She won't have to return tonight.
    j. I will be able to swim in three months.

112. a. will be playing
    b. will be preparing
    c. will be running
    d. will be making
    e. will be practicing

113. a. What will you be doing at four o'clock?
    b. What will he be doing then?
    c. What will she be doing that day?
    d. What will you be doing this afternoon?
    e. What will they be doing tomorrow evening?

114. a. will have finished
     b. will have sent
     c. will have done
     d. will have called
     e. will have moved

115. a. Singing
     b. traveling
     c. getting lost
     d. Traveling
     e. driving
     f. Waiting
     g. going
     h. talking

116. a. going
     b. taking
     c. working
     d. telling
     e. smoking

117. a. We want to go bowling.
     b. They like to go fishing.
     c. He has to go shopping.
     d. She hates to go camping.
     e. She wants to go dancing.

118. a. What do you feel like doing?
     b. Do you feel like swimming?
     c. No. I felt like swimming yesterday.
     d. Today I feel like dancing.

119. a. Would you mind taking off your hat?
     b. Would you mind saving my seat?
     c. Would you mind helping us?
     d. Would you mind lending me $100?
     e. Would you mind taking me home after the meeting?

120. a. cleaning
     b. driving
     c. dancing
     d. trying
     e. training
     f. running

121. a. They appreciated her coming.
      b. She regrets his resigning.
      c. She loves his dancing.
      d. They don't like her singing.
      e. His cooking is pretty good.

122. a. to lose
      b. to learn
      c. To manage
      d. To forget
      e. to hurt
      f. to help
      g. to use
      h. to be
      i. to study

123. a. to buy
      b. to play
      c. to marry
      d. to finish
      e. to stay
      f. to save

124. a. I'm going to the store to buy milk.
      b. They are going to Aisha's house to see her.
      c. Melissa is not strong enough to lift that box.
      d. Danny is old enough to get his driver's license.
      e. It takes (me) twenty minutes to drive home.
      f. It takes Jackie two hours to clean her room.
      g. I am glad to hear your good news.
      h. I am sorry to hear your bad news.

125. a. driving
      b. to talk
      c. take
      d. to sleep
      e. taking
      f. go
      g. get up
      h. to wake up
      i. waking up

126.   a. helping
       b. to postpone
       c. wash
       d. to have
       e. to learn
       f. seeing
       g. go
       h. to talk
       i. to drive
       j. clean
       k. to find
       l. hearing
       m. to tape
       n. living
       o. shopping
       p. doing
       q. working
       r. losing

127.   a. dancing
       b. to call
       c. to write
       d. shopping
       e. working
       f. to earn
       g. to find
       h. to help
       i. to graduate
       j. to wear
       k. wearing
       l. listening *or* to listen

128.   a. Molly asked, "Are you coming with us?"
       b. Sam said, "I'm not going anywhere."
       c. "I will wait here," he told her.
       d. Then he added, "Don't worry about me."

129.   a. was going
       b. wanted
       c. couldn't
       d. didn't want
       e. wanted
       f. would bring

130. a. had gone
     b. had wanted
     c. had done
     d. had played
     e. had brought

131. a. Steve said that Martha was clever.
     b. Mrs. Adams said that Jessica wanted ice cream.
     c. The children yelled that they couldn't swim.
     d. The lady reported that they hadn't done it right.
     e. Jerry said that he wasn't going to drive.
     f. Joan asked if Sam was going to work.
     g. The reporter asked if they had finished yet.
     h. He asked later when they were going to finish.
     i. Dad asked where she had gone.

132. a. Ralph said, "I'm going home."
     b. "Are you tired?" asked Judy.
     c. "I'm exhausted because I've been working all day," Ralph told her.
     d. "You deserve a rest," Judy replied.
     e. "How many hours have you worked?" asked Ralph.
     f. "I have worked eight hours," replied Judy.
     g. "I think I will go home, too," she said.

133. a. Do you know where her house is?
     b. Do you know why she is leaving?
     c. Do you know where Monica lives?
     d. Do you know where Freddy bought that hat?

134. a. I don't know who that lady is.
     b. I don't know when the party is.
     c. I don't know where the buses are.
     d. I don't know what Katrina does.
     e. I don't know why they went home.

135. a. Can you tell me where the president's office is?
     b. Can you tell me who her boyfriend is?
     c. Can you tell me where Main Street is?
     d. Can you tell me what time it is?
     e. Can you tell me when they got here?
     f. Can you tell me why they left?
     g. Can you tell me when you are going to begin?

136. a. where to go
      b. how to get there
      c. who(m) to call
      d. when to leave

137. a. He is adorable, isn't he?
      b. We aren't finished, are we?
      c. She is afraid, isn't she?
      d. They are cold, aren't they?
      e. You like ice cream, don't you?
      f. He wants a drink, doesn't he?
      g. I haven't been there, have I?
      h. You have performed already, haven't you?
      i. He hasn't called us, has he?
      j. He was there, wasn't he?
      k. You went to the game, didn't you?
      l. He tried to help you, didn't he?
      m. They didn't like the dessert, did they?
      n. He hadn't seen the movie, had he?
      o. She had been working all day, hadn't she?

138. a. David gives her money. / David gives it to her.
      b. Helen draws him pictures. / Helen draws them for him.
      c. Sandra mentioned it to him.
      d. Robin asked her a question.
      e. Paul explains them to the students.
      f. Richard built her a house. / Richard built it for her.

139. a. get
      b. get
      c. getting
      d. getting
      e. get
      f. get   getting
      g. got
      h. got

140. a. I'm going to have my hair cut.
      b. We have our grass cut every week.
      c. He has his oil changed regularly.
      d. He has his shirts ironed.
      e. She had her house cleaned last week.
      f. We had the damage repaired last year.
      g. We are going to have our house painted next week.

141.   a. ask
     b. ask for
     c. lend
     d. borrow
     e. asking   lend

142.   a. talk
     b. speaks
     c. speak
     d. talked

143.   a. come   bring   take
     b. come   bring   take
     c. going
     d. going   taking   brings

144.   a. say
     b. Tell
     c. tells
     d. says   tell

145.   a. do
     b. do
     c. makes
     d. do   make

146.   a. wish
     b. hope
     c. wish
     d. hoped
     e. wish

147.   a. looking at
     b. watching
     c. looks
     d. looks like
     e. look alike

148.   a. I am not understood.
     b. That teacher is loved.
     c. These rugs are made in Iran.
     d. She is cared for.
     e. He is called a lot.
     f. They are being helped.

149. a. I was not understood.
      b. That teacher was loved.
      c. These rugs were made in Iran.
      d. She was cared for.
      e. He was called a lot.
      f. They were being helped.
      g. This poem was written in 1865.

150. a. I haven't been understood.
      b. She has been cared for.
      c. He has been called a lot.
      d. They have been helped.
      e. The bank on the corner has been robbed.

151. a. Call me!
      b. Send me a letter, John.
      c. Don't leave, Mom.
      d. Don't drive fast, Erin.
      e. Let's dance, Pat!
      f. Let's go to a movie.
      g. Let's not argue.
      h. Let's not play tennis today.

152. a. How do you start the machine?
      b. How do you get to Center Street?
      c. Where do you park?
      d. How much do you have to pay to ride on the metro?
      e. Where can you mail letters?

153. a. You put a quarter in the slot and push the start button.
      b. You go straight ahead, then turn left.
      c. You park on the street.
      d. You mail your letters at the post office.

154. a. Adam to erase the blackboard.
      b. Jessica to pick up the toys.
      c. Amy and Lisa to put away the crayons.
      d. David and Brian to put the chairs in place.
      e. Reza to put the trash in the wastebasket.

155. a. She wanted him to erase the blackboard.
      b. She wanted her to pick up the toys.
      c. She wanted them to put away the crayons.
      d. She wanted them to put the chairs in place.
      e. She wanted him to put the trash in the wastebasket.

156. a. that he be quiet
     b. that we be responsible
     c. that she be careful
     d. that you come home
     e. that he get a tutor

157. a. I wish I had a ticket.
     b. I wish he went to school.
     c. I wish she didn't work on weekends.
     d. I wish we had money.
     e. I wish they didn't leave their dirty dishes in the sink.

158. a. I wish they hadn't gone home early.
     b. I wish you hadn't called me at 6:00 A.M.
     c. I wish she hadn't quit her job.
     d. I wish he hadn't found out the truth.
     e. I wish we had told him in time.

159. a. If I had a lot of money, I would take a trip to Europe.
     b. If she were here, I would dance with her.
     c. If he had a diploma, he could get a job.
     d. If we were lucky, we would win the lottery.

160. a. If I had had a lot of money, I would have taken a trip to Europe.
     b. If she had been here, I would have danced with her.
     c. If he had had a diploma, he could have gotten a job.
     d. If we had been lucky, we would have won the lottery.

161. a. If I walk, I get tired.
     b. If he reads, he falls asleep.
     c. If she drinks milk, she gets a stomach ache.
     d. If he is awake, he watches T.V.

162. a. If I go home early, my wife will be happy.
     b. If I get a vacation in August, I will go to Asia.
     c. If he marries her, he will move to California.
     d. If they buy that house, they will make a beautiful garden.
     e. If we move in February, we will give you our furniture.

163. a. If I went to the beach, I would buy a bathing suit.
 b. If she bought that dress, she would have to lose ten pounds.
 c. If he won the lottery, he would buy a fabulous new car.
 d. If we took a trip around the world, we would visit you.
 e. If they got married, they would have a lot of problems.

164. a. in
 b. under
 c. on
 d. next to
 e. behind
 f. against

165. a. in
 b. of
 c. in
 d. on
 e. at

166. a. toward
 b. away from
 c. onto
 d. through

167. a. in   in   on   at   in
 b. since
 c. for
 d. at   by
 e. until   for
 f. on
 g. at

168. a. in   on
 b. in   on   in

169. a. for   at   up
 b. on
 c. in   in

170. a. by
      b. for
      c. with   by
      d. from
      e. in   from
      f. in   of
      g. by
      h. without
      i. from

171. a. Who(m) did you go to the movies with?
      b. What is she thinking about?
      c. What street do they live on?
      d. What city does he live in?
      e. Who(m) did you talk to?

172. a. at
      b. for
      c. to
      d. with

173. a. in
      b. by
      c. on
      d. in
      e. in
      f. With
      g. on
      h. on
      i. in
      j. in
      k. at   at

174. a. about
      b. for
      c. in / with
      d. from
      e. of
      f. with
      g. of
      h. to
      i. for
      j. about
      k. in / with
      l. from

175. a. about / of
     b. about
     c. at
     d. of
     e. with
     f. to
     g. on
     h. to
     i. with
     j. for
     k. in

176. a. watch out / look out
     b. dropped off
     c. got away
     d. show up
     e. hangs around
     f. Keep out
     g. start over
     h. check in
     i. get along
     j. find out
     k. get up
     l. give up

177. a. Please throw it away.
     b. Are you going to pay him back?
     c. I wrote it down.
     d. We will look into it.
     e. You need to hand them in.
     f. May I try it on?
     g. I had to ask for it.
     h. She had to clean it up.
     i. He tried to do it over.
     j. She likes to pick them out.
     k. They ran out of them.
     l. We will have to call them back.
     m. Try to get over it.
     n. They called it off.
     o. Do you think you can catch up with them?

178. a. here
     b. away
     c. anywhere
     d. upstairs
     e. there   downstairs   high   low   everywhere
     f. underneath

179. a. late
       b. ago
       c. next week
       d. soon
       e. recently / lately
       f. anymore
       g. still

180. a. tonight
       b. later
       c. Then   afterward / then / later

181. a. Today
       b. Yesterday
       c. the day before yesterday
       d. Tomorrow
       e. the day after tomorrow

182. a. This morning
       b. this afternoon
       c. this evening

183. a. last
       b. this   next
       c. this   next
       d. last

184. a. once
       b. again
       c. times
       d. twice

185. a. 25 percent of the time
       b. 100 percent of the time
       c. 5 percent of the time
       d. 0 percent of the time
       e. 80 percent of the time
       f. 60 percent of the time

186. a. well
       b. carefully
       c. fast
       d. quickly
       e. easily
       f. hard
       g. busily

h. ably
i. late
j. responsibly
k. early
l. badly
m. slowly
n. better than
o. more slowly than
p. faster than
q. more easily than
r. worse than
s. more carefully than
t. more quietly than
u. less capably than
v. the most responsibly
w. not as easily as
x. not as well as

187. a. hardly
  b. really
  c. somewhat / a little
  d. almost

188. a. average
  b. bad
  c. better than average
  d. excellent

189. a. I'm going outside.
  b. He's going to New York tomorrow.
  c. Yes, they are still sleeping.
  d. Yes, I have already finished.
  e. No, I haven't finished yet.
  f. No, she doesn't take lessons anymore.
  g. She seldom practices.
  h. They usually play in the afternoon.
  i. Sometimes my friend calls me in the evening. /
    My friend calls me in the evening sometimes.
  j. He paints very well.
  k. John is pretty tall.

190. a. and   and
  b. or
  c. but
  d. yet
  e. and   not only   but also

f. or
g. and
h. so
i. but
j. for

191. a. Kathleen is happy, and Glenn is too.
     b. Jack works hard, and Mike does too.
     c. Emily left yesterday, and Jeremy did too.
     d. Val was cooking, and Renee was too.
     e. Sue isn't tired, and Joel isn't either.
     f. Kevin didn't come, and Scott didn't either.
     g. Carolyn wasn't driving, and Bob wasn't either.
     h. We didn't see them, and Gayle didn't either.

192. a. Kathleen is happy, and so is Glenn.
     b. Jack works hard, and so does Mike.
     c. Emily left yesterday, and so did Jeremy.
     d. Val was cooking, and so was Renee.
     e. Sue isn't tired, and neither is Joel.
     f. Kevin didn't come, and neither did Scott.
     g. Carolyn wasn't driving, and neither was Bob.
     h. We didn't see them, and neither did Gayle.

193. a. both   and
     b. not only   but also
     c. neither   nor
     d. whether   or not
     e. either   or

194. a. before
     b. after until
     c. While
     d. because
     e. so that
     f. Although / Even though
     g. rather than
     h. although / even though

195. a. first
     b. Second, / Next, / Then
     c. Next, Then / After that,
     d. Next, Then / After that,
     e. Meanwhile
     f. After
     g. Finally

196. a. and / as well as
      b. In addition / Plus
      c. Furthermore
      d. On top of that
      e. Moreover

197. a. she is a good friend of mine. (one possible answer)
      b. it's the best pot roast I've ever had. (one possible answer)
      c. it was the most fun I've had for a long time. (one possible answer)

198. a. on the other hand / in contrast
      b. otherwise
      c. nevertheless / still
      d. but / however,
      e. instead

199. a. in other words / that is
      b. for example
      c. specifically
      d. I mean
      e. that is / in other words

200. a. anyway
      b. after all
      c. after all
      d. In any case

201. a. although / even though
      b. even if
      c. although / even though
      d. even if

202. a. in the end
      b. In summary / In short
      c. In short
      d. In conclusion

203. a. sixty-four
      b. three hundred and seventy-seven
      c. four thousand, five hundred and forty-one
      d. twenty thousand, three hundred and two
      e. four hundred thousand and one
      f. six million, three hundred and twelve

g. six and a half miles

h. one and three-quarter acres

i. ten dollars and thirty-four cents

j. five thousand, four hundred and twenty-eight dollars and twenty-one cents

k. ten million dollars

204. a. Thursday is before Friday.

b. Wednesday is between Tuesday and Thursday.

c. Saturday and Sunday are the weekend.

d. August is before September.

e. April is after March.

f. Independence Day in the United States is on July 4th. / the Fourth of July.

205. a. It's five o'clock.

b. It's six-oh-five / It's five after six. / It's five past six.

c. It's seven-ten. / It's ten after seven. / It's ten past seven.

d. It's eight-fifteen. / It's a quarter after eight. / It's a quarter past eight.

e. It's nine-twenty. / It's twenty after nine. / It's twenty past nine.

f. It's ten-twenty-five. / It's twenty-five after ten. / It's twenty-five past ten.

g. It's eleven-thirty. / It's half past eleven.

h. It's twelve-thirty-five. / It's twenty-five to one. / It's twenty-five of one.

i. It's one-forty. / It's twenty to two. / It's twenty of two.

j. It's two-forty-five. / It's a quarter to three. / It's a quarter of three.

k. It's three-fifty. / It's ten to four. / It's ten of four.

l. It's four-fifty-five. / It's five to five. / It's five of five.

206. a. pleasant weather

b. electricity in the sky

c. a flow of water over usually dry land

d. cold weather

e. a loud noise

f. winds over 75 miles per hour

g. hot weather

h. a circular storm

207.   a. It's (nine) o'clock.
     b. I'm (writ)ing.
     c. I'm (tired).
     d. I'm (tired) because I have been (study)ing.
     e. I have answered (five) questions.
     f. I'm going to (rest).
     g. I was (work)ing.
     h. I was at (my office).
     i. I arrived there at (8:30 A.M.).
     j. (Shirley, the office manager,) was there.
     k. She was (working at her computer).
     l. She had been there (twenty minutes).
     m. I ate lunch at (one-fifteen).
     n. Yes, I had. / No, I hadn't.
     o. I was (happy).
     p. I was happy because I had (finished all my work).
     q. Yes, I did.
     r. Yes, I am.

Appendix

Weights and Measures

Weights

U.S. Standard Weights	Metric Equivalents
16 ounces = 1 pound	.454 kilogram (almost half of a kilogram)
2,000 pounds = 1 ton	907.18 kilograms
1.102 short tons	1 metric ton
Abbreviations	
ounce = oz.	pound = lb.

Liquid Measures

U.S. Standard Measures	Metric Equivalents
1 cup	236 milliliters
2 cups = 1 pint	473 milliliters
2 pints = 1 quart	.9464 liter
4 quarts = 1 gallon	3.7854 liters
Abbreviations	
cup = C.	quart = qt.
pint = pt.	gallon = gal.

Dry Measures

U.S. Standard Measures	Metric Equivalents
1 teaspoon	5 milliliters*
3 teaspoons = 1 tablespoon	15 milliliters*
¼ cup	60 milliliters*
½ cup	120 milliliters*
Abbreviations	
teaspoon = tsp. or t. tablespoon = T.	cup = C.

*These measurements are approximate.

Linear Measures

U.S. Standard Measures	Metric Equivalents
1 inch	2.54 centimeters
12 inches = 1 foot	30.48 centimeters
3 feet = 1 yard	.9144 meter
5,280 feet = 1 mile	1.6 kilometers

Abbreviations

inch = in. or ″	yard = yd.
foot = ft. or ′	mile = m.

Square Measures

U.S. Standard Measures	Metric Equivalents
43,560 square feet = 1 acre	4,047 square meters
640 acres = 1 square mile	2,590 square kilometers

Abbreviations

square feet = sq. ft.	acre = ac.

Temperatures

U.S. Standard /Fahrenheit For Weather:	Celsius/Centigrade
−10	−23
0	−17
32	0
50	10
68	20
86	30
104	40

Normal Body Temperature:

98.6	37

For Cooking:

212 (boiling point of water)	100
250 (low oven)	121
325	163
350 (moderate oven)	177
375	190
400	204
450	232
500	260

Abbreviations
° = degrees F = Fahrenheit C = Celsius or Centigrade

Common Abbreviations

Time Expressions

A.D.   *anno Domini*—the years counted for present time
B.C.   before Christ—the years counted backwards from
       present time
A.M.   *ante meridiem*—before twelve o'clock noon
P.M.   *post meridiem*—after twelve o'clock noon

Personal Titles

Mr.   the title for a man
Mrs.   the title for a married woman
Miss   the title for an unmarried woman or young girl
Ms.   the business title for a woman
Dr.   the title for a man or woman with an earned
       doctorate degree
Rev.   the title for a member of the clergy
Sr.   senior—used after a man's name when his son has
       the same name
Jr.   junior—used after a man's name when his father
       has the same name
Ph.D. Doctor of Philosophy—used after the name of a
       person who has earned that degree
M.D.   Doctor of Medicine—used after the name of a
       medical doctor
D.D.S. Doctor of Dental Surgery—used after the name of
       a dentist
LL.D. Doctor of Laws—used after the name of a lawyer
       who has earned that degree
Note: Choose one title or the other: Dr. Donald Lawrence
or Donald Lawrence, M.D.

For Report Writing

cf.   *confer*—compare
e.g.   *exempli gratia*—for example
et al. *el alii*—and others
etc.   *et cetera*—and so forth
i.e.   *id est*—that is
N.B.   *nota bene*—note well

Irregular Verb Forms

Basic Form	Past Tense Form	Past Participle
be	was, were	been
become	became	become
bear	bore	born
beat	beat	beaten
begin	began	begun
bend	bent	bent
bet	bet	bet
bind	bound	bound
bite	bit	bitten
bleed	bled	bled
blow	blew	blown
break	broke	broken
breed	bred	bred
bring	brought	brought
build	built	built
burst	burst	burst
buy	bought	bought
catch	caught	caught
choose	chose	chosen
cling	clung	clung
come	came	come
cost	cost	cost
creep	crept	crept
cut	cut	cut
deal	dealt	dealt
do	did	done
dig	dug	dug
draw	drew	drawn
drink	drank	drunk
drive	drove	driven
eat	ate	eaten
fall	fell	fallen
feed	fed	fed
feel	felt	felt
fight	fought	fought
find	found	found
fit	fit	fit
flee	fled	fled
fly	flew	flown
forbid	forbade	forbidden
forget	forgot	forgotten
forgive	forgave	forgiven
forsake	forsook	forsaken
freeze	froze	frozen
get	got	gotten
give	gave	given
go	went	gone
grind	ground	ground
grow	grew	grown
hang	hung	hung

Basic Form	Past Tense Form	Past Participle
have	had	had
hear	heard	heard
hide	hid	hidden
hit	hit	hit
hold	held	held
hurt	hurt	hurt
keep	kept	kept
know	knew	known
lay	laid	laid
lead	led	led
leave	left	left
lend	lent	lent
let	let	let
lie	lay	lain
light	lit	lit
lose	lost	lost
make	made	made
mean	meant	meant
meet	met	met
mistake	mistook	mistaken
pay	paid	paid
put	put	put
quit	quit	quit
read	read	read
rid	rid	rid
ride	rode	ridden
ring	rang	rung
rise	rose	risen
run	ran	run
say	said	said
see	saw	seen
seek	sought	sought
sell	sold	sold
send	sent	sent
set	set	set
shake	shook	shaken
shed	shed	shed
shine	shone	shone
shoot	shot	shot
show	showed	shown
shrink	shrank	shrunk
shut	shut	shut
sing	sang	sung
sit	sat	sat
sleep	slept	slept
slide	slid	slid
sling	slung	slung
slit	slit	slit
speak	spoke	spoken
speed	sped	sped
spend	spent	spent
spin	spun	spun
split	split	split

Basic Form	Past Tense Form	Past Participle
spread	spread	spread
spring	sprang	sprung
stand	stood	stood
steal	stole	stolen
stick	stuck	stuck
sting	stung	stung
stink	stank	stunk
strike	struck	struck
strive	strove	striven
swear	swore	sworn
sweep	swept	swept
swim	swam	swum
swing	swung	swung
take	took	taken
teach	taught	taught
tear	tore	torn
tell	told	told
think	thought	thought
throw	threw	thrown
understand	understood	understood
upset	upset	upset
wake up	woke up	waked up
wear	wore	worn
weave	wove	woven
weep	wept	wept
win	won	won
wind	wound	wound
withdraw	withdrew	withdrawn
wring	wrung	wrung
write	wrote	written

Index